John Stewart.

PRAISE FOR *SPIRITUAL DIARY*

"Bulgakov's *Spiritual Diary* is a uniquely precious document. Here we glimpse, not events, but, traced on his soul in prayer, his inner life of exile, unworthiness, overarching providence, and constant recourse to the Mother of God—all disclosing the 'sophianic' as inner truth. A superb translation, greatly enhanced by the translators' introductions and notes."

—**ARCHPRIEST ANDREW LOUTH**, author of *Introducing Eastern Orthodox Theology*

"We owe these two translators our thanks for bringing this remarkable document into English. Bulgakov's metaphysical genius is beyond question, the profundity, rigor, and comprehensiveness of his thought unparalleled in modern theology; but here is something more. In these pages, one is granted entry into his private devotions, meditations, and prayers, and one discovers that the source of his majestic intellectual achievement was a fervent (and mystical) inner spiritual life. The genius is still on full display, but in a new and especially affecting register."

—**DAVID BENTLEY HART**, author of *Kenogaia (A Gnostic Tale)*

"This translation of Sergius Bulgakov's *Spiritual Diary* is a precious gift to Christians of all traditions, especially to those who have already discovered him as one of the preeminent theologians of the 20th century. Written in 1924–1925, it reveals Bulgakov's intimate conversations with God at the crucial stage in life when he found and followed his calling to be a loving pastor with personal 'colorful' relationships, and not some 'self-appointed prophet.' At the same time, his 'prophetic thirst for Truth' engendered real dialogue between Eastern Orthodoxy and Western Churches. This emphatic translation of the *Spiritual Diary*, together with the insightful memoirs of his spiritual daughter Sr. Joanna Reitlinger and the brilliant biographical and theological introductions, dispels any misattribution to Bulgakov of philosophizing theorization or neglect of the gravity of sin. If Bulgakov is right that holiness does not mean sinlessness, but rather fulfilling one's calling by resisting the great sin of despair in the face of evil and one's own sinfulness, his *Spiritual Diary* is itself an outstanding example of just such 'holiness at work.'"

—**REGULA M. ZWAHLEN**, University of Fribourg

"A particularly lustrous offering to our present golden age of Bulgakov studies comes in the spiritual diaries of Bulgakov himself, newly available in English. Bulgakov is revealed for the reader in his ministrations to the dying, his ecstatic thoughts on and experiences with prayer, his self-doubt, his devotion to the Mother of God, and his intimacy with the liturgy. The result is a fuller, richer understanding of Bulgakov than his scholarly works alone can afford, but which complements and illumines that work. Translators Roosien and De La Noval offer a beautiful portrait of Bulgakov as a man whose creative intellect was, in his own words, one with his 'enflamed heart.'"

—**CARRIE FREDERICK FROST**, Western Washington University

"This spiritual diary offers a truly personal insight into the reflections of one of the profoundest theologians of the twentieth century. It unveils the inner dimensions of Bulgakov's spiritual life, enabling us to appreciate ever more the depths of his theological vision. Consider it a necessary companion to any study of Bulgakov."

—**FR. JOHN BEHR**, University of Aberdeen

"Sergius Bulgakov's *Spiritual Diary* is at once demanding and generous, learned and plainspoken, stricken and full of real hope. It will provide both provocation and consolation to those trying to understand what it might mean, in this modern world, to live a life in Christ. The editors have done a great service in making this book available to an English-speaking audience."

—**CHRISTIAN WIMAN**, Yale Divinity School

SPIRITUAL DIARY

SERGIUS BULGAKOV

SPIRITUAL DIARY

Edited, Introduced, & Translated by
MARK ROOSIEN *and* ROBERTO J. DE LA NOVAL

Foreword by
BISHOP ROWAN WILLIAMS

Angelico Press

First published in the USA
by Angelico Press 2022

For information, address:
Angelico Press, Ltd.
169 Monitor St.
Brooklyn, NY 11222
www.angelicopress.com

paper 978-1-62138-850-0
cloth 978-1-62138-851-7
ebook 978-1-62138-852-4

Book and cover design
by Michael Schrauzer

Cover image: Yuliya N. (Sr. Joanna) Reitlinger,
"Father Sergius in the Forest near Paris." France.
Early 1930s. Paper, gouache. Collection of the House of
the Russian Emigration (Moscow). Used with permission.

Dedication

to Iva
a mi madre, Maria

CONTENTS

FOREWORD

SERGII BULGAKOV'S THEOLOGICAL AND metaphysical thought attracted controversy throughout his life, as indeed it still does; but it is striking that even those who were critical of his ideas—people like Alexander Schmemann and Vladimir Lossky—acknowledged his devotion and integrity as a priest, while those who had known him directly as a spiritual father—the Zernovs, Sister Joanna Reitlinger, and many more—unhesitatingly bore witness to the depth of his spiritual discernment and his personal holiness. This book provides a unique insight into Bulgakov's inner life, and helps us to understand something of this near-universal recognition of his spiritual stature. As the invaluable biographical preface to this text makes clear, the journal begins in the aftermath of a period of intense inner turbulence. Bulgakov, struggling to come to terms with the colossal trauma of the Revolution, had asked hard questions about the responsibility of the Russian Church for the collective apostasy that had overtaken the country, and wondered—too audibly for comfort—whether this was the effect of the division between Eastern Christendom and the See of Rome. He had briefly thought—fantasized?—about his own vocation as a bridge-builder, drawing East and West together, and as the prophet of a new and transformed ecclesial consciousness. But reality had kept breaking in, both in the shape of domestic sufferings and crises, and in the recognition of the intensity of the suffering of those still in Russia (including his son Fedya and some with whom he was deeply bound in spiritual companionship, Fr. Pavel Florensky above all). The journal represents something of the costly process of finding a new center of gravity in the daily duties of the priesthood and in the daily remembrance of mortality that went with this.

Bulgakov had not initially thought of himself as primarily a pastor; but circumstances made him one. The experience of accompanying people on their deathbeds, including friends and colleagues, comes sharply into focus in these pages as a central aspect of his priestly ministry—or, better, his priestly *identity*. He finds himself repeatedly standing with men and women in the moment when the door opens into the new depth of reality and the new immediacy of love that is the gift of death. His priesthood is crucially, in that moment, a simple bearing witness; his task is to accompany, and to testify to the Christian community what death actually is. The journal returns several times to this centrality of death in his thinking and praying; and it is the very opposite of morbid negativity. Only in loving action in the present moment, the doing of what is there to be done for the sake of God's Kingdom, however apparently routine or humble, do we truly align ourselves with God's loving will. And that is a kind of death for our self-dramatizing fancies, our dreams of perfection and success. We must learn simply to give ourselves into the moment, recognizing that divine love surrounds us and enables us, in failure and in success, in death and in life. If we really know how to live in faith, we know how to die; if we understand the promise of death, we know how to live. This is the Gethsemane we must inhabit, both unutterably costly (Bulgakov never forgets that his friends in Russia literally confront the daily prospect of suffering and death at the hands of the regime) and the one place where peace is to be found.

These reflections do not give much by way of direct reference to the intellectual patterns that Bulgakov was developing and maturing in his theology. But it would certainly be fair to say that anyone trying to understand where the heart of his "sophiological" speculations is located would learn a great deal from the way he writes here about this sacrificial embrace of the given moment. His sweeping cosmic vision of Holy Wisdom uniting God and creation is not—as superficial readers imagined and still imagine—some bland tidying-up of the world's complexity, unpredictability, and agony. Quite the contrary: if we find the grace to act here and now in love, whatever the darkness of the surroundings and the total obscurity of the outcome, we affirm simply that we live in a world where the divine gift or presence depends on nothing but itself, and works unceasingly in the depths of reality. Holy Wisdom, divine Sophia, is, as Bulgakov often indicates in his longer works, a "kenotic" action, the self-outpouring of divine life into the otherness and contingency of the created world, holding nothing back in its commitment to live and work and heal "anonymously" within the universe—but also urging us forward, as humans who are charged with the dignity of transformative labor and the making of meaning, to bring Wisdom to light in words and acts, supremely in the work that is liturgical worship.

What surrounds us is love. "Sophiology" is nothing if it is not a way of declaring this conviction, and Bulgakov's meditations make this plain. And one aspect of the love that surrounds us which will probably strike a Western reader as unfamiliar is Bulgakov's thinking about guardian angels. It mattered intensely to him to have a particularly intimate spiritual friend (Florensky in his earlier years, Sister Joanna later on); and his language about his guardian angel suggests that he saw these human friendships as a kind of near-sacramental image of the fact that God has given each of us a non-human companion, a witness who stands in the nearer presence of God, whose love for us is exactly what we most long for in a human friend—selfless generosity, fidelity, truthfulness. God's own selfless, faithful, truthful love is always mediated to us in the unique and personal forms of relationship within the created world. And if it is true that we are never left without that love, even in circumstances of extreme human abandonment, must we not suppose that God gives us an unseen and in most respects unimaginable "friend" to assure us that our struggles and pains do not go unwitnessed? This is not the child's "imaginary friend," an invented playmate, but a wholly mysterious anchorage for our own unique personal history in the loving witness of an invisible other within the community of all created beings.

Meanwhile, the priest's task too is to offer that "anchorage" of loving witness for all with whom he ministers. Bulgakov's exploration of this calling is not the least important element of these pages. The journal will amply confirm the judgment of those who have testified to the way Bulgakov lived out his priestly vocation. But it will also help Bulgakov's readers see a bit more clearly (as the prefatory essay on the theological hinterland of the journal makes plain) how his picture of the sophianic cosmos was grounded in his own prayer and self-examination, and in the episodes of visionary clarity recorded here. For all its brevity, this is a genuinely significant text for understanding one of the greatest Christian minds of the twentieth century. It is a real gift to have it available in an excellent translation and with such illuminating essays on its biographical and intellectual context.

Bishop Rowan Williams
Cardiff, Pentecost 2022

TRANSLATORS' PREFACE

WE HOPE THAT THIS INTIMATE volume of spiritual reflections contains something for multiple audiences. Those looking for a deeper explication of its context and themes may consult our scholarly introductions on the historical and biographical, as well as theological, aspects of this work. Those who wish simply to skip ahead to the *Spiritual Diary* and Sr. Joanna Reitlinger's memoirs of Bulgakov may do so without any loss in understanding, for we have provided through the main text's endnotes all the information that is immediately necessary for comprehension.

THE TEXT

Bulgakov's *Spiritual Diary* (*Dnevnik Dukhovnoi*) was one of the several diaries Bulgakov kept during the years following his ordination to the priesthood in 1918.[1] It was never published in his lifetime.[2] Not until 1998 did the *Diary* see the light of day, in a single volume, in Bulgakov's homeland of Russia.[3] Before this publication, however, the full text of the *Diary* appeared in France, in 1996–1997, in the pages of *The Herald* (*Le Messager; Vestnik*), the journal of the Russian Christian Student Movement.[4] The latter version has served as the base text for our volume. Ours is the third translation of the *Diary* into a foreign language, coming after a Czech translation in 2009[5] and a Polish version in 2014.[6]

The Russian text of the diary printed in *The Herald* is a copy of the original made by Mother Blandina, the beloved spiritual daughter of Fr. Bulgakov.[7] We have been unable to locate Mother Blandina's transcription of the *Diary*: neither *The Herald* publication nor the 2003 Moscow printing of the *Diary* explain how they accessed Mother Blandina's transcript. Nor have we been able to ascertain whether the original diary notebook can be found in the Bulgakov archives at St. Serge Orthodox Theological Institute. The need for the digitization of this archive is felt acutely today by scholars of Bulgakov the world over.

The ordering of the *Diary* in *The Herald* publication presents some confusion to the reader, as the entries do not appear in chronological order over the three issues in which they were published. In our translation we have set the entries in their proper sequence, though of the two entries for *10/23.I.1925*, we cannot discern which was written first. The *Diary*, furthermore, appears to be incomplete: the editors of *The Herald* relate that a 1928 inset to the diary is now missing.

The concluding section of this volume contains the memoirs of Sr. Joanna Reitlinger. For our translation we used the Russian text published by *The Herald* in 1990, roughly two years after Sr. Joanna's death.[8] We are grateful to the editors of *The Herald* for granting us the permissions for these memoirs. The *Spiritual Diary* is in the public domain, as is every work written by Bulgakov.

TRANSLATION PHILOSOPHY

One of the challenges of translating Bulgakov's academic, theological works is to capture his sometimes dramatic shifts in tone from the analytical and argumentative to the poetic and rhapsodic. Due to its uniqueness in Bulgakov's oeuvre as a diary of spiritual reflections, the *Spiritual Diary* confronted us with a new challenge: to find a *third* voice which is neither analytical nor poetic, but rather devotional. In order to convey his unique voice in this text, we strive to keep the structure of Bulgakov's syntax as close to the Russian as English will allow, and to retain the length of his sentences. Whereas translators of Bulgakov sometimes break up his sentences for the sake of clarifying his complex theological ideas, here we prioritize tone and feeling. We also follow the older English convention of using the word "man" to translate the Russian *chelovek*, and the singular male pronoun in references to the human person. While we recognize the problems this poses in contemporary English, this rendering more accurately captures Bulgakov's own style and thinking in his early-twentieth-century context.

Bulgakov liberally and fluidly quotes the Bible in the *Spiritual Diary*, using different registers of language. When he lifts a direct quotation from the Bible in Church Slavonic (the translation used in Russian Orthodox liturgy) we use the King James Version to translate it, unless indicated otherwise. More often than not, however, Bulgakov simply references the Bible using a combination of the Russian Synodal Translation approved by the Russian Orthodox Church in 1876, and his own antiquarian, "Slavonicizing" phraseology, a telltale sign that he is quoting from memory. We have tried to capture this by translating directly from Bulgakov's text, using, for example, "You" and "Thou" to indicate changes in register from the more familiar to the more reverential. Finally, Bulgakov often draws from biblical verses or stories while adhering to the biblical text only loosely; we have hunted down these intertexts and left a trail of references for the reader in our parenthetical notes within the text of the *Diary*. Additionally, all endnotes are ours. They are intended to illuminate the text for readers unfamiliar with Bulgakov's historical context, with his broader theological vision and that of Orthodox Christianity and liturgy, and with the episodes of church history and the lives of the saints that he discusses. The native language of Bulgakov's heart was Scripture and liturgy; we trust our notes make this apparent.

We have preserved Bulgakov's convention for marking the date of each diary entry. Each entry has two dates: the first from the Julian Calendar, which to this day is still the official calendar of the Russian Orthodox Church, and the second from the Gregorian (civil) Calendar, which is thirteen days ahead of the ecclesiastical calendar. Thus, for example, the first entry 8/21.III.1924 means March 8 according to the Russian ecclesiastical calendar, and March 21 according to the civil calendar. Lastly, to communicate where there are lacunae in the text, we have used the following symbol: <...>.

BULGAKOV THE MAN, BULGAKOV THE PRIEST

Beyond the scholarly contribution this volume represents, we offer the *Diary* and Sr. Joanna's memoirs as a gift to our fellow Christians. For Orthodox Christians, this volume represents a look into the soul of a teacher whose theological writings make up a rich part of their modern spiritual patrimony. We hope that when readers meet Bulgakov in the intimate pages of his diary, the pastor's heart which produced the extraordinary speculative vision of sophiology will gain a renewed and sympathetic hearing, especially as sophiology has once again become a focus of theological interest and debate in the academy. For in these pages readers will find Bulgakov forging his sophiological synthesis in the furnace of life's trials, both intimate and personal as well as epochal and world-historical. We hope that reading Bulgakov's *Spiritual Diary* will mediate an encounter with a priest whose pastoral presence so impacted many of the shining lights of twentieth-century Orthodox Christianity in the West.[9]

But Bulgakov belongs to Christians of other traditions too. At its heart, the *Diary* reveals a Christian soul laying itself bare to God's creative and re-creative work in the midst of the drama of world and personal history. Therefore, we believe that every Christian, and indeed every person, regardless of religious identity, may be able to draw something of value from this *Diary*. As Bulgakov himself writes in this text, "we would not know that we ourselves, each of us, harbors this possibility—to be simply a human being, a son of God, living among our fellow man—if we always remained surrounded by those of our own tribe" (*22.V/4.VI.1925*).

Because our goal with this volume is to present Bulgakov the man, the Christian, and the priest, we thought it right to conclude the book with a portion of the memoirs of Sister Joanna Reitlinger, Bulgakov's spiritual daughter and collaborator. These memoirs from 1945–1946—just a few years after Fr. Bulgakov's death—relate her recollections of him as a mentor and spiritual father. In them the reader will discover, among other stories, Sr. Joanna's first encounter with Bulgakov, details concerning his relationship to his academic work, his practice of hospitality and care for his friends and associates, his usual catchphrases, and his thoughts on the pursuit of holiness. These anecdotes fill in the picture of Bulgakov we gather from reading his *Spiritual Diary* and his other, deeply learned, though also passionately devout, theological works. Yet our inclusion of Sr. Joanna's reflections in the volume should not, however, be taken as a sort of hagiographical exercise—something that Fr. Sergius himself would not have endorsed. Indeed, we find that his spiritual authority is displayed best precisely in his self-dispossession: "Fr. S. warned against looking too intently for a 'teacher,' against ascribing him too much meaning: 'for one is your Teacher—Jesus Christ,' in the words of the apostle [*sic*]."[10]

BULGAKOV AS SPIRITUAL FATHER: MOTHER BLANDINA AND SR. JOANNA

A word should be said concerning Mother Blandina and Sr. Joanna, because of whom we possess these testimonies of Fr. Sergius. Bulgakov knew Mother Blandina already in Simferopol, during his internal exile in Crimea (1918–1922) and before their common exile to Europe.[11] Yet this was long before Mother Blandina had taken her monastic vows, when she was still Aleksandra (Asya) Obolenskaya, a young woman in her twenties who spent her time with Yuliya Reitlinger, the future Sister Joanna—another woman whose life would be radically changed by meeting Bulgakov. Mother Blandina's relationship with Bulgakov continued in exile, where she was an original member of the Russian Christian Student Movement in Belgrade; in fact, she was one of the students who in 1923 gifted Bulgakov the notebook that became the *Spiritual Diary*. For the rest of Bulgakov's life they maintained a lively and heartfelt correspondence.[12] In Bulgakov's final days, Mother Blandina (together with Sr. Joanna) cared for Bulgakov after he suffered a stroke, and she was a witness of Bulgakov's "transfiguration" and Taboric illumination before his death.[13] It is quite fitting, then, that Mother Blandina would be the one to transcribe the notebook that she gave to Bulgakov in her student days, though the date in which she undertook this task is unknown to us.

Yuliya (later Sr. Joanna) Reitlinger (1898–1988), born in St. Petersburg, also met Bulgakov in Crimea during his years of internal exile there. Their acquaintance in Crimea sparked a life-long relationship. She, too, moved to Prague and lived there from 1922 to 1925, studying iconography at the Academy of Fine Art. Together with the Bulgakov family, she moved to Paris in 1925, and made monastic vows in 1935, taking the name Joanna, in the chapel of St. Sergius Theological Institute where Bulgakov was dean.[14] The two friends served as mutual inspirations for one another throughout their relationship, which is evident in their frequent correspondence. For more, see the biographical introduction.[15]

It is our hope that readers will go on to learn more about these women and how they creatively carried forward Bulgakov's legacy in their own way, in their own time.

ACKNOWLEDGEMENTS

WE WOULD LIKE TO EXPRESS OUR GRATITUDE to friends and colleagues whose contribution to this volume proved invaluable.

Dr. Yury P. Avvakumov and Dr. Claire Roosien provided several insights into thorny passages in this volume, and our translation is far richer because of it. We the translators hold sole responsibility for any mistakes or inaccuracies in our text that may remain.

Thanks belong as well to Dr. Regula M. Zwahlen, whose labyrinthine knowledge of Bulgakov and Bulgakov studies, as well as her generosity in supplying digital versions of difficult to find texts, have enriched this volume in sundry ways.

As the Right Rev. Dr. Rowan Williams was among the first to begin the work of bringing Bulgakov's thought to the attention of the Anglophone theological world, we cannot imagine a better person to introduce this volume. We are overjoyed and deeply grateful for his collaboration with us in this work.

John Riess, our editor at Angelico Press, deserves much gratitude for his enthusiasm for this project and for his patience with us in the process of completion. Angelico is a beacon for important, new theology, and we are so pleased to be publishing with this press.

Mark Roosien
Roberto J. De La Noval

THANKS GO FIRST TO MY DEAR FRIEND AND collaborator, Mark Roosien. It has been a genuine pleasure to work on this volume together and to draw from your deep well of learning in the process. May we enjoy many more years of friendship and fruitful labor!

I am eager to express my gratitude to my mentor and friend, Yury Avvakumov, for helping me develop my Russian skills over the years. His erudition, together with his life of personal integrity and Christian witness, makes clear to me what it means to have a scholarly vocation.

Claire Roosien offered her expertise in the Russian language, as well as her hospitality as Mark and I worked late into the night in their home. Thank you!

For reading this text through, and many others of mine besides, I wish to thank Sonya Cronin. With friends like you, life is more fantastical.

Sofia Ruiz-Castañeda has been a faithful companion throughout much of this project, and for that I am deeply grateful. Her faith is Bulgakov's, and my life is so much richer for it. Thank you.

Finally, I am grateful to my mother, Maria, who has given me, and continues to give, so much. The "love of Love" that Bulgakov holds up in this text is her native disposition. For that reason, I dedicate this book to her.

Roberto J. De La Noval

FIRST, I WANT TO THANK MY GREAT FRIEND and co-translator, Roberto. I was only vaguely aware of this text's existence when Rob asked if I would consider translating it with him. It didn't take too much convincing once I read the first few entries. Working with such a careful translator and lover of language as he has opened my eyes to the joys of collaborative work. Chief among those joys is the friendship we have shared.

I want to thank Dr. Robert Porwoll for reading a draft of the translation and my biographical introduction, and for his insightful comments.

Special thanks go out to Claire, for her unending love and support.

Much of this work took place during the evening hours, which occasionally deprived my daughter Iva of bedtime snuggles and conversation. By way of apology and as a token of my love, I dedicate this translation to her.

Mark Roosien

BIOGRAPHICAL INTRODUCTION

BECOMING FATHER SERGIUS:
Bulgakov Between Russia and Paris

Mark Roosien

FR. SERGIUS BULGAKOV HAS JUSTLY acquired a reputation as one of the greatest religious thinkers of the twentieth century. While his theological writing has garnered a wide readership in the Western world over the past few decades, the man himself, his charismatic personality, and his prophetic yearnings, are still relatively unknown and little discussed. The present volume, Bulgakov's *Spiritual Diary*, written in Prague from 1924 to 1925, offers a profoundly personal glimpse into the heart of this pastor and theologian in his formative, early years as a priest. It reveals how his ideas, which some have criticized as excessively abstract, concretely shaped his life and personal spiritual journey.[1]

Born into a priest's family in Russia in 1871, Bulgakov left his family's Eastern Orthodox Christian faith as a teenager and became a well-known Marxist economist and professor before the age of thirty. However, beginning around the year 1900, Bulgakov experienced a series of intellectual and spiritual conversions, eventually returning to the faith of his ancestors.[2] He was ordained as a priest in the Russian Orthodox Church in 1918 at one of the most tumultuous moments of Russian history: the Bolshevik Revolution. Due to his opposition to Bolshevism, he was expelled from Russia in 1922 along with many other intellectuals and clergy. After three years of transitory living in Constantinople, then in Prague, he and his family settled in Paris in 1925, where he led the St. Sergius Orthodox Theological Institute as its first dean. He would remain in Paris until his death in 1944. It was there that he wrote most of the theological works for which he is best known.

Commentators on Bulgakov's life and thought often pass over in silence the years between his exile from Russia in 1922 and his arrival in Paris in summer 1925. Yet these years were absolutely crucial to his development both as a theologian and as a priest. This period of uncertainty, upheaval, and deep inner struggle was the crucible in which was forged not only Bulgakov the thinker, but also Bulgakov the pastor and prophet.

Bulgakov's *Spiritual Diary* is a record of the inner life of a man finding his place in history: not just local history or even ecclesiastical history, but world history. With the recent rise in translations of Bulgakov's theological works into English and other European languages, Western readers are beginning to see just how important a thinker he was. But Bulgakov was not merely a great thinker; he was also a "great man" in the classic sense—unfashionable today—in which William James used the term: one who "brings about a rearrangement, on a large or a small scale, of the pre-existing social relations."[3] Such a description of Bulgakov is justified because he, more than any other figure in modern times, ushered in the first genuine encounter between the Eastern and Western Churches since the Middle Ages. And he knew it.[4] Yet even beyond his unique role in history as an apostle of the East to the West, Bulgakov was a "great man" because he was a "good shepherd": a shepherd of souls and a steward of the mystery of Christ entrusted to him as a priest of the Church.

Above all, it is this pastoral side of Bulgakov, which has not often been seen by the wider world, that the *Spiritual Diary* unveils. If Bulgakov's theological treatises represent the "outside" of his concept of God in the world, then the *Spiritual Diary* represents the "inside." For this reason, the present volume is supremely important for anyone who wants to understand Bulgakov and his work. He did keep other diaries, primarily in the years immediately before and during the time that he was writing the *Spiritual Diary*. In those diaries, Bulgakov recorded the events of each day, the trials of family and professional life in emigration, and occasionally jotted down theological ideas. Those diaries are invaluable for understanding Bulgakov's early years as a priest-theologian and for contextualizing the *Spiritual Diary*.[5] Accordingly, I draw on them extensively in this introduction. But among all of Bulgakov's writings, including those daily journals, it is the *Spiritual Diary* that provides the most vivid glimpse of the luminous, though sometimes shadowy and disturbing, depths of his heart. It was also a one-time endeavor. Never again did he write a spiritual diary of this kind after 1925.

To appreciate the *Spiritual Diary* in all its significance, it is necessary to understand the circumstances of Bulgakov's life between his ordination to the priesthood in 1918 and his eventual relocation to Paris to assume deanship of the St. Sergius Orthodox Theological Institute in the summer of 1925.[6] These years of exile, dislocation and relocation, as well as physical and mental illness, took a toll on Bulgakov and his family and friends. His struggles took place, of course, within the broader context of upheaval in Russia and throughout the world: war, revolution, rapid modernization both capitalist and communist, the rise of far-right political movements—the list goes on. Amidst the conflicts and struggles that swirled around Bulgakov, the *Spiritual Diary* is an island of introspection, an attempt to make solid, spiritual meaning from the "Heraclitean fire" around him and, indeed, inside him.

REVOLUTION AND PAPISM: BULGAKOV AFTER ORDINATION

Bulgakov had a keen awareness that his life and work would have a formative influence on the encounter between the Christian East and West, although his conception of that influence changed over time. From around 1900, he was among the leaders of the spiritual wing of the Russian *intelligentsia*, the intellectual vanguard of the Russian Empire. It was comprised of poets, professors, scientists, philosophers, as well as theologians.[7] Bulgakov's ordination to the priesthood in 1918, along with that of his friend and mentor Fr. Pavel Florensky seven years earlier in 1911, was seen, by others and by Bulgakov himself, as the coming-of-age of the *intelligentsia*, its "enchurchment." As Bulgakov reflected six years after his ordination, "When I was ordained, I had, by the way, the sense that, in me, a new page in the history of the *intelligentsia* was turning over, that in me it was consecrated and enchurched. At that time, perhaps, it was still a proud and vain feeling, but now, having gone through abjection, it remains essentially the same. It was not only a facet of my life, but that of Russia's."[8]

At the time of his ordination, Bulgakov saw his ministry as a "sacerdotal" one as opposed to a "pastoral" one. He wrote to

Florensky later that he had imagined his role to be that of a *zhrets*—a priest who offers sacrifice—not a *pastyr'*, a shepherd of souls.[9] As a "priest" in this sense, Bulgakov saw it as his chief duty to offer the eucharistic sacrifice of the Body and Blood of Christ in the liturgy.

Bulgakov also saw his mission as a prophetic one. In August–September 1922, he wrote to Florensky and recalled how, together, they had planned to usher in a new historical era for Orthodox Christianity: "We knew that now the *axis* of Orthodoxy and global history was passing through us, and we felt ourselves called and sent to do the work of Orthodoxy. This was not a personal prophetic calling from God like the prophets had... our goal was not to found just another theological school which would be a little better than our existing theological academies. Our goal was rather to initiate a *new epoch of religious consciousness*."[10] If this seems grandiose, that is because it is. But one has to keep in mind that the first two decades of the twentieth century were heady days for the Russian Orthodox Church. The Church was preparing for a council that promised vast changes and reforms—though many of these reforms were thwarted by the Russian Revolution.[11] Bulgakov, Florensky, and other members of the *intelligentsia* saw on the horizon an open, free, and intellectually serious church for the modern age. The school that Bulgakov hoped to create with Florensky was to be "no mere school; it was a *new* consciousness, a new Church, which is also at the same time the old Church in its genuine essence."[12] Such were his ambitions immediately following his ordination in 1918, though they did not remain so forever.

The dream of a "new religious consciousness" in Orthodoxy did not come to fruition—at least not then. Whatever plans Bulgakov and Florensky had for a new Russian theological academy were dashed by the Revolution and the Bolshevik rise to power. Unable to remain in Moscow, Bulgakov moved his family to the city of Simferopol in Crimea in 1918, where he taught political economy and theology at the local university. However, with the Bolshevik capture of the city in 1920, he was forced to move further south, eventually settling in the Crimean coastal town of Yalta, on the Black Sea. There he assumed pastorship of an Orthodox parish.

The seeming compromise of the Russian Orthodox Church with the atheistic Bolshevik regime broke Bulgakov's spirit. Orthodoxy, especially Russian Orthodoxy, he complained to Florensky, was "weak" and "flabby." He concluded that the Russian Church was unable to cope with, let alone resist, the pressures of modernity. According to the diagnosis he laid out in a long letter to his mentor, the problems with Russian Orthodoxy stretched all the way back to its very inception. By the time Kievan Rus' received Christianity from the Byzantines in the tenth century, the Byzantine Greek tradition had already been seriously weakened from centuries of separation from the Latin-speaking world. For its part, Slavic Orthodoxy never established true contact with the West and so suffered intellectual and spiritual impoverishment. That was why it was floundering before the challenge of modernity, which had emerged from Western principles and ideas that the Russian Orthodox Church never fully encountered and had not equipped itself to take up or resist. He wrote to Florensky that the Russian Church was fragile; its clergy, spineless; its spirit, parochial: "This sorry outer condition is only a disclosure of the nature of our ecclesiality engendered by 'Greco-Russianism,' that is, national particularism instead of catholic supra-nationalism.... Our clergy are *spineless* and to that degree also impotent, not in the sense of personal weakness of character but rather of the fragility of their church."[13]

For Bulgakov, Orthodox ecclesiology, with its parochialism and nationalism, had exhausted itself in history. The Russian Church's collapse under Bolshevism confirmed it. But more importantly for him at this time, it was also a *theological* dead end. Orthodox ecclesiology, Bulgakov came to believe while in Yalta in 1921–1922, was terminally ill. The church's entire ecclesial life, its culture, and even its theology, was sick. Boldly, Bulgakov declared that the reason for this was that the Orthodox Church was schismatic:

> For I know all the positive qualities of the Russian Orthodox priesthood that many on the outside cannot see, and I consider myself personally blessed to find myself in its ranks. And yet the "Greco-Russian" Church is nonetheless in *paralysis*. Now, I absolutely don't mean that "paralysis" which our church liberals, along with Dostoevsky, used to speak about. Instead, I mean an internal, purely logical paralysis: flabby muscular tissue caused by weakness of the heart muscle, a rupture from the center of unity in the Church, a schism.[14]

While in Yalta, Bulgakov penned a scathing critique of Orthodox ecclesiology, canon law, and ecclesial culture in a book titled *At the Walls of Chersonesus*, which remained unpublished in his lifetime.[15] His proposed solution to the problem of Orthodox ecclesiology was reunion with the Roman papacy. By reunion, Bulgakov did not mean that the Orthodox should simply convert to Roman Catholicism. Rather, he advocated for a mutual partnership of the Christian West and East in which each would retain their native particularities yet unite under the Pope of Rome.[16] His vision was not unlike that of Pope John Paul II decades later, who would describe reunion between the Christian East and West as the Church breathing with its "two lungs."[17] For Bulgakov, Orthodoxy needed to unite with its separated brethren in the West and come under the headship of the Roman pontiff in order to revive itself and indeed, remain true to itself.

What is important about this stage in Bulgakov's intellectual journey for the purposes of the present introduction is the role he conceived for *himself* in the enormous task of reuniting the Eastern Orthodox and Roman Catholic Churches. Quite simply, he saw himself as a primary catalyst for the world-historical event of church reunion. He wrote in Yalta in September 1922, "Thanks be to the Lord, for He has given me His light and revealed His will—here in this year my eyes were opened, and there was accomplished in me my revolution and union with Rome which, if only I stay the course, will constitute for me a vocation and ministry for the remaining years of my life."[18] Through his prophetic leadership, the Christian East and Christian West would finally unite and complete one another. Only together could they form a spiritual bulwark strong enough to withstand the stormy sea of modernity in both its communist and capitalist degradations.

In the long and agonizing letter to Florensky already referenced, he explained the position that he would outline in greater detail in *At the Walls of Chersonesus*. He spoke of himself as unavoidably drawn to papism not only as a result of his intellectual investigations, but also because of his own personal calling from God. This calling replaced the calling he and Florensky had earlier imagined for themselves, to revive the Orthodox Church's self-consciousness through enchurching the *intelligentsia*. Reprising the sense of prophetic mission he shared with Florensky when they were together in Moscow, he wrote, strikingly, "Today I feel far more *personally* called than I did then."[19]

BULGAKOV AND FLORENSKY

In view of Bulgakov's shifting sense of his role in history away from the vision he had previously shared with Florensky, it is useful to address directly his relationship with his one-time mentor. It is only a slight exaggeration to say that for many years Bulgakov venerated him as a saint, during Florensky's lifetime. Florensky was a genius, not only equipped with the God-given abilities of a Da Vinci-esque polymath, but was also extraordinarily well read, original in thought in both scientific and humanistic spheres (in addition to writing important works of philosophy and theology, Florensky had dozens of scientific patents to his name), and a pious Orthodox Christian and priest.[20] Bulgakov described Florensky in his Yalta diary in June 1922 thus: "He, of course, is one of a kind; he is a miracle of human thought and genius—he himself knows this about himself, and this, liberating him from every trifling and earthly thing, gives him the power and consciousness of superhuman freedom. He is in fact the Übermensch, but at the same time he is a Christian—a saint."[21] Florensky was everything to Bulgakov, everything he wished he could be. One can see Bulgakov's desire to imitate Florensky in his 1917 book *Unfading Light*, a theological work that was written in a mellifluous style typical of the Russian Silver Age, but was not as experimental and daring as the theological writing of Florensky.[22] Though an important book in its day, it did not reach the literary and philosophical heights of Florensky's celebrated and controversial 1914 book, *The Pillar and Ground of the Truth*, an undisputed milestone in Russian religious thought.[23]

Bulgakov's sharp turn towards the papacy cut strongly against the grain of Florensky's views on ecclesiology. He undoubtedly surprised Florensky in the letter outlining his commitment to the Pope of Rome. In sending the letter, Bulgakov hoped against hope for Florensky's approval—or at least his authentic engagement with Bulgakov's ideas.

But he never received a reply from Florensky, who had remained in Moscow and all but disappeared from his life and from the world outside Russia, after the Revolution. The lack of reply from

Florensky devastated Bulgakov. He valued Florensky as his true "Friend," capitalizing Friend in references to Florensky in his writings during that time. Such was his "slavish" (his words[24]) devotion to his priest-Friend.[25] Later, as we will see, the rank of Friend would be assumed by another: Yuliya Reitlinger.

ROME AND NEW ROME

Without Florensky's acknowledgment, let alone approval, Bulgakov set off to carry out his prophetic, world-historical task of church reunion. He wrote about it (privately) and even commemorated the Pope of Rome in the Divine Liturgy (secretly). He occasionally met with Orthodox churchmen and theologians to gauge their support for his ideas, but rarely found a sympathetic ear. Nevertheless, throughout his time in Yalta from 1921 to 1922, he remained convinced that his prophetic mission was to facilitate the reunion of the Roman Catholic and Eastern Orthodox Churches, despite difficult odds and trying historical circumstances. He wrote in April 1922, "Onto my shoulders, weak and feeble as they are, has fallen such a back-breaking and unbearable load: how to make the work of my remaining days the question of the division of the Churches—a question hopeless from a [merely] human perspective. For here I must simply resign myself unto the grave, perhaps fruitlessly."[26] Despite the historical and intellectual crisis that precipitated his sense of mission at that time, Bulgakov's days in Yalta would turn out to be the calmest of the early 1920s.

With the Bolshevik advance to the city, Bulgakov was exiled from Yalta in December 1922. He relocated, along with most of his immediate family, to Istanbul/Constantinople. It was a painful and undesired move, and one that entailed much uncertainty. The Bulgakovs remained there for a few months in a transient state. Bulgakov wrote copiously in his diary during this time. (He was still a year and a half away from starting the *Spiritual Diary*.) Although it was a difficult period of transition, he was energized by the prospect of meeting both Greek Orthodox Christians and Roman Catholics to discuss his ideas on church reunion and to find partners in his efforts. New faces might, at the very least, provide a welcome relief from his familiar Russian Orthodox circles in which even the most "enlightened" were stubbornly hostile to the papacy and ideas of reunion with Catholicism.

However, what he found in Constantinople dashed his hopes. He admittedly did not expect much from the Greek Orthodox, whose clergy he regarded as too ignorant and obstinate to understand his sophisticated ideas. And indeed, it turned out that the Greeks were not at all amenable to his ideas on church reunion. They did not see it as a pressing task. Bulgakov came to despise his Greek co-religionists (it seems the feeling was mutual). Attending their liturgies and observing their way of life, Bulgakov doubted whether Greeks and Russians even shared the same religion. "This is not just manners," he wrote in January 1923, a few weeks after his arrival in Constantinople, "this is a different faith, this liturgical heresy.... Indeed, if, as they say, the spirit of Orthodoxy is in the liturgy, that precisely this spirit unites us and distinguishes us from the heterodox, then where is the unity of spirit, prayer, sacraments that unites us with the Greeks? I repeat, this is a different faith, this national rite of the Greeks."[27] Greek Orthodox liturgical practice in Constantinople differed significantly from the strict and stately Russian practice. For Bulgakov, this difference was not merely one of style, but of religion. Because of the great importance that Orthodox Christians place on standardized worship for expressing church unity, the "aberrations" of Greek Orthodox liturgy suggested to Bulgakov that there were deeper discrepancies between the national churches of world Orthodoxy. This misgiving further detached from him a sense of belonging to a universal, catholic church.

Finding little in common with the Greeks in Constantinople, he sought intellectual camaraderie with local Roman Catholics. Here, too, however, Bulgakov found only disappointment. Even the most intellectually skilled and ecumenically minded Catholics did not understand or sympathize with his perspective. More often than not, they tried to convert him to Catholicism, which greatly annoyed him.[28] What the Catholics he met in Constantinople did not understand was that Bulgakov was not interested in converting to Catholicism; he sought to unite the churches, keeping both intact—under the Pope of Rome.

In Constantinople as in Yalta, Bulgakov found almost no one with whom he saw eye-to-eye, and this isolation distressed him. With no one to share his vision on either side of the Orthodox-Catholic divide, Bulgakov felt completely alone in his ideas. And more importantly, he began to doubt his calling as a prophet of the future united Church. After only a month in Constantinople, he wrote, "Is it not unwise and pointless to strive to unite that which cannot be united? Is it not a different biology, different lungs, like fish and birds, which breathe underwater and in the open air [respectively]?"[29] In March 1923 he took his ideas about church reunion to Archbishop Anastasii (Gribanovsky) of Kishinev and Khotyn', who was the administrator of the Russian Orthodox churches in the Constantinople district. Although he did not agree with Bulgakov, he was a man with whom he could speak freely. The archbishop gave Bulgakov a healthy dose of realism: not only did he himself hold an "absolutely rock-solid position" against the idea, but so did all Russian bishops, clerics and laity, not to mention all the Eastern patriarchs and the entire Slavic part of the church. After this meeting, Bulgakov mused that dreams of church reunion were easier for Vladimir Solovyov, the 19th-century Russian philosopher whose views on church reunion strongly influenced Bulgakov's at this time.[30] Solovyov, after all, was just a layman, without the responsibility of a cleric, and those were different times, before the turmoil of revolution and world war.[31]

Over the course of the next few months, Bulgakov began to think that the prophetic task of church reunion was not his to undertake, at least not at the high level he had imagined. He wrote in March 1923, "Maybe I have gone down a false path altogether.... I keep beating my head against the stone wall and I'm going to perish. But my God, what can I do? Teach me, enlighten me."[32] To add to this sense of uncertainty, Bulgakov became convinced that he only had a few years left of his life to carry out his mission. His health was not good. His prophetic task was quickly becoming, in his mind, a dying task.[33]

Toward the end of his time in Constantinople, Bulgakov began to pull away from Catholicism, little by little. Attending Roman Catholic liturgies, he found them, especially the services of Holy Week, to be lacking, especially in comparison to the grandeur and sobriety of Russian Orthodox worship.[34] In Bright Week, the week following Pascha, he wrote that he had become convinced it was not God's will for him to "make noise" and "demonstrate" for the reunion of churches. Though he still believed in church reunion, now was not the time. After all, he wrote, was not Patriarch Tikhon of Moscow, persecuted by the Bolsheviks back in Russia, "awaiting his Golgotha day after day"? Russia was suffering and all he could think of was the papacy?[35] He felt a deep sense of shame in the fact that he was not participating in the suffering of his fellow countrymen.[36]

BULGAKOV IN PRAGUE: NEW BEGINNINGS

Amidst the gloom of Constantinople, a shaft of light opened onto Bulgakov's life. He received an invitation to move to Prague and take up an appointment as professor of Church Law and Theology at Charles University, teaching classes in Orthodox theology, church history, and canon law. The prospect of teaching the future leaders of the suffering Orthodox Church renewed in him a sense of purpose and personal calling.

Bulgakov and his family took their leave of Constantinople on April 15, 1923 and set off for Prague. As he reflected on his time in Constantinople and his task ahead, he wrote that his views had changed in the four months since arriving at the old East Roman capital. While *en route* to his new home, he wrote, "All that touches on the Catholics and the Vatican here takes on a more complex and concrete light. In any event I have freed myself from the naïveté with which I formerly related to the question, and yet at the same time I feel much firmer on my ecclesial soil. It is only by standing on this soil that I can do something for the Church and the fatherland and can think about the reunion of the churches ... and at the same time I need to confess my own faith firmly."[37] He was finding his footing once again in the soil of the church of his birth, the Eastern Orthodox Church.

In Prague, Bulgakov was a man wholly committed to his students, the same students who gave him the notebook in which he penned the *Spiritual Diary*. His enthusiasm for teaching overshadowed his previous enthusiasm for church reunion. He wrote in May 1923, "What kind, young faces; how in need they are of help, tenderness, love, care. Being face to face with this immense task somehow calms down my 'Catholic' anguish—it is above all them that I need to serve."[38] Things progressed well enough in Prague, and regular contact with other Russian émigrés strengthened his bond with the Russian Church: "Every morning I wake up with depression and thoughts about Russia, about Fedya [his son, who had remained in Russia], about the suffering patriarch [Tikhon] and all the other martyrs that are suffering there, and here we are prospering. I have to somehow suffer with Russia, struggle with her in a spiritual way, at the very least."[39] As his feeling of solidarity with Russia grew, his sense of connection with Roman Catholicism faded: "I'm not the papist I was when I left Russia [that is, Yalta]," he wrote in June 1923.[40]

Even as Bulgakov gradually distanced himself from the dream of reunion with the Roman Catholic Church, he still retained the conviction that his was a world-historical, prophetic mission for the church. But now that it was becoming clear that such a mission was not going to take place in the sphere of church reunion, he wondered what, in fact, his mission was. He wrote in September 1923, "Day after day I read books on Catholicism with one single conclusion: to be free from the self-hypnosis I fell into and am now freeing myself from. But is this the kind of work I can devote the rest of my life to?"[41] While in Prague, he and other Orthodox intellectuals made plans for reviving the Brotherhood of St. Sophia, a dormant organization dedicated to Orthodox thought, that had started in Russia in 1919.[42] Despite this exciting new project, Bulgakov began to feel alone and old, and worried that he was about to die without having carried out his life's great task, whatever that might be.

Although he had resigned himself to Florensky's silence, he still thought about him, that man who was able to accomplish so much more in his life than Bulgakov ever could: "To work and achieve like that? I can't. It's too late, since I have squandered my whole life in error. It's too late to undertake a serious endeavor. And furthermore, I have no one who listens to me, even though I have a sort of audience. I believe that only Yuliya Reitlinger [more on her below] listens and hears me internally—others, I don't know. She, truly, is benefitting from this hearing, thanks to the richness and depth of her own nature."[43] He was putting away his former sense of calling, but where was he going? In December 1923 he wrote a particularly heart-wrenching entry expressing his deep sense of uncertainty: "Everything is hazy in my soul, and I can't even understand myself anymore. The main thing is that I then had the conviction that God had sent me. And, it turned out, that was a delusion, which I did not know how to discern. Or, perhaps the last word has not been spoken! It feels so heavy, and difficult, difficult, difficult!"[44]

DE PROFUNDIS

Bulgakov's situation grew worse when a new tragedy struck: his wife Elena Ivanovna contracted an illness of the gallbladder, which confined her to the hospital for weeks.[45] Her serious and protracted illness had a profound effect on Fr. Sergius. His diary entries from this time (in his daily journals, not the *Spiritual Diary*, which he would not begin for a few months) betray the thoughts of a man utterly unmoored and humiliated that he had just recently imagined some great, world-historical task for himself. He wrote on New Year's Day, 1924, "A year ago I was languishing from my Catholicism and my fight with it from the Orthodox perspective; now this [Elena's illness]! My future is closed off with an impenetrable veil, I can't see anything. But I've already stopped asking. I have come to a halt and quieted down, I've stopped tormenting myself, but once again I am unable to find myself."[46] He constantly accused himself of being at fault for her illness. He wrote on January 3, 1924, "The Lord is angry with me for my sins and is punishing me through the illness of Nelichka [Elena]."[47] He connected his wife's illness with his own perceived sins against God and against the church in straying into papism. He felt a tremendous sense of guilt for her sufferings, and spent many days and nights in anguish by her side.

As Elena's health declined, Fr. Sergius became convinced that she was going to die. One of the most agonizing passages in his diary was written on the evening of January 13, 1924: "The pus from the wound stinks like a corpse (and I had the tactlessness and flippancy to say this to her). The night was horrible, and so was the morning. Mentally, I have already buried her."[48] This was perhaps the lowest point in Bulgakov's life. He was intellectually alone and adrift, having abandoned his former ambitions as delusions of grandeur. Now his beloved wife, too, was dying, leaving this wreck of a man to pick up the pieces and guide his children, traumatized as they were through years of uprooting and exile.[49]

BULGAKOV THE PASTOR

But Elena did not die. Against all odds, she recovered, and though she did not return to full strength she would live out the rest of her life with her husband. Her recovery pulled Bulgakov out from the depths of despair. He could once again envision a future. It was then, I believe, that Bulgakov fully realized the meaning of an intuition that he had expressed to Florensky in his long letter from 1922. He had stated then that he knew that his calling was not merely to be a *zhrets*—a priest in the sacerdotal sense—though he conceived of it that way at the time of his ordination. He knew that his calling was to be a *pastor*:

> You might remember our conversation before I became a priest, when we discussed my ordination and I said that I aspired to celebrate the mysteries: "I want to be a priest who offers sacrifice [*byt' zhretsom*], not be a pastor." Elena, however, kept objecting to this understanding of priestly ministry. At that time, I, together with you, considered her view completely wrongheaded, but today I think that she was right. An Orthodox priest is not only one who offers sacrifice, but also a pastor, a shepherd.[50]

The seeds of Bulgakov's realization of his pastoral calling were already planted in 1922, and they sprouted occasionally during his time in Constantinople as well. He wrote in February 1923 after disappointing discussions about church reunion: "Will I be saved through prophesying [about the reunion of the churches]? I cannot and should not. For me prophesying is but one element [of a greater life], but prophesying by itself is a dilettantism of life, bankruptcy. I need to find myself in history, realize myself in my priesthood. And I am banging my head against a wall. God, help me, a sinner, reveal to me my path!"[51] And again, four months later, in Prague, he wrote, "The most precious thing to me is the priesthood."[52]

Even though Bulgakov had written these words before, it was only now, in the wake of his wife's illness, that he fully came to terms with the idea that his role in the church was to be a pastor, and not some self-appointed prophet. He recollected fondly his simple pastorate in Yalta as one of the happiest times in his life: "A year ago on this day I said goodbye to my dear parishioners in Yalta. I don't remember if that was in heaven or on earth: the dark church, full of people, quietly crying... I made a terrible effort not to cry or go into hysterics... I spoke about the joy of pastoral service, which is higher and holier than anything else I know."[53] He was ready to dismiss his "prophetic" sense of calling as a delusion, and one for which he was embarrassed. He wrote in late January 1924: "I feel embarrassed, after all that I built has turned out to be an illusion, or more to the point, a delusion. I need to humble myself to the last, but I know not how, and all the while seize up in some kind of powerlessness... The only thing that saves is the unspeakable mercy of God—the priesthood; at the altar of God everything petty and personal burns away—thanks be to the Lord!"[54]

Bulgakov knew that the time had come to fully commit to his pastoral calling and make it his own. Now was the time to live into this calling.[55] A sense of joy and peace is palpable throughout his diaries after this acceptance, especially after Elena's recovery. Contrasted with the utter despair of the entries in his daily diary during his wife's illness, the following passage from early June 1924 shows the lightness and freedom of a man who has fully integrated his calling: "I have the feeling that I have always been a priest, that I have never not been a priest, that the priesthood is my eternal reality. What a great and blessed feeling."[56]

WRITING THE SPIRITUAL DIARY

Bulgakov began writing the *Spiritual Diary* in early 1924, at the time he was rediscovering his calling as a pastoral one. The entire diary is quite clearly written against that background. Bulgakov speaks of pastoral visits, liturgies, prayers, his own sense of unworthiness to celebrate the mysteries of God—all the stuff of Orthodox pastorship and very little of the grandeur of church reunion or a "new religious consciousness."

The difference between the *Spiritual Diary* and the other, daily diary he kept concurrently is that in the *Spiritual Diary* the encounters and external circumstances of Bulgakov's life are muted as Bulgakov seeks what is universal within them. While there is plenty of introspection in the daily diary, in the *Spiritual Diary* Bulgakov seeks wisdom on a higher register, in order to understand spiritually what is going on around him.

Was the *Spiritual Diary* intended to be read by others, or was it a purely private endeavor? It is difficult to answer this question. The first several entries in the *Diary* seem to simply reflect Bulgakov's private, spiritual thoughts, and are tightly connected with people and events in his life. But within a few months of writing, around the beginning of June 1924, the entries begin to address a reader. Bulgakov writes to "you," or "we," or "man" in the abstract. As the *Diary* continues, the reflections gradually take on a universal quality, as he dispenses wisdom and insight for various situations.

To further contextualize the *Spiritual Diary*, it is useful to compare it with two other Russian works in the genre. The universalizing and didactic moments of the *Spiritual Diary* will remind some readers of St. John of Kronstadt's *My Life in Christ*.[57] This spiritual diary, written in the late 19th century, contains prayers, reflections, and especially teachings about how to conduct oneself in prayer and meditation. St. John was famous throughout Russia and this book was widely read; there is no doubt that Bulgakov was familiar with this text. What distinguishes Bulgakov's *Spiritual Diary* from *My Life in Christ* above all is the presence of Bulgakov himself in the diary: the writer is very much present, even as external circumstances often take a back seat to his spiritual reflections. Ironically, despite the title given to St. John's diary, *My Life in Christ*, the author himself—his personality, his struggles, the circumstances of his life—is consistently effaced. Unlike Bulgakov's *Diary*, John's *My Life in Christ* reads as though it could have been written by any wise spiritual writer at almost any time and place in Christian history.

One may also compare the *Spiritual Diary* to another well-known text in the genre by Fr. Alexander Elchaninov: *The Diary of a Russian Priest*.[58] That diary, written by a Russian Orthodox priest in France and one-time student of Bulgakov, features the same rootedness in time and place as Bulgakov's, in distinction from the timelessness of St. John of Kronstadt's text. Yet, more than Bulgakov's *Spiritual Diary*, Elchaninov's reflections and jottings relate quite directly to the particular features of modern, Western society. In this way, it is somewhat less didactic and universalizing than the *Spiritual Diary*. Further, Elchaninov's *Diary*, like St. John's, contains very little of the penitential and sometimes agonizing tone that Bulgakov strikes in his *Spiritual Diary*.

Bulgakov's *Spiritual Diary* never loses its personal flavor. Bulgakov's personality and the circumstances of his life persist "behind" the text. Importantly, so do the people around him, who subtly shaped the formation of the text through their influence on Bulgakov's life at the time of writing. Chief among those people is Yuliya Reitlinger.

BULGAKOV'S RELATIONSHIP WITH YULIYA REITLINGER

Yuliya (later Sr. Joanna) Reitlinger has been mentioned once or twice in this introduction already. She played no small role in Bulgakov's journey of self-discovery. Bulgakov had been her spiritual father since his days in Crimea in the early 1920s. Their friendship blossomed in 1924 during the time Bulgakov was writing the *Spiritual Diary*.[59] Indeed, it was in 1924 that Bulgakov began to refer to Reitlinger as his "Friend," a word which, when capitalized in Bulgakov's works, had previously referred to Florensky.[60]

Reitlinger was an enthusiastic lover of "the desert"—that is, of the ascetic life. (Bulgakov once opined that she was destined to be a fool-for-Christ one day.) She was also an inspired artist and iconographer who showed Bulgakov the things of the Spirit that previously he had only known abstractly. Her presence as a conversation partner was also important for Bulgakov intellectually. According to him, she completely understood his ideas about Sophia, unlike many others.[61] He wrote in April of 1924 that her receptivity to his ideas was an intellectual and creative boon for him, one that he needed in order to be inspired to think and write. After Pascha that year he reflected,

> What a great difference between this Pascha and the two that came before it: in Constantinople, it was a nightmare for me, a simultaneous intoxication with Catholicism and with episcopal autocracy. In Yalta, it was bright and joyful, but commonplace. Here [in Prague]—I have literally grown wings in my soul, because around me and with me stands the [iconographic] oeuvre of Yuliya, receiving her impulses from me, and that's why new thoughts and ideas have sounded and matured in my soul once again.[62]

Reitlinger was a primary interlocutor for Bulgakov not only intellectually, but also personally. She, unlike Fr. Pavel Florensky, his former "Friend," did not require that he discover his calling and identity in her, but rather in himself. He wrote in May 1924, "In this fateful hour a friend has been sent to me, one who does not allow herself to be 'targeted' [to become the center of attention], like Fr. Pavel. On the contrary, she gives me some incomprehensible strength and the leeway to lean on *myself*."[63] In the *Spiritual Diary*, one can discern what it meant for Bulgakov to find his mission and calling by turning inward. In an important way, Reitlinger helped him discover his pastoral voice and mission. In turn, Bulgakov's sophiology deeply informed her own thinking and artistic practice.[64]

Their relationship, though intensely deep, remained chaste. Their closeness, however, would be a cause of consternation for Bulgakov's wife and children on more than one occasion.[65] He protested against their suspicions in an entry in his daily diary from October 1924: "[My] friendship with Yuliya is on a different, spiritual-artistic plane, it's like a special escape of the soul." The fact that he felt he was being forced by his family to alter his relationship with Reitlinger was very painful for him, but he also realized how painful it was for his wife to see him so close to another woman: "On the cross is now being crucified my intimate life, but along with me my dear, my beloved Nelichka [his wife Elena], is also being crucified."[66] Later that month, Bulgakov took concrete measures to distance himself from Yuliya, notably by disallowing her to attend his lectures. He confessed in his daily diary that it was a costly sacrifice, as her presence in the class invigorated him. Yet, he wrote, "It's what God wants. This is clear to me with certainty, and I cannot go against the will of God. But it did torment my heart."[67]

THE BROTHERHOOD OF ST. SOPHIA

The Brotherhood of St. Sophia also played an important role in Bulgakov's life during the writing of the *Spiritual Diary*. A major venture for Bulgakov, it was also a source of great turmoil for him, and may have contributed to the anxious tone of some of the entries in the *Diary*. As the leader of the Brotherhood and its elder statesman, Bulgakov was subjected to close scrutiny by those inside and outside the group. His former commitment to the papacy had severely damaged his reputation among his Orthodox peers.[68]

In February 1924, Bulgakov received a letter from the historian and later professor of Russian history at Yale University, George Vernadsky, informing him that he would not join the Brotherhood. He was alarmed by Bulgakov's former advocacy for church reunion under the Pope of Rome and his continuing openness to the West. Vernadsky believed that the future direction of the Brotherhood under Bulgakov's leadership would be a "synthesis" of Orthodoxy and Catholicism—a prospect he wanted nothing to do with. Bulgakov perceived Vernadsky's refusal to join the Brotherhood as a personal betrayal. He wrote, "There was a time, and not long ago, when [Vernadsky] loved me and trusted me fully, without exception, and would walk alongside me and behind me everywhere without asking. Since then, he has 'elementarized' himself... in the sphere of ideas he is settling on the plane of the most rudimentary 'Eurasianism.'"[69]

The reference to Eurasianism is revealing. Eurasianism was an ideology rooted in 19th-century Russian thought and the ideas of German philosopher Oswald Spengler, that placed Russia's history and cultural identity more within the sphere of the exotic and mystical "East" than in the cold and rational "West." It was an anti-Western, anti-Semitic, and in some ways anti-intellectual movement that nevertheless appealed to many Russian émigrés who felt that the Bolshevik Revolution occurred due to Western (and Jewish) influence. Bulgakov would have no truck with it.[70] The younger theologian and sometime spiritual child of Bulgakov, Georges Florovsky, eventually declared that he, too, was leaving the Brotherhood, perhaps because he was drawn to the Eurasianists (whom he would later disown).[71] In a diary entry lamenting Florovsky's decision to leave the Brotherhood, Bulgakov wrote that the Eurasianists were growing in size. While they had an ostensibly inclusive worldview, an "inner Panmongolism," they nevertheless succeeded only in painting themselves into a corner of "growing isolation."[72] Bulgakov believed that Eurasianist isolationism and hostility toward the West was a dead end for the Russian emigration, and for Orthodoxy more generally, and that it could not form the foundation for a new intellectual and educational endeavor. But the more that movement grew, the more alone he felt: "I need to carry my cross; I'm not the first and I'm not the last, and what's more, in the end, I'm not alone. But what will become of the brotherhood? I myself cannot imagine."[73]

PLANS FOR PARIS AND THE PROBLEM OF SOPHIA

In June 1924, Metropolitan Evlogy (Georgievsky), one of the leading bishops of the Russian emigration and Bulgakov's immediate ecclesiastical authority, discussed with him the possibility of founding an Orthodox seminary in Paris and making Bulgakov the dean.[74] Bulgakov considered this idea to be unrealistic, given his tainted reputation, but was nonetheless intrigued. He wrote that while many church authorities suspected his orthodoxy, "Met. Evlogy calls me to become the *dean* of a spiritual school under his rectorship in Paris. And here to overhaul the voice of the Church! What nonsense! On the other hand, it is a new and unexpected argument *for* [moving to] Paris!"[75]

Bulgakov's theological reputation threatened the possibility of his deanship at the future seminary in Paris. His former papism was not the only thing that brought him under suspicion by others in the Russian emigration. His developing theory of sophiology also drew criticism. Late in 1923, Bulgakov became convinced that the only alternative to papism as a binding force in the church was a robust theological embrace of Sophia, the Wisdom of God. For him, Sophia represented an inner principle of unity and conciliarity in the church, in contrast to the outer principle of papal authoritarianism. He wrote in November 1923,

> Right now, in my soul—completely unexpectedly, but powerfully and naturally—there stands an antithesis: Sophia or the papacy? Horizontal or vertical? For me it is clear that the Church-Sophia does not bow to the pope; but losing this [sophianic] feeling, the papacy becomes inevitable, or [alternatively] a Protestant idealism. Now it has become clear to me why in recent years—with surprise—I lost the concrete sense of Sophia and came to see her like the majority of adherents to Orthodox 'seminary (that is, a basically poor version of Catholic) theology' see her—as philosophical fiction and something useless. And on the soil of this lack of sophianic feeling and my inner fright in the face of Bolshevism, papism appeared. For me it is so clear that it happened this way. Clearly, I did not overcome the Bolshevik temptation—a strong hand simply freed me from it. The Lord pardoned me of my Bolshevik-Catholic seduction through the prayers of parents and holy saints.[76]

Having renounced the task of church reunion under the papacy as his primary intellectual occupation, Bulgakov dove back into sophiology. He had developed his sophiology in preliminary fashion in *Philosophy of Economy* (1912) and *Unfading Light* (1917), but had now arrived at a new and deeper theological vision. Bulgakov formulated his new ideas on Sophia throughout 1924 and published them in early 1925 in an article entitled "Hypostasis and Hypostaticity: Scholia to *The Unfading Light*."[77] This article was extremely important for the future of Bulgakov's thought, and contained some of the core ideas that he would develop in his two theological trilogies.[78]

As an initial missive in what would become a massive oeuvre dedicated to sophiology, his article provoked opposition. Bulgakov's theological speculations in *Unfading Light* had already marked him among fellow Orthodox theologians as dangerous.[79] In this new article, Bulgakov distanced himself from some of his more controversial opinions but articulated an idea that was no less troubling for some readers. Namely, he drew a distinction between God *in* Himself (God as Trihypostatic subject) and God *for* Himself (God in His self-revelation to Himself). Bulgakov wrote that God does not close Himself up in a "Luciferian" love of self—an *I* that never encounters a not-*I*—but is always already disclosing Himself to Himself. The Father's begetting of the Word is a certain "utterance" or "declaration," which the Son "answers" in the Holy Spirit. Each Hypostasis discloses itself to the other two. Far from being locked in unknowable obscurity, God reveals Himself in positive content that can be known, even by His creation. This content is the "Glory" and the "Wisdom" (Sophia) of God. Sophia is shared by all three hypostases, since they each reveal themselves to themselves, though each hypostasis reveals itself in a special way. Sophia is not a "fourth hypostasis" in the Trinity, but rather the "hypostaticity" shared by the Three Hypostases, which are always "hypostasizing" in their paternity, filiality, and motherhood-daughterhood. She is not a divine Person; she is Divinity itself, the eternal self-revelation of the Hypostases and their self-consciousness. If God is Hypostatic Love, Sophia is the Love of Love. She is the world in God (as the divine ideas about the world) before the world's creation.

It was this latter aspect of Bulgakov's new ideas on sophiology that was so controversial among his peers. For many, the notion of a "divine world" co-eternal with God (though, again, not God *in Himself*) smacked of pantheism and was tantamount to a rejection of the doctrine of creation *ex nihilo*. (Bulgakov had not yet fully articulated the crucial difference between Divine Sophia and created Sophia, which addressed some of these concerns.)[80]

Bulgakov's new, bold ideas about Sophia were evidently being discussed in the Russian émigré community even before the final publication of the article. The discussion was generally negative, further damaging Bulgakov's reputation. He wrote in his daily diary that various bishops knew of his ideas and opposed them.[81] Despite this episcopal opposition, Bulgakov remained firm, sure that his pursuit of the question of Sophia was now his calling and his path with the same surety he once had about his calling to reunite the churches.[82]

Bulgakov's self-assurance in his quest and refusal to renounce his ideas on Sophia threatened to bring about serious consequences. He wrote in February 1925, after the article's publication, that the Eurasianists rejected it and publicly cast doubt upon his *bona fides* as a truly orthodox theologian. This public doubt threatened the creation of the academy in Paris of which he was to be the dean:

> Everything related to the Academy is at a standstill, and with this discrediting of me it will get even worse. And yet, in all humility, I, searching myself, find that I could not and should not go about things otherwise. Other essays of mine, perhaps, were incorrect because of lazy thinking, and here, in this one, there also proved to be a stumbling block, eliminated by me too late, but, in essence, I feel this to be my destiny, my fate, whatever it costs me. *I could not* and *should not do otherwise.*[83]

Bulgakov worried about the potential ecclesiastical ramifications of intellectual exile: "It even occurs to me at night that, perhaps, not only is my academic career ending, but my ecclesiastical one as well."[84] But no matter; this was to be his last stand.[85] Sophiology was for him the way in which he would live out his (now fundamentally pastoral) calling. Yet despite Bulgakov's worries, the academy in Paris, the St. Sergius Orthodox Theological Institute, forged ahead for launch, with Bulgakov as dean. Writing during a visit to Paris in early April 1925, he was overjoyed to learn that the new theological academy had already accumulated students enrolled for the fall term.[86]

CONCLUSION

Bulgakov wrote this in the last page of his daily diary in Prague on June 29, 1925, just before he left for Paris to begin a new chapter in his life:

> "It is good for me that thou hast humbled me"! [Ps 119:71 Douay-Rheims]. I arrived here with prideful ideas about church reform, about the union of the churches, of my nearly prophetic mission, but I leave here with a deep awareness of my sinfulness and infirmity. Illusions have scattered; I see myself stripped and poor, but I commend myself to the will of God, who delights in me this way. I want to live out the rest of my life in peaceful and obedient fulfillment of my daily work, with no prideful pretensions, and feel freedom and joy because of this.[87]

These words were the result of soul-searching and desperate attempts to find inner meaning amidst the trials of life. The *Spiritual Diary* is the record of how he got there, what depths of introspection were required for him to discover his true calling, and to persevere in his pursuit of it. In this sense, the *Spiritual Diary*, though an utterly personal piece, resonates as universally as his theological works. Through them, the reader can gain insight into what it means to find one's calling in the midst of the fires of life.

It is important to recollect once more that the *Spiritual Diary* was written before the major theological works for which he is best known. What does that tell us about his theology? I would argue that, at the very least, it means that his work, his sophiological "system," was the product of a man who was not simply an academic theologian but a *priest*—a pastor and spiritual father. The *Spiritual Diary* is sophiology at its source: lived experience.

On the sixth anniversary of his ordination, Bulgakov reflected that in his self-discovery as a pastor, he had not, in fact, abandoned his prophetic mission after all. Rather, his mission, his theological and educational task, was ever to be carried out *through* this pastoral calling:

> I feel this special, prophetic-priestly nature of mine and carry it in myself as a higher calling, as both cross and glory—not in human pride, but in Divine election, of

> which I am unworthy in my wretchedness. But the gifts of calling are irrevocable. From this comes both all my divergence and friction with the prevailing trends, and these eternal misunderstandings and suspicions from all sides. From this comes even now the story I am now beginning on the question of Sophia—everything, everything comes from this.[88]

In the *Spiritual Diary* we see the soul of Bulgakov, the humble priest, the spiritual guide, the man who stands in wonder—on every page!—at the activity of God in the world. Wonder! Is not that what sophiology is all about? It was that fundamental vision, that of wonder, that he elsewhere transposed into the language of theology.

THEOLOGICAL INTRODUCTION

"LIKE AN ARTIST BEFORE HIS FACE":

Sophianic Self-Creation in the Spiritual Diary

Roberto J. De La Noval

If Bulgakov is known for any of his theological teachings, it is certainly his sophiology, or his doctrine of Divine Wisdom, Sophia. This doctrine states that the divine essence, or *Sophia-ousia*, is the Tri-hypostatic God's concrete self-manifestation that, while perfectly hypostatized as Father, Son, and Holy Spirit, nonetheless possesses its own life of responsive love to the Trinitarian persons.[1] It is this relative "independence" of Sophia in God that grounds the relative "otherness" to God of the creaturely world, which in its essence is the divine *nature* immersed in nothingness and awaiting its hypostatization in human persons, whose humanity is ultimately and already always assumed by the divine person of the incarnate Son. As might be expected, opinions vary on the merits of this central aspect of Bulgakov's theological vision. Yet what should not be forgotten in any consideration of Bulgakov's sophiology is the anthropological basis of the doctrine. Sophia's delight, after all, is "in the children of men" (Prov. 8:31), and the most expansive context in which Bulgakov's doctrine of Sophia functions is the teaching on *Divine-Humanity*, namely humanity's inherent divinity and divinity's inherent humanity, both of which are consummately on display in Christ, the *theanthropos*, the *bogochelovek*, the God-Man.[2]

Whereas his younger contemporaries who would become leading lights of the Neopatristic movement in Orthodox theology, such as Georges Florovsky and Vladimir Lossky, spoke easily and enthusiastically of humanity's destiny to be divinized by participation in the divine energies, Bulgakov emphasized that the human person *in her very beginnings* is already a "created god."[3] Human persons "proceed" from God as "fourth creaturely hypostases" in the Trinity,[4] for they are the "outpourings of His essence."[5] Unlike other creatures,[6] humans are created directly through divine spiration, for God breathes his own Spirit into Adam (Gen. 2:7) to make him a living being. If the Godhead dwelt bodily in Christ, then this was only because humanity itself was ontologically capable of it: *humanum capax divini.*[7] Accordingly, the human person herself is already a moment of divine revelation, a Sophianic unfolding of the divine nature within the ontological limits of creaturehood.[8] It would not be an exaggeration to say that the key biblical text for all of Bulgakov's sophiology, and not just his theological anthropology, is Genesis 1:26–27: humanity made in God's image. The reciprocity of those imaged—both God *and* humanity—reveals the divine dignity of the human person and the human lowliness of the divine Persons, who come to dwell with us in the one dynamism of God's eternal life.

So vaulting an anthropology was destined to draw criticism. How could such an emphasis on humanity's divinity not obscure the doctrine of humanity's sinfulness? How could it not dull the sense of a desperate and existential need for redemption for every single person? These were some of the questions raised by Bulgakov's critics in the wake of the ecclesiastical condemnations of his sophiology in 1935, in the controversy known as the "Sophia Affair."[9] One such critic was John (Dmitrii Alekseevich) Shakhovskoi, the future Orthodox archbishop of San Francisco, who satirized Bulgakov's theological anthropology with a comical retelling of the story of Job from a purportedly sophiological perspective:

> Job sits on his dung heap, pulling off his last tatters and cutting his hair, but then the sophianic idea approaches him and begins haughtily to adorn him: "Come now, things aren't really so bad; you are good, you bear the image of the Creator within you, you are capable of *creativity*!" Poor Job (and man)! How wrongly they think of you and, once again, how they fail to understand you, these new friends of yours, so much the opposite of your former insensitive comforters![10]

Similarly, another of Bulgakov's critics, the widely-respected philosopher Nikolai Sergeevich Arsen'ev,[11] judged that Bulgakov's sophiological anthropology transforms salvation history from a true "drama" into a mere "odyssey" whose positive conclusion is already decided in advance.[12] By contrast, Bulgakov's frequent collaborator, the existentialist philosopher Nikolai Berdyaev, faulted the historic mainstream Christian tradition, both Eastern and Western, for its neglect of humanity's original and logically prior *creative* vocation.[13] Berdyaev puts his finger directly on the question here: is *creation* or *fall*, *creativity* or *redemption*, the center of gravity for Christian anthropology and so for an understanding of Christian mission in the world?

Where among these options does Bulgakov's theology lie? Does his sophiology in fact erase the reality of sin through an overreaching view of the human person? A reading of Bulgakov's *Spiritual Diary* reveals quite the opposite: the gravity of sin is mixed into the very foundations of Bulgakov's theological anthropology, and the latter cannot be understood without it. The following entry exemplifies the point:

23.XI/6.XII.1924

> *In wisdom Thou hast made them all.* Lovely is Your world, Lord, and everything is lovely within it. And—strange for me to say it—lovely too is my own bodily nature, lovely because You created it. How often we lose heart on account of our sinfulness, which obscures from our very selves our true image! Satan is a slanderer, and he slanders both us and—to do us harm—God's creation as well; he implants confusion and faintheartedness within us, and as a result faintheartedness and laziness grow in our souls. We lose ourselves, we refuse to wage battle against ourselves for the sake of our very selves; but God, who created all things in wisdom, by the same wisdom created each of us as well. God's Wisdom was an artist before His face, and she artistically formed our image as well, which we, like spiritual artists, must also form. Do not turn away from the work that is yours, for everything is from the Lord: your gift comes from the Lord, and your work is for Him. Fulfill your responsibilities to the gift of your

> life, to the gift of this world. Do not let God's world become a temptation for your heart on the pretext of the world's sinful state. If you disrobe yourself of your life now, then you will stand naked in the age to come as well. Therefore cursed be he that doeth the work of the Lord neglectfully. But the work of our life is God's work, and the Lord has entrusted to each his own talent, and from each will He demand its harvest.

This passage, a concise summary of the *Diary* as a whole, will serve as our hub from which we depart and to which we return in the following five sections: *Beauty*; *Despondency*; *Judgment*; *Election*; and *The Cross*. Given the critical developments in Bulgakov's theology that occurred around the time he was writing the *Spiritual Diary*, the emphases on display in these pages provide a significant interpretive key for much of Bulgakov's later speculative sophiology. Let us look more closely at the theological landscape of the *Diary* to discover Bulgakov's vision of the human person as a participant in God's creation *and* redemption, a vision of human life as an unceasing project of *sophianic self-creation*.

BEAUTY

In this life, we do not come to beauty clean, or with ease; the world's beauty remains too bright for darkened eyes to see. Yet in its foundations and its manifestation, the world *is* beautiful, divine beauty in matter, and at times, this beauty breaks through. Nature by right bears the secret of beauty, although it is the experience of art that most of all removes the veil of opacity which sin has lain over God's world, that reveals humanity's original creative vocation to cooperate with the Spirit in bringing new beauty to life. Bulgakov writes: "The joy of creativity. Before my eyes was accomplished a miracle of human creativity in the Lord and for the Lord: pure virgin hands outlined icons of the Savior and the Ever Virgin, the fruit of profound awe and quiet prayer but also of constant, self-denying labor."[14] Just like Divine Wisdom in Proverbs 8, which in "perceiving the revelation of divine creativity feels joy and rapture through it,"[15] so too Bulgakov rejoices at human creativity, here in the work of iconography. Creativity is a miracle, a quasi *ex nihilo* event that introduces something new into the world.[16] Of course, this novelty is relative to the created foundations of finitude, which set the parameters within which life develops and within which the human person can do creative work; all creativity is ultimately *co*-creativity with God. "The Lord gives strength. He sends inspiration, and by the Holy Spirit beauty is imprinted."[17]

It is indeed the Spirit who bestows beauty, for as Bulgakov would develop in his later pneumatology, the Spirit is the Trinitarian person most associated with God's glory, with the making visible of the Son as Divine Wisdom, both hypostatically in the Godhead as well as in creation, which is the "incarnation" of the multiform divine ideas that eternally reside "within" the Logos.[18] And beauty is nothing other than manifestation of a divine idea now clothed with flesh and made present for our praise. The world's beauty is *objective*, not merely a subjective projection, for it is directly intuited by those whose eyes are purified; as such, beauty speaks to us of our Creator and thereby calls us to Him.[19] "I was looking through the window at a blushing field, reddening foliage, and a blueing sky, and my soul was beside itself in the sweet languor of love for the Lord and for His world."[20] This summons, in fact, was the path of Bulgakov's own return to the faith of his childhood.[21] Since the creation of the world, God's beauty has been visible, and so to refuse this beauty is to sin. "And it is simply blindness and sluggishness of soul to wait for some specific moment in order to stop and say [to life]: you are beautiful!"[22] Our blindness to beauty requires the healing of the Spirit, and so Bulgakov throughout this diary implores God for the gift of illumination that he may see the beauty of every moment. When we love God above all, the world is revealed to us in its true splendor.[23]

In this revelation we discover the highest beauty in creation, the human spirit itself. Only the "gaze of love"—a gift of the Spirit—discerns the infinite riches of the human soul.[24] Deep cries out to deep, and the Spirit who searches the deep things of God permits us for our part to recognize the depths in every human face. And what is this depth? It is the human heart's *love*. Love and its deifying power is the major melody of the *Spiritual Diary*. "O human heart, seat of the image of God in man! What is more beautiful and more sweet than you, what is more joyful than love?"[25] Love and the image of God in humanity are one, for God is Love. Thus does God's priest, who by the grace of priesthood serves as a conduit of God's love, see in the penitent not merely the sin but also the divine image, God's beauty inscribed in human flesh.[26] Yet nowhere is this beauty more apparent or more overwhelming in its objective power than in the saint, the lover *par excellence.* In their holiness the saints reveal the beauty of love by inspiring responsive love in our hearts. That is, they reveal to us *ourselves.* "We ourselves do not know what we possess from God, and then suddenly a saint—through his own soul—manifests to us our own power and our own beauty in all our infirmity."[27] This is how beauty saves the world.

But what is this self that the Spirit reveals to us through the beauty of the saints? It is our "ideal image" in the mind and heart of God, the *sophianic self.* This brings us again to Bulgakov's teaching on Divine Wisdom, or his sophiology. Bulgakov's writing on Sophia is multifarious and complex, evolving over time in response to new discoveries and challenges, but the ecclesial-ascetical core of the teaching remains stable throughout his entire theological career. At the heart of the doctrine is the insight that God's creative intent for the world, the ideal-image or *sophianic* image in which God rejoices, struggles in this life to become a reality on account of human sin and rebellion. Bulgakov can consider the question of Sophia in abstraction from sin, of course, in a theoretical mode; we may call such a perspective the "creative" as opposed to the "redemptive." In the creative framework, which is the state of things before the Fall, the world in God's original design constituted the "the artistic re-creation of the eternal ideas that together make up the ideal organism, the divine Sophia, the Wisdom that existed with God before Creation and whose joy is 'with the sons of man.'"[28] This is God's art: to take the ideal-images of creaturely realities, plunge them into nothingness, and let arise the world of becoming in matter, in which the ideal-images function as causes but also as *norms* for creaturely existence (both "forms" and "entelechies," in the Platonic and Aristotelian language Bulgakov borrows).[29] Such a world is by definition incomplete, for the balance between "nothing" and "being" is unstable, and creation can revert to chaos should the garden not be properly cultivated, if matter is not transfigured so as to become transparent to its sophianic basis.[30]

Yet no part of God's earth is as metaphysically unstable as the human being. For unlike the other creatures who do not share in rational freedom, each person is created "incomplete," awaiting the subject's *own* self-creation: "The world was only precreated in the human being, who had to create himself from his own side with his own freedom and only then enter into possession of the world, having brought to realization the general plan of creation."[31] Ascesis, then, was proper to humanity even before the Fall. Had humanity rejected the temptation to elevate the creature above the Creator, the divine likeness would have shone through, making art and ascesis one. When the divine image, the ideal-image, will be fully manifest in creatures, then the gap between ideal and real is overcome, and matter clothes the intelligible world of God's creative ideas in *resurrection* flesh.

That path, however, represents the road not taken, and so is only hypothetical; the redemptive framework must be our concrete base of operations. Accordingly, the creative task given humanity in our creation—to transform the material world so that God's ideal may become perspicacious in it—is now identical with the task of working out our salvation. To pursue this task is both to participate in our redemption by Christ and to cooperate in completing God's initial creative work. For Bulgakov, then, in a fallen world there is no real distinction between the creative and the redemptive tasks. Anticipating the language of later Orthodox liturgical theology,[32] Bulgakov compares the creative work of the iconographer to the work of liturgy, when "people begin to do all things in the Lord," when "the entirety of life becomes praise, becomes liturgy."[33] Here we find the ecclesial-ascetic context of Bulgakov's ideas on Divine Wisdom, or Sophia. And the goal of this teaching is to help Christians to cooperate with God in releasing their ideal image from the stone of sin and death—precisely the work reflected in Bulgakov's personal struggles in the *Spiritual Diary*.[34]

DESPONDENCY

Whereas in later writings on beauty Bulgakov will highlight the temptation that the world's beauty can produce in a soul not given over to the Creator,[35] here in the *Spiritual Diary*, the danger, both in Bulgakov's programmatic theological statements and in his prayers, lies on the opposite pole: we *fail* to see our innate and God-given beauty—hardness of heart and sinful flesh hide it from us—and so we despair.

As God's creatures, made in the divine image and likeness, we are beautiful *in*, or despite, our infirmity, the weakness of sin that corrupts and overshadows divine beauty and that reaches even to our experience of our very bodies. We are subject to passions that distort our incarnate life, and these invite us to mistake the *flesh* for the *body*. As Bulgakov would write some years after concluding the *Diary*, "The body is not flesh that suppresses and shuts off the light of the spirit. On the contrary, the body is the image and self-revelation of the spirit."[36] When Bulgakov expresses puzzlement in the *Diary* over the beauty of his own body ("And—strange for me to say it—lovely too is my own bodily nature, lovely because You created it"[37]), we catch a glimpse of the difficulty of existentially appropriating the crucial distinction between fallen flesh and blessed embodiment as revealed in creation and in Christ's resurrection. At times in this diary, Bulgakov asks God's help in order to hate himself,[38] and though it is not difficult to understand the theological context (as articulated immediately above) in which such a prayer can arise, it is also not unreasonable to sense in these passages that Bulgakov's response to his passions, and so to his body, at times becomes theologically erroneous and psychologically damaging. In fact, Bulgakov writes explicitly against self-loathing in this diary, perhaps in response to his own personal tendencies in this direction: "We need abhor neither others nor ourselves, for this is just as much a sin when it is directed at one's neighbor as when directed at oneself."[39]

True self-knowledge would show us our sophianic beauty, but it would also reveal to us the depth of our sin. Such transparent vision of ourselves, therefore, comes with its own temptations. "Lord, teach me the humility of the publican, grant it to me to come to hate myself in my filth, but preserve me from *despondency* and *terror*."[40] If the beauty of love is the main theme of the *Diary*, then despondency and its temptations sound as the counterpoint; indeed, despondency is "greater than all sins."[41] Bulgakov follows the tradition of Eastern monastic writings, in which *acedia*, if not numbered as the first, is regularly listed among the most fatal of the vices.[42] Yet *acedia* in both the Western and Eastern Christian ascetical traditions is difficult to define precisely, for this vice exists somewhere between sloth and sorrow.[43] The *Diary's* "despondency" definitely belongs with the latter; it is the sin of despair, often in the face of God's allowance of evil and suffering, but more often in the face of one's own sinfulness. The first aspect of "despondency" in the *Diary* will concern us later, but for now we pause to discuss despondency as paralyzing shame in response to our personal sin.

There are biographical roots to this accentuation of despondency as shame. From reading his other journals penned in the years before the *Spiritual Diary*, it becomes apparent that Bulgakov was a man who lived with debilitating shame, usually with regard to perceived failure, and often when comparing himself to other figures he idealized (such as his mentor, Fr. Pavel Florensky).[44] This should be kept in mind as we read Bulgakov's entries on self-hatred in the *Diary*.[45] In Bulgakov's thinking, shame is constitutive of the experience of remembering past sins. Shame, in fact, is found in the *Diary* far more often than guilt, and when the latter does appear, it mostly concerns the guilt of others and not of Bulgakov himself. Bulgakov's writings on despondency born of shame therefore invite us to read him in light of the twentieth-century's psychological type of the "divided" or "depleted" self, a self consumed far more by shame than by personal guilt.[46]

The "divided" or "depleted" self struggles to accept the gap between one's idealized image of self-perfection and one's actual state, and the shame provoked by this unwelcome realization produces in the person a crushing paralysis that can spawn myriad other vices and devices—such as pride—to keep the truth of oneself at bay.[47] Given the prominence in Bulgakov's thought of the notion of a person's "ideal image" as the sophianic self, we may wonder whether the *Diary's* concern with despondency can be understood as the function of a psychologically damaging ideal of human normativity, one made far worse by the notion that such an ideal is in fact *God's* and not merely our own. There can be no doubt that such a normative ideal may be and has been used—both through self-condemnation and in external judgment—to crush those who fail to meet it (which is all of us). Yet Bulgakov's writings on despondency in connection to the sophianic self serve a different purpose: to keep hope in God's forgiveness together with the humbling knowledge that we are not yet perfected. The former should lead to grateful and confident repentance, and the latter to *proportionate* shame and strenuous religious effort.[48] In other words, Bulgakov's theology of despondency keeps the *ideal* in view while forswearing the *idealization of the self*.[49] For this reason, Bulgakov's transposition in the *Spiritual Diary* of the sin of despondency into a contemporary register speaks powerfully to other "depleted selves" whose chronic shame chokes their development into the selves God created them to be.

Let us look then more closely at the *Diary's* teaching on this affliction. Despondency is that vice which tempts us to put down the artist's brush and to leave our ideal image unmanifested. "We lose ourselves, we refuse to wage battle against ourselves for the sake of our very selves." When defined in this manner, despondency's risk becomes apparent. For the Christian life is meant to be perpetual repentance, faithfully confronting oneself with the fact of one's own sin. But if despondency looms in the face of the enormity of sin, then, paradoxically and perversely, the knowledge of sin itself transforms into a new temptation, and a Satanic one at that. "In a fit of its despair [the soul] repeats the Slanderer's slander and thereby slanders itself."[50] It is a mark of the subtlety of the Tempter's designs that in this fashion he can corrupt the instrument of salvation, self-knowledge, by turning it into a stumbling block to the sinner. Simply put, the full and clear knowledge of our sins is too heavy for most of us to bear: "What a heavy thing this is—*to see oneself*. Truly, a man cannot bear this for long, he seeks to forget, to turn his back to himself; only ascetics, men of strength, have endured this unremitting vision of their sins, this unremitting repentance."[51]

This temptation to despair is especially grievous when we turn a backwards glance to our lives, when we recognize how much we have left undone for the Lord.[52] This proleptic anticipation of the verdict of the Dread Judgment proves harmful to the sinner here and now who does not experience this vision alongside an equally unadulterated vision of God's *love*; in so doing, the despondent sinner assumes Christ's role as Judge, judging himself prematurely ("Judge not that ye be not judged"). And if this vision of God's compassion does not attend our self-judgment, the fear of punishment will cast out love as despair usurps love's rightful throne.[53] Paradoxically, it is our *pride* that reveals itself in this despair, as if through a mask, when we consider ourselves so uniquely sinful that we are unworthy of God's universally prescribed remedy: repentance and patience.[54]

When this despair makes its home in us, genuine repentance becomes impossible, and its counterfeit, self-pity, dominates any time we look back on the past or turn our eyes forward to the work the Lord has given us to do. "My days are winding down, and all the more clearly and mercilessly I hear the coming verdict: slothful and wicked servant! And I see my whole life, mired in narcissism, idleness, and laziness, laziness... If only I could devote myself to some work, *any* work, to the point of sweating blood, if only I could escape self-pity at least for a *moment* for the sake of the Lord and His work!"[55] The idleness and sloth so integrally connected with *acedia* in the ascetic tradition manifest in the *Diary* as the inevitable consequence of despair; seeing its mountain of sin, the soul sighs, "Why bother?" But all the while, the threat of judgment, of the coming verdict, stands before us.

JUDGMENT

Memento mori fills these pages. What shall be the verdict of the Just Judge? Seen in this light, Bulgakov's writings on despondency reveal the pitfalls that may attend a thoroughgoing "eschatological mood" in the Christian life,[56] and so it is fitting that in the course of the *Diary*, his attention turns to eschatology and specifically to the Final Judgment. Bulgakov's theology here of eternal torments and universal salvation serves, in a fashion, as an antidote to the damaging beliefs about God's love for humanity that operate in moments of deepest despondency.

To understand Bulgakov's doctrine of eschatological judgment in the *Diary*, we need only recall the refrain of the *Brothers Karamazov*: we are, each of us, "guilty before everyone, for everyone and everything."[57] Or, in Bulgakov's words: "[U]pon each one of us hangs the fate of the entire world."[58] Our individual deeds enter into world history, and we are each a crucial factor in the historical causality that joins all humanity together. In Bulgakov's mind, for example, it was his generation that bore the blame for the fate of the children currently being raised in an atheist Russia, deprived of their birthright of a Christian upbringing. These children could not be *personally* guilty of the blasphemies they would imbibe with their mother's milk, just as the children of previous generations had no special merit for the contingency of being baptized and raised by Christian parents.[59] For this reason the Lord commands us *not to judge*—we are too quick to assign personal guilt when we cannot possibly know the true culpability of another. But God *can* judge, and He will judge all humanity together, for God alone can grasp the sundry ways in which our fates are intertwined and by which we are responsible for one other.

It is a point of interest that Bulgakov—in contrast to the more typical notion of a personal post-mortem judgment followed at the end of time by the universal judgment—imagines two *corporate* eschatological judgments that contextualize the individual within her human community. First, there is the preliminary judgment following immediately upon death, in which we are judged together with our closest circle; even in personal judgment, no man is an island.[60] Then will the secrets of our hearts be disclosed, in the full view of those dear to us. Our masks will fall away, and we shall be known by them as we are known. In one final offense against our neighbors, we will disillusion and grieve those who loved us but lived in ignorance of the falsehood in our souls.[61] Afterwards, at the end of time, comes the universal judgment, in which the more limited intelligibility of our historical action and responsibility finds its true and proper context in the universal scope of all world history. Not for nothing does Matthew 25 depict the final judgment as a judgment of the *nations* and then of individuals. When we stand before the Just Judge, the impact of our life on the historical unfolding of humanity will then crown or condemn us.

For Bulgakov, the Dread Judgment is nothing other than the final confrontation with the truth of our lives: *it is this self-knowledge that lights the fires of hell in the soul of the sinner.* There is no avoiding this final unmasking of the human person. Unlike some twentieth-century thinkers who understood hell as God's generous allowance of sinners to go their own way, into the infinity of eternity, locking the door to hell from the inside while nursing forever their delusions of self-sufficiency,[62] Bulgakov came to see the matter differently. In the vision of eschatology depicted in the *Diary* and in his later, more thoroughly argued works, hell exists because God does in fact judge the sinner: *every* knee shall bow, and no one can escape the *dies irae.* Justice will be done. Bulgakov further specifies that God's eschatological judgment to damnation will not be received as if from some external source, whose legitimacy and truthfulness the sinner could, in principle, deny in perpetuity. No, the sinner must in the end acknowledge the justice of the Judge, lest God not become for the sinner "all in all" (1 Corinthians 15:28).

The sinner will agree with God's final judgment because the *sinner himself is the agent of that judgment.* This occurs through his conscience, the "voice of God in the human heart" that "denounces falsehood and sin, tears off masks, strikes at vices."[63] This means that the unavoidable unmasking that constitutes the Final Judgment begins here, today, whenever the voice of God speaking through us reveals, with all the imperiousness of self-condemnation, the cracks in our facade. Unmixed yet undivided, God's judgment and our own bring to light today the truth of what we have made ourselves thus far,[64] and at the eschatological Dread Judgment, conscience itself will look back on the entirety of our life and render a verdict.[65] Accordingly, the Dread Judgment is *divine-human,* both transcendent in its origin—for it is *God* who renders eschatologically impossible our earthly evasions of conscience—and immanent, insofar as we, with our own free agency, speak God's judgment over ourselves.[66]

The Christian's posture towards this final self-judgment is one of great fear. In the words of the Kontakion for the Sunday of the Last Judgment: "When You, O God, shall come to earth with glory, all things shall tremble and the river of fire shall flow before Your judgment seat; the books shall be opened and the hidden things disclosed! Then deliver me from the unquenchable fire, and make me worthy to stand at Your right hand, Most Righteous Judge!" Repeatedly in the *Diary*, Bulgakov projects himself into this eschatological judgment and expresses trepidation concerning God's verdict on his life.

> O, dreadful hour of death and dreadful judgment of God! How can I stand before Your face? How I will grieve over my life lost in laziness, in idleness, wasted away in self-love—what a total mistake, what a sin, what a failure it will seem! How far away will stand everyone near and known to me, and then my conscience alone and none other will unroll its impartial list! How meaningless will appear then what now appears so important and necessary, how fleeting all these earthly disturbances, but over them all and in them all there will be pronounced only one dreadful verdict: God gave you a long life, gave you strength and health, gave you friends and people close

> to you—how and for whom did you spend this life, what mark will it leave in the world? And there is no answer besides one final, impotent regret, the eternal torment of the good that was left undone.[67]

The content of this eternal torment, the substance of its fire, is *regret.* Here Bulgakov echoes a venerable stream of Eastern Christian thinking on hell found in classical ascetical writers such as St. Isaac of Nineveh.[68] For this tradition, hell is simply one modality in which God's love may be received, just as heaven is another. As the sun hardens mud but melts ice, so too shall the soul, depending on its state, experience God either as torment or bliss. To be more precise: for Bulgakov in this *Diary*, it is not that God *directly* causes the torments of hell, for it is the sinner's own self-isolation from divine delight that makes a torment for him the joy of the blessed, who by contrast do not flee in their shame from God's eschatological face. And, *horribile dictu*, we can know something of the pain of fleeing God even today. "One can experience these torments of hell here, in this life, immediately after sin, while still in the captivity of sin. The wretched sinner is judged not by an external judge, not by a dictate from God, but by sin itself, by his very self. The torments of hell—this is the *power* of sin in your own self, this is the shame, the unbearable shame of sin, the shame of deceit, the shame of desecrating what is holy, near, and dear."[69]

Bulgakov's eschatological entries in the *Diary* explicate theologically the Eastern Christian iconic tradition of depicting the final judgment. In such images Mary, the Mother of God, mournfully pleads for sinners, whereas Christ remains seated on the throne with stern expression. Thus Bulgakov writes that Christ and His Mother, the Most Holy Theotokos, will bring God's anger *and* mercy in the judgment:[70] the Father's "two hands"—the Son as justice and the Spirit through the Ever Virgin's mercy—accomplish the universal salvation of the world on that Last Day. Why are these two, anger and mercy, divided between the Son and the Spirit/Mary? Surely not because God is divided in Himself, requiring the intercession of someone outside the Godhead to secure a more merciful outcome to the Final Judgment. It is Christ the "Compassionate One," after all, who reveals His "dread glory" and so lights the fires of the eschatological tribunal, as Bulgakov prayed every Lent in the Great Canon of St. Andrew of Crete.[71]

I suggest that this partitioning of anger and mercy takes on particular meaning if read in light of the *Diary's* consistent theme of the pitfalls of despondency and of the human inclination to doubt God's absolute love. Because it is *we* who will perform God's final judgment on ourselves, either of these two in isolation—justice or mercy—would prevent us from executing a true judgment that could make possible our eschatological repentance and salvation; hence the symbolic meaningfulness of apportioning between the Son and the Mother the divine attributes most relevant to judgment. As Bulgakov had written some years earlier, the Son's role in the judgment is to manifest to us in His person the "immanent norm of *humanness*, which at the same time proves to be the measure of Christ."[72] Upon receiving the vision of the human norm of life in Christ, the human person freely judges by its light her work of sophianic art, her life, fashioned in freedom.[73] The realization of how we have failed to co-create the likeness of our divine image triggers in us *anger*, manifested as Christ's anger at the sinner—perhaps the same anger that despondency transmutes, namely self-directed anger on account of our sins.[74] For the ascetics of the early church, the passions could be mobilized to work against the other passions;[75] but for the despondent sinner, the passion of anger at his sin is "frozen" as inordinate shame ("the torments of hell—this is the *power* of sin in your own self, this is the shame, the unbearable shame of sin") and therefore fruitless.[76] At the Dread Judgment, however, this self-anger cannot remain stunted as paralyzing shame and self-pity because its downward inclination is stopped by the complete mercy and compassion of the Mother of God.[77] Anger is therefore freed to *move* the sinner to eschatological repentance, throughout the unknowable aeonic time in which the judgment shall occur.[78] And it is mercy and the promise of God's compassion that makes such a transformation possible.

Note how this eschatological balancing of anger and mercy works to realize God's goal of re-creating the sinner and revealing his divine likeness precisely *through* his human freedom. The prospect of justice without compassion sinks the honest soul into the pit of despondency already in this earthly life, and the application of mercy without justice, without bringing forth the fruits of repentance as a new self, renders otiose our God-given freedom and responsibility. Therefore the Spirit, as the perfecting hypostasis of the Trinity, takes the eschatological justice delivered by the Son through our own self-condemnation and sublates it into the mercy and compassion of the tearful Mother of God.

Because Mary is the Disconsolate Mother as long as sin remains on earth—the sin that is the continuing crucifixion of Her Son in His human brothers and sisters whom She now calls her own—this eschatological role properly belongs to her.[79] And until the day when God shall wipe away every tear, Mary weeps. Yet these tears are the dew of the Holy Spirit, for she is, *par excellence*, "the Bearer of the Holy Spirit," the "Holy Spirit Himself manifested as a human being."[80] It is not that Mary's humanity is an *incarnation* of the Spirit, as Christ's humanity is for the divine Word. Rather, what is in view here is the maximal transparency of Mary's humanity to the Spirit, so that if you have seen the Mother, you have seen the Spirit; conversely, where the Spirit is, there too is the Theotokos. Thus at the eschaton, she will manifest the Spirit as Christ's Co-Judge, and through her compassion and the Son's purifying, just fire, she will answer the prayers of the faithful: "Through the intercessions of the Theotokos, Savior, save us."[81]

ELECTION

If Bulgakov's theology of universal judgment and reconciliation provides a template for how to pursue self-judgment in repentance without succumbing to despair, it also reveals the absolute necessity of humility in the Christian life. Genuine humility uses lapses into sin as an occasion for greater softness of heart, for growing closer to God and to our fellow sinful neighbors.[82] But despondency signals the perseverance of a pride that refuses to learn the true meaning of temptations. It is scandalized by human weakness and failure, it does not see itself in the disciples of Christ who scattered and deserted their Lord on the Gethsemane night.[83] When viewed with the eyes of pride, the sheer contingency of human existence, and the presence or absence of the natural and supernatural powers that condition our moral efforts, constitute insurmountable stumbling blocks.[84] Only a profound grasp of the concrete situation of humanity as *captives of sin* burns up the pride of self-idealization and prevents despondency from choking the spiritual life. Like the cross itself, whose original use for destruction was transformed into a channel of divine love through Christ's self-offering and resurrection, temptation can also become a good by serving as an instrument of self-knowledge and therefore of knowledge of God. "Before the fall you did not know the power of sin within, you were proud in your righteousness, which was merely the absence of temptation. Now you have been humbled, because you have come to know your nothingness."[85] All the good we possess is from God; the rest, our weakness, is ours.[86]

Only this kind of self-knowledge saves, only this knowledge leads to humble prayer and awe before the mystery of election. This is not a predestining election to *eschatological* salvation or damnation—Bulgakov's affirmation of universal salvation rejects this sort of predestination, as we have seen. This election concerns instead the historical destinies that the Lord sends to human persons, the concrete gifts and life circumstances, personal and societal and global, that determine how they pursue their sophianic self-creation.[87] Yet in the *Diary* the predominant referent of this kind of election is God's election of some to suffer grievous harm, including the suffering of grave temptations:

> Why and for what reason were the apostles plunged into this temptation [in Gethsemane], which the Lord, calling them to prayer, warned them about (pray that ye enter not into temptation)? The Lord wished to make manifest the *weakness* even of those whom He elected out of all people to do His work, those who by God's grace found in themselves the strength to serve Him. Here every kind of Luciferian pride in man is exposed. *There is not and cannot be* a person who could remain invincible against temptations and tribulations, against the power of sin. And holiness is a special gift, a mercy of God; it is from God. How great a mystery is human destiny! The Lord enclosed all in disobedience in order to have mercy upon all! Oh, the depth and the riches of the wisdom and knowledge of God, how unsearchable His ways![88]

As we turn the pages of the *Diary*, we witness Bulgakov's gradually deeper acceptance of this mystery of Providence and of election to suffering, to perseverance, and to liberation. This acceptance is the only cure for the other variety of despondency in the *Diary*, the kind waiting on the wings of horrendous evil and the suffering it brings—including especially the spiritual suffering of rending aporia in the face of God's selective miraculous interventions in history. The rationale for God's historical bestowal of grace to some and not to others remains unfathomable; human reason cannot penetrate it. We are confounded because we know that God does not tempt, and that He has given us a guardian angel, a kind guide,[89] to protect us from Satan's attacks and snares.[90] *Yet this defense can be taken away*; like Job, we can become the victims of Satanic attack by God's permission, and it is not given to us to know why one is left defenseless and another is protected by divine grace.

In the *Diary*, Bulgakov's meditations on the mystery of election find their most urgent catalyst in the contemporary Soviet persecution of the Church and in the incalculable suffering of the Russian people.[91] "How long, O Lord, how long will your anger burn against the Russian land? Wherefore have You abandoned it to desecration and corruption? Why do you endure the satanic rule of the atheists? You know the weakness of our nature, You know that human patience has its limits. Why then do You allow us to be tempted beyond our measure, why do You permit this to the point of an inevitable fall?"[92] Ultimately, for Bulgakov, it is God who has brought the Soviet affliction upon the Russian nation.[93] Just a few years prior, Bulgakov had understood the Bolshevik cataclysm as a divine punishment representing the inevitable outcome of Rus' fateful acceptance of a defective—that is, *non-Catholic*—form of Christianity at its baptism nearly a millennium before. In this outcome Russia was not guiltless, especially since she ignored the prophets that God sent to call her to reconciliation with Rome, prophets like the pro-union philosopher and theologian, Vladimir Solovyov.[94] Here in the pages of this *Diary*, however, Bulgakov's views on the origin of Bolshevism have changed, and whatever guilt the Russian Church and the Russian people may bear in Bulgakov's mind accordingly recedes as the *mysterium iniquitatis*, and its sister mystery of election, swallow the horizon.[95]

For Bulgakov, Russia's election to suffering was most visible in the Church's martyrs—among whom he was not counted. He felt acutely the contingency of his situation in Europe: had he not been exiled from his homeland, he too, like his beloved Patriarch Tikhon, could have been assigned a martyr's lot. The repeated discussion we find in the *Diary* on the weakness of human faith and flesh, its absolute dependence on God's gift of endurance, and the mystery of why that gift is granted to some and not to others, suggests Bulgakov's existential pondering of how he would have faced the threat of death. (Not that Bulgakov had proved himself a coward in the years before his exile; his choice to pursue ordination when he did, as it became apparent what Bolshevik rule in Russia would mean for Christians therein, witnesses to his character and to his love for God and the church.) The fate of Judas, who is never named in the diary but whose apostasy Bulgakov would study in great detail years later, haunts these contemplations of Russia's calamity.[96] "How many of our Christians, if only they had been born in another age from this persecution would never have been confronted with the problem of apostasy or martyrdom but would have lived blessed lives of faith until the very hour of death." These words from Shusaku Endo's Fr. Sebastião Rodrigues would fit quite naturally in the *Spiritual Diary*.[97]

As Rowan Williams has observed, in tragic theater we learn the humility of accepting our general impotence to save those whose fate is tied to our own through the bonds of empathy. "[W]e are still learning the solidarity that comes out of recognizing the sheer distance between actual human persons, so that our stillness in the face of represented pain becomes a forced acknowledgement of our habits of avoidance and denial and a confrontation of the helplessness in the presence of catastrophe that we regularly experience and avoid reflecting about."[98] So Bulgakov, by witnessing the sad spectacle of Russia's destiny, came to accept the mystery of Russia's election to deathly persecution—as well as the fact that the Lord had chosen for him not to undergo it. "Faced with these chosen ones who are now being crucified on Russia's cross, how it confounds your soul that you are not with them! But you should not be confounded, if what is happening is God's will. It is not given to us to choose our lot..."[99]

But this acceptance of our own mysterious lot cannot and should not lead to coldheartedness, to forgetting, to a contraction of our love. There is a duty of "unceasing remembrance," and it is fulfilled in prayer. To forego it is to sin against love and against our brothers and sisters; to fulfill it is to allow the "inexplicable mercy of Providence" that has spared us their fate (certainly not because we are somehow worthy!) to make their suffering salvific for us.[100] Only we must pray, and then even our impotence is overcome in the mystical body of Christ, where our charity is identical with the Son's, because it is the Spirit of the Son who pours it into our hearts.

What sustains this pained prayer in the face of evil and God's allowance of it? The example of Christ, who remained nailed to his cross, with no legions of angels coming to save him.[101] In the theological works of his final years, Bulgakov would insist that the inscrutability of divine revelation refers not to the *what* of God's goals, which are definitively revealed in Scripture ("the Lord enclosed all in disobedience in order to have mercy upon all") but only to the *how*.[102] The fruit of Christ's passion—the salvation of the world—gives Bulgakov confidence in that whatever God's hidden reasons for permitting tragedy on earth, the ultimate purpose of Providence is the good of all. "[W]e do not know God's paths and we do not know the paths of this love"—yet still these paths are paths of *love*.[103]

THE CROSS

That the whole of God's purpose is love inspires us to trust that God's creative work with us and with the world is not in vain, that we must strive to bring to fruition the task of sophianic self-creation and not succumb to despondency. Nothing would be more deadly for us, therefore, than to believe that this work is already accomplished in *time*. If despondency over our sinfulness and our agonizing incomprehension before the mysteries of divine election keep us from our artistic-ascetical work, so too does pride, the refusal to admit the chasm that exists between our current image and our true sophianic image. We foster in ourselves this self-deception from our earliest days and so put aside the work that must be done to mold ourselves into God's ideal image.[104] "God, who created all things in wisdom, by the same wisdom created each of us as well. God's Wisdom was an artist before His face, and she artistically formed our image as well, which we, like spiritual artists, must also form." We are already formed; we are not yet formed. Both are true, albeit in different registers; in God's eternity we are always fully "sophianized," possessed by God as the future for which sake he created the world; it is this future that shall be revealed on the Last Day, when in unison with God we will acclaim over the world: "Very good" (Gen. 1:36). And yet *in time* we must still form ourselves here below. This is the creative task, as well as the dignity, of the everyday: God's invitation to us to participate "in the destinies of people, of the world, the opportunity to build up one's own soul."[105] Between the Scylla of despondency and the Charybdis of pride, there is only one path to sophianic beauty that avoids either extreme: Christ's cross, the *via crucis.*

We reveal our true image by crucifying the flesh—whatever in our life that prevents love of God, of self, and of neighbor. As we have seen, in the *Diary* this battle of Spirit versus flesh often takes the form of repudiating the *logismoi,* or tempting thoughts, which would deter us from repentance and hope. In many of his entries, Bulgakov draws on the wisdom of the ascetical tradition, as well as on the psalms' detailed mapping of the geography of the soul, in order to illuminate the day-to-day experience of sophianic self-creation. We train our bodies in this life, Bulgakov says, and so too should we train our souls—meaning here our *emotions*—to avoid violent vacillations, so that the spirit can pursue love without impediment.[106] This is not equivalent to "wrapping ourselves in the toga of Stoic dispassion and indifference," which Bulgakov considers nothing more than "pride and hypocrisy."[107] On the contrary, Bulgakov's approach highlights the vital role of feelings in Christian discipleship and the need to give them their due, to acknowledge them, to earnestly pray for what we sincerely desire.[108] For without this sense of self, there is no true *sacrifice* to the Lord, nothing that is "ours" to offer up. What is more, if we ignore our feelings, there will be no progress in the Christian life: without attending to our instinctive responses and using our freedom to cultivate, over time, certain feeling states (such as cheerfulness), the fruit of Spirit proves more difficult to grow, and the seeds of grace that the Sower always sows fall on rocky ground. Therefore, the daily setbacks that reveal to us our impatience and irritability should be turned by our spirit into opportunities to strengthen our souls.[109] The task is ours to take up the *voluntary* crosses that life presents us.[110]

Only if we have undergone such training, both bodily and emotional, will we be able to say, when the decrees of Providence and election come to us as something external and unwilled, that we are perplexed but not in despair. In those moments, we are being summoned to Gethsemane. According to Bulgakov's later writings,[111] Gethsemane is the mystical core of Christ's passion. If so, it is there that we can expect to learn what it means to daily carry the cross, and Bulgakov brings out these implications of his doctrine with fullest pastoral force in the *Diary*.

> [I]t is necessary to cultivate in oneself an acceptance of *whatever* the will of God may be. And this is the feat of faith, of sweating blood. The Son of God accepted through his humanity the inscrutable will of the Father as a law *external* to him: "Not as I will, but as Thou wilt." And He, as a man, wanted for Himself something other than what was necessary according to God's will. And life is *always* like this.[112]

Inexplicable suffering sets the conditions for the ultimate act of ascesis and sophianic self-creation—submitting our will to God's without falling into despair. This cross is intrinsic to sophianic self-creation, for even Christ in his humanity could not bypass it on the road to deification. The *feat of faith* accomplished by Christ in Gethsemane and then made flesh on the cross shows us the way in which we must walk. Accordingly, it also shows us the one temptation that will necessarily attend this self-crucifixion: the temptation to evade or to come down from our cross. This seduction comes in various forms. It may be that we refuse to give up what is most dear to us, our "Isaac" on the mount, in response to God's command,[113] or we may resist the purification of our loves that can only occur by crucifying our loves, by examining whether in relationships we remain trapped in the orbit of seeking solely *our* interests, yet under the clever guise of care for the other.[114] It is possible we fear the sufferings that come from bearing Christ's name, and so we seek human praise instead of obeying God.[115] Perhaps we strain to escape crucifixion by shutting out of our minds the sufferings of those whom we love yet whose geographical distance allows us to forget them.[116] All this is to "make peace with the world" and so effectively to renounce the cross.[117]

Or—and here is the most *theologically* sophisticated temptation—we may attempt to unmount the cross by convincing ourselves that God is not in ultimate control of events, thereby granting our inquiring mind relief from its questions about God's responsibility for allowing the evils that transpire on earth. Theoretical distinctions between primary and secondary causality, and between direct divine action and divine permission, are vital and justified in pursuit of intellectual and moral coherence in our speech about God. Eventually, however, these distinctions give way to the hard implications of Job's agonies: Satan may be the aggressor, but God oversees the entire affair.[118] This fact confounds the intellect and scandalizes the heart. "But you, fearful and despairing, see not a Father but only an evil torturer in the heavens."[119] Thus does Bulgakov chide himself, confessing the presence of the scandal within his own heart as well.

Here is the crux of the matter: God is omnipotent; Providence guides history to its end; thus our free actions—and they truly are free[120]—are either allowed or not allowed onto the paths of history to the extent that they serve the manifestation of this divine wisdom, for God possesses history's outcome already in the eternity that is Divine Sophia.[121] This is a hard teaching, but Bulgakov was not a man to shy away from a logical conclusion. As we have seen, only the promise that God works all things together for good, and that the imprisonment of all in disobedience serves in the end for the gift of mercy upon all, renders God's kenotic allowance of earthly suffering *morally* intelligible for the Christian, who makes his act of faith in God's goodness any time he utters the word "Father" in prayer.[122] Yet this divine silence must remain *intellectually* unassimilated for us who are hoisted on the cross *in medias res*. "In situations like these, ignorance need not attempt to understand by straining its proud intellect, for the intellect is powerless. It is with a broken and humble heart, with patience and prayer, that we must penetrate the meaning of the destinies given by the Lord; will not the Lord reveal His will?"[123]

In such moments, in order to offer God everything we have in our love, God demands of us a *sacrificium intellectus*, a turning away from the innate human quest for understanding. The spiritual battle ensues for the believing heart in a feat of *prayer*, and Christ's surrender in Gethsemane shows us best how to express this love for God beyond all understanding: "*not my will, but thine.*"[124] The crucifixion involved in this self-offering becomes most acute for us when we try to fulfill the Apostle's injunctions to always give thanks:

> My heart burns, my soul grows faint, God, my sweet, good, great God. I must thank you for everything: for joy and for grief, for life and for death, for bliss and for trials, for people's love and hatred. But at times my poor heart is confounded: how can I thank You for famine, for spiritual captivity, for slavery and woe, for the ruin of those nearest to me, for the ruin of my nation, for the desecration of my homeland? Would this not be a lie and hypocrisy, an abomination before the Lord? I stand speechless in the face of these disasters, in the face of these droughts and famines that the Lord has sent to innocent people, to infants.[125]

In the *Diary*, Bulgakov reaches no answer to this perplexity: how to thank God "for all things,"[126] including the unspeakable calamities that God permits to unfold. The question is particularly acute for the priest, who offers the Eucharistic, or thanksgiving, sacrifice to God. Yet Sr. Joanna Reitlinger tells us that by the end of his life, in the midst of the tragedies of the Second World War, Bulgakov found a way to make this sacrifice of praise: "'Can I sincerely offer up to God [my Eucharistic thanksgiving] for this?' And suddenly the answer resounded within me: 'Yes, I can [give thanks]...for Christ, who suffers in them and with them!'"[127]

By inviting us to this Gethsemane feat of faith, the Father asks nothing of us that he did not undertake himself when he delivered his Son to a fate that was, in the eyes of the world, "severe, inscrutable, and cruel, for what could be more cruel and inscrutable than to send the Son to the Cross, to give Him up to agony?" Hence we must daily work on ourselves to prepare to make this sacrifice and not to fall into despair.[128] Then our sacrifice will be one with Christ's, a genuinely Eucharistic sacrifice, in which fire from heaven consumes us without destroying us. This sacrifice is the culmination of sophianic self-creation, when we strive to love what God wants for us, concretely, and not what we would want for ourselves. For if in relationships with others we fulfill the law of love by denying ourselves and no longer seeking "our own,"[129] then the same holds true in the life-long task of loving *ourselves*, the sophianic self that is identical with God's creative intent for us. In this sacrifice we love truly not only ourselves but also God, not as we tend to imagine Him (that is, as the giver of everything that would satisfy our presently limited desires), but as He is in infinite love and wisdom. When we hand ourselves over to the hammer and chisel of the divine decree by humbly submitting to the divine will, then, and only then, will our eternal form in God's wisdom becomes manifest: "In this lies a higher wisdom and a higher obedience."[130]

Bulgakov's *Spiritual Diary* presents a stark vision of the cross that frames the Christian life. There is no calm reassurance in its vision of the human person, purportedly free of any tragedy or drama because of God's eternal possession of us in Divine Sophia. Critics of sophiology's anthropology on this score miss the mark when they fail to understand that sophiology's "creativity of the cross" is *ascetic*; as Bulgakov reminds us when speaking of iconographic creativity, this beauty arises only from "constant, self-denying labor."[131] This sophianic vision flips the matter on its head: precisely because God so possesses us and all creation in Divine Sophia, this means that our high calling demands of us nothing less than everything, until God shall be "all in all."[132] But Bulgakov never lets us forget that sophianic self-creation is co-creation *with* God, together with the angels, and the saints, and all who love us. Our guardian angel keeps watch over us with prayer and encouragement.[133] The saints grow into the infinity of love by loving us in response to our prayers.[134] The Theotokos sends us the Holy Spirit.[135] To enter into Christ's cross and to allow God to transform us and to release our divine beauty is to love *love*. But the love of Love is another name for the Holy Spirit, and so the cross is far more than just the death of our flesh. It is our entry into trinitarian joy.[136] "Train yourself to love love, endure the work of love, carry the cross of love, and it will become ever easier and more joyful for you. Herein lies the very mystery and power of the cross, the power of Christ's meekness and humility, making the yoke easy and the burden light."[137] There is a peace that passes all understanding, that undergirds and outstrips the *sacrificium intellectus*, that knows already the resurrection even on Great and Holy Friday. To find this peace is the purpose to which Christ calls us. Bulgakov reminds us that we need only follow.

SPIRITUAL DIARY

Dedication

To dear Father Sergius.
On the Feast of St. Sergius, September 29.[1]
Belgrade. Přerov. Prague.[2] 1923.[3]

N. Zernov[4]
Iosif Rietoriya[5]
V. Zenkovsky[6]
Sofia Zernova[7]
K. Euler[8]
A. Obolenskaya[9]
K. Reitlinger[10]
Y. Reitlinger[11]
P. Novgorodtsev[12]
G. Shumkin[13]
Ark. Struve[14]
S. Bezobrazov[15]
A. Obolensky[16]

PRAGUE, 8/21.III.1924

Last night, after being grievously impressed by the vanity of this age, by failure and by personal bitterness, I arrived home in a poisoned state, and all night—both in sleep and out of it—I languished and mourned. I felt myself submerged in a deep darkness, and as often happens, my whole life seemed to me a mistake and a failure. And I felt in me and on me the breath of *death*: it came and went and had possession of me. I prayed, I called out to God, but I lacked the strength to break forth from these depths. I had a dream: we were headed somewhere, and we were being exiled, and with us was a newborn, feeble, unfortunate child, and my heart was faint from pain and pity for this child. In that state I awoke—dead, languishing—and I began to pray. At first prayer was difficult, but later my heart was miraculously reignited. The Lord had mercy on me, and I felt in my heart one joy, one love, and one agony: to give away everything, everything for the Lord, to accept everything from the Lord, to bear everything given by the Lord. My Christ, grant me one thing: to love You, to dissolve in this love. My light, my Most Sweet Jesus! My Joy, my Delight! Do not abandon this cold, dead heart, You who raise the dead!

PRAGUE, 9/22.III.1924

This whole day a darkness covered me, and in vain I called out from the depths to the Lord [cf. Ps. 130:1]. But the evening brought a ray of light. The wife of Pr. K-R died.[17] She was, or rather considered herself to be, an unbeliever. The Lord granted her to commune—by my sinful hands—in the Holy Mysteries. Even in her final confession she prattled on about her unbelief, but her beautiful, pure, true heart already loved and knew the Lord. And before death she requested that there be placed in her coffin the napkin with which she had wiped her lips at communion. My joy, my dear: it is the Lord Himself who has come to sup with you. And I will place for you in your coffin not only the napkin but also the glass chalice and spoon with which you communed. Shield yourself with these from demonic provocation and proceed valiantly to the Final Judgment! So here she lies: dear, bright, serene, as if sleeping; her soul has fluttered away like a bird and is somewhere here among us. And I felt that my wretched heart was touched by the Lord through the hands and prayers of the newly departed

Ekaterina, and my heart began to palpitate from this joyful call. Just are You, O Lord, and just are Your ways [Rev. 15:3].

10/23.III.1924

After unrest and turmoil of heart cease, the Lord grants His light and peace and joy. The heavens are opened, the storm clouds dissipate, and what just yesterday seemed dark and dismal now shines with heavenly joy. Nothing has changed, only that the Lord touched my heart, and it rejoiced anew. Of all the things people hold dear, none is necessary: not talents, not successes, not accomplishments. All these are imaginary riches for oneself. There is one fortune and joy that God grants equally to every person: one's own life, created in God, and a heart capable of loving and of rejoicing in love.

O human heart, seat of the image of God in man! What is more beautiful and more sweet than you, what is more joyful than love? For God is Love, and the one who loves abides in God [1 John 4:16]. O joy! O joy of joys! The song of love resounds in the loving heart, and it melts away in bliss. "I sleep, but my heart is awake"; at its door the Groom knocks [Song of Sol. 5:2].

12/25.III.1924

The Lord has given us a spiritual sword—prayer; yet how difficult it is for us to wield it when our hearts grow lazy and cold. Man hurries to quickly bypass prayer and to undertake the day's work, he hurries away from prayer. And only when he overcomes this laziness of his heart, when his heart is ignited by prayer, does he see that he is hurrying to nowhere and for nothing, that there is nothing on earth more needful and sweet than prayer.

14/27.III.1924

God has granted me the joy of seeing the pure creativity of a feminine soul.[18] And my soul is filled with surprise at God's miracles, and with thanksgiving. My heart trembles and knows neither words nor thoughts; it desires—little maggot that it is—to melt and to dissolve in the ocean of divine love surrounding us. O, the love of God, Love itself, and our human love, the love of Love—they are immeasurably distinct, yet every drop spills out into this ocean. And may it be, may even the drop of my heart be poured out into this sea, my Lord, my Joy, my most sweet Jesus!

15/28.III.1924

The Lord grants a new day of life, a new possibility to love Him, to please Him, to build oneself up as a temple for Him [cf. 1 Cor. 3:16–17]; He grants new joy in life. He as it were creates His world anew through this joyful day. We must daily feel this new blessing from God, this new creation of the world, we must stir up in our hearts gratitude and tenderness. When in morning prayer you thank God for this day that He has given, then with joyful surprise you look upon this day, upon these clouds, upon this world, given to you once again. And then unwittingly you look also upon the end, when with the beckoning of God's right hand this world will be taken from you and there will no longer be new days; then only the old days, which you wasted in vanity, will be visible in the mirror of your soul.

19.III/1.IV.1924

What is more beautiful than a pure human soul turned towards God? I have spent these past days at the bedside of one dying,[19] and witnessing his prayerful ecstasies, I felt myself unworthy to stand in this holy place, for the Lord was here [cf. Gen. 28:16]. It is as if the gates of eternity have been thrown open, and reaching us through them—light and the song of bells and joy, joy forevermore...

21.III/3.IV.1924

Out of the depths have I cried unto thee, O Lord [Ps. 130:1].[20] When sorrow overwhelms the heart and gloom descends on the soul, You, O Lord, only You are my comfort and my refuge. I grasp at the hem of Your garment [Matt. 9:20], and my grief subsides, and joy, graced joy, floods my heart. And I feel that nothing can take this joy from me. But when in my cowardice I let go of the hem of this garment, I drown [Matt. 14:30].

Lord, hear my voice and help all orphaned and grieving souls. How lofty is the ministry of priesthood—to stand at the side of the grieving and dying, to witness their struggle and the light of their soul, to pray with them and for them. I was at the bedside of a young consumptive woman, and my soul grieved and I trembled from pity and tenderness before this flower of life cut down. The Lord is nigh unto all them that call upon Him [Ps. 145:18].

23.III/5.IV.1924

Blessed are the meek [Matt. 5:5]... These words of the Lord concerning the blessedness of meekness come to the heart when the temptations of arrogance, rashness, and anger visit the sinful soul; and they are always visiting it. And how sweet it is not to give oneself over to these feelings, what freedom and joy does meekness provide. Not for nothing did the Lord say of Himself that He is meek and lowly of heart and that He grants peace to our souls [Matt. 11:29].

26.III/8.IV.1924

At the bedside of one dying... How lofty and blessed is the priestly ministry. The Lord grants it to the priest to stand at the gates of eternity when they open to receive a departing soul, and the priest himself sees into these open gates, and this sight is like an indictment, and yet at the same time like a call that refreshes the soul by entering into it. This vision should introduce into the soul an unceasing remembrance of death as well as a consciousness of the proximity of these two worlds. And all the more so when a just person departs in peace, in full consciousness and fully given over to God's will, as has just happened now... Speaking to the priest, he says of himself: "My heart is ready" [Ps. 57:7], and he forces the priest to self-examine: is his heart ready and, if not, why not? The parched soul is refreshed by heavenly dew, you feel the nearness of the Lord and His hand upon you, and the heart burns with love and joyful surprise. There is no death: there are only two worlds, or rather one, yet for the time being it remains, for us, divided.

28.III./10.IV.1924

At the bedside of one who is dying in the Lord.[21] There is no anxiety about death, none of its rending horror, but there is joy, bliss, and readiness to obey the Lord's command to cross over to that other world, which is as subservient and near to the Lord as this world is. Standing before the face of eternity and losing the sense of one's own heaviness... Oh, how this frees the soul, how it fills it with heavenly rapture... And in the face of *this*, how insignificant our earthly circumstances appear. We have been ripped out of Russia, *our* spiritual homeland, and yet *what does this matter* when before us we have our *common* spiritual homeland? And not once did my departing companion reminisce or express any feelings about his exile, for before him stood his homeland according to the flesh, his kin, as well as his homeland according to the spirit, a priest, in whom this Russian land dwells. And it is with this homeland and from this homeland that he goes forth to his spiritual homeland. There, it is nothing like it is here; there are different dimensions, a different vision of things. Blessed be God who has vouchsafed for me, unworthy as I am, to see and to experience all these miracles.

5 / 18.IV.1924

The joy of creativity. Before my eyes was accomplished a miracle of human creativity in the Lord and for the Lord: pure virgin hands outlined icons of the Savior and the Ever Virgin, the fruit of profound awe and quiet prayer but also of constant, self-denying labor.[22] How lofty and holy is this work! The Lord gives strength. He sends inspiration, and by the Holy Spirit beauty is imprinted. Human art brings Him satisfaction, and blessed is he who can and who wishes to devote this art to Him. And if this creative work—done in a small corner and imperceptible to the world—pleases the Lord, then what blessedness will come if people begin to do all things in the Lord, if the entirety of life becomes praise, becomes liturgy. Yea, *come*, come, Lord Jesus! [Rev. 22:20].

18.IV / 1.V.1924

Holy Week and Christ's Pascha are marvelous and manifest miracles of God that appear every year, like the stirring of the waters at the pool of Siloam [John 9:7]. These are the highest mountains to which the long ascent of Great Lent leads, and their heights are not even felt once a person scales them. The soul is aflame and burns everything with a blazing fire in the marvelous days of Holy Week, and in dying it experiences bliss, and in bliss the soul dies. And afterwards this flame suddenly and immediately transforms and turns into the paradisiacal, luminous, and gladdening white Paschal fire, neither scorching nor burning.[23] If people alien to the Church knew this, how they would be ignited, how their souls would begin to shine. And this manifest miracle of God's grace is both salvific and merciful. Everything is transfigured, and this already just *is* the dawn of transfiguration; everything appears in a different light, full of grace and sanctified from within. The mercy of God: so dreadful and yet so sweet. At times the soul wishes as if to be set free from the body in sweet release [cf. Phil. 1:23], to give itself over to God, to come to rest. And this light of the Resurrection, which suddenly blazes forth on Pascha night and displaces all colors and hues, clothing everything in a white that no fuller on earth knows [Mark 9:3]—how it enters the heart and merges there with the white fire, and it burns, and it shines. O joy of joys, most sweet Jesus!

6/19.V.1924[24]

We must love the *work* of prayer and never slacken in it. People seek spiritual pleasures, and if grace ever shows its face to them, when it is taken away from them they languish and their soul grows cold. But the work of prayer—persistent, never slackening, tenacious—is the expression of our active love for God that strives to bind our sinful being and bring it to the altar. The Kingdom of God is taken by force [Matt. 11:12]. And this work never remains unjustified [cf. Matt. 11:19]. At times you pray but the heart remains cold and callous, the tongue wooden. And yet, if you force yourself and make absolutely no concessions nor grant any indulgence to your laziness, after prayer the soul feels itself renewed, resilient, and strengthened.

The same thing also happens when you attend church services and the experience is accompanied by a certain coldness; after this too do you feel yourself strengthened. Therefore, work, brothers, and even you, wicked servant [Matt. 25:26], work. For work is love, and the one who does not work and is lazy in love—his heart is cold.

19.V/1.VI.1924

What a miracle prayer is! The sinful and unworthy human being, in mad audacity, sends forth his prayers, lobs his words to heaven, and it happens that the prayer *is heard*; the heart of the one praying knows this when he prays sincerely. This does not mean that our *every* wish is immediately fulfilled as we would want; this may in fact happen—and then the prayer is immediately miracle-working—but it may also not happen. But a prayer that is sincere and heartfelt *always* has an effect and is *always* fulfilled:

it is *always* miracle-working, for it is animated by the all-powerful and dreadful Name of God.[25] Pray, O man, learn to pray, and great strength, joy, and tranquility will be with you. Do not deny the power of prayer on account of sinful weakness, do not say to yourself that God will not hearken to one so weak and sinful. He hearkens to every praying heart, and the heart hearkens to the God who hears it. And God is not somewhere far off, high in the heavens [Deut. 30:12; Rom. 10:6]; He is here, in your heart [Rom. 10:8], everywhere that His Name is called upon with awe, for He is in this Name.

Oh, what a mercy of God is prayer! Teach yourself the breath of prayer, entrust yourself to prayer, learn to undertake nothing without prayer, and it will be well with you! [cf. Eph. 6:3]. Pray both in sorrow and in joy, in necessity and in thanksgiving, and you will feel the Lord holding your hand, and you will never be alone... I have set the Lord before me [Ps. 16:8], where does my help come from? My help comes from the Lord, the maker of heaven and earth [Ps. 121:1–2].[26]

26.V/8.VI.1924

Today on my way to the liturgy, in the early morning, I walked through the streets of the city made fresh after the night. I thought: God provides this morning in His world. Everything within it lives in boundless breadth and depth. Innumerable creations: people and birds, fish in the deep and leeches on Everest, all creatures clean and unclean [cf. Lev. 11]—everything sings praise to God this morning, and He fills everything, and everywhere He is near... And He is near also to you, and you were created in this world as a part of it, no less than the others were you counted worthy of existence; you are a citizen both of this earth and of these stars, and of all endless things, both great and small. And you can and therefore must attend to the song of the world borne to you from all sides, you must attend to the glory of God that fills heaven and earth [Isa. 6:3]. For here there is no other *then* or *there*; there is only the immovable *here* and *now*. All life, until the Lord should extinguish this light of your life, is an unceasing *now*. And what a sin against oneself and against the world, what cowardice you expose in yourself when you escape to that *then*. See, it is here, now, that the Lord and His Glory are near, that eternity is near, as well as this infinite world of God's: the angels sing glory to God, and all creation does too. How to feel this in a single moment, the beating of the world's heart and myself as a drop of the warm blood of the world rushing through the world's body? How can I set the Lord always before me? [Ps. 16:8]. But I can and I desire to: help and teach me, Lord!

28.V / 10.VI.1924

Every day begins a new life—like every page of this diary—and it reveals a new boundlessness to God's mercy. God allows us to love and to pray to Him, to rejoice in love and to live. Yet how lazy is this heart of mine, which desires to put off the effort of this day and thinks to itself: not this ordinary day, but some other day... "tomorrow." And meanwhile at every moment of life we have *everything*: God, and the world, and our own soul. And it is simply blindness and sluggishness of soul to wait for some specific moment in order to stop and say: you are beautiful!

In truth, every moment of life is *equally* beautiful, for God bestows it. And so do not be lazy, my soul, know this and put it into practice... And when the moments are taken away, when the fires of life are extinguished, then you will see *just how* beautiful, how truly beautiful each moment was, and then it will be too late... Lord, expand my heart to know how beautiful is this moment of life You give us, to rejoice, to give thanks to You; in this joy all earthly grief will dissipate.

30.V / 12.VI.1924

What a miracle love is! Lord, You have filled your world with miracles, the whole world is one miracle of Your goodness and wisdom. But even this miracle pales before the miracle of Love, before the miracle of the human heart.

You, Subsistent Love, have placed in man your image, have placed in him the ability to love, as well as the power of love, and the thirst of love, and the bliss of love. There is no bliss more powerful, more inexplicable than love. Earthly life cannot contain it, it fills the soul to the brim and spills out onto the whole world, it frees the soul from the shackles of this life.

Love is as strong as death [Song of Sol. 8:6]. Death in this world is stronger than life, for it cuts life off; but love is stronger than death: it breaks life open, but it also ignites life in eternity. Love always bears eternity in itself, it is the living revelation of eternity, for God Himself is Love [1 John 4:16]. Eternity—this just is love, and the voice of eternity, the revelation of eternity in the human heart, is love. How marvelous are Your works, Lord! [Ps. 139:14] You created the world, but You also created that which is higher than the world: love. All you who are blind and deaf—understand the *mystery* of love in Christ and in the Church, understand the bliss of love. The Lord is the Bridegroom, the Beloved of my soul; the Church is my beloved bride. Love is bliss insatiable, thirst unquenchable, jealousy as fierce as the grave [Song of Songs 8:6]. And this love is never satisfied, it is ever flaring up and filling the soul to the brim. Such is my love for my Lord and such is my Lord's love for me, for every one of his creatures. Love is Divine—it is a boundless ocean; an unsearchable abyss; a flame inextinguishable, blazing for eternity. Love is the joy of joys, the bliss of bliss.

6 / 19.VI.1924

"Steady me ... for I languish with love. His left hand is under my head, and his right embraces me" (Song of Songs 2:5–6). This is spoken of love, in the Song of Songs, concerning the human soul. And when there dawns upon the soul this white, sweet fire of love that does not sear but rather gladdens, the soul experiences such an unearthly bliss that it trembles and wishes to break free from the body. And it becomes apparent that of all the bliss, of all the goods that the Lord has prepared for man, the highest bliss is the bliss of love. To love with divine love is possible even for man, or rather it is possible in human love to find this divine love, because, for people and among people, there is nothing more lofty, more unconditional, more holy than love. God-Love[27] created people for love, and the bliss of paradise *is love*, blazing and burning hot beyond all limits and drowning in the ocean of divine, tri-hypostatic love.

And then it becomes clear that the entire New Testament is about love, the love of God for the world, for fallen creation, the love of Christ for the Church and for every human soul, the love of the tri-hypostatic God—to this love God unites, and desires to unite, creation. "We will come to him and make our abode with him" [John 14:32]. And the Holy Spirit-Comforter is the joy of triumphant love; comfort is love, and those who love are fanned and comforted by the Holy Spirit, they feel within themselves the heart of Christ loving them and through them the entire world. That is why when the fire of love is kindled in one spot, it spreads through the entire world, it embraces everything and everyone...

8/21.VI.1924

Love and prayer, prayer and love: only these two are the wings of the Christian life. When you stand at prayer and your heart grows enflamed from love for your sweet and dear fellow-travelers in life, then this flame spreads through the whole world, and the soul is plunged into the ocean of love, into the bliss of love, and it burns with so blissful a fire that the soul grows faint from this bliss. O sweetness of sweetness, O joy of joys, my most sweet Jesus! Enflame me with Your fire, enkindle my soul, burn it in You.

10/23.VI.1924

Oh, what a miserable sinner am I, but what great gifts and blessings from God I have been granted! This evening I shuddered and squirmed like a worm, and my soul died from bliss at the breath of the Holy Spirit. I felt this breath, I knew it, I loved and rejoiced with the unearthly bliss of the joy of love. And I came to recognize that the Holy Spirit is love, and that the revelation of the Holy Spirit is the bliss of love. When the Lord, according to John's Gospel, promised the Comforter, He gave a new commandment as well: "Love one another" [John 13:34], and this command pertains to the reception of the Holy Spirit, and the new promise is His perfect joy, and this joy is joy in the Holy Spirit.

This evening—for the first time—I came to know this by experience, and the Holy Spirit was with me, and I grew faint, and cried, and trembled, and loved everyone and everything, my heart expanded and boiled over, and I grew faint from love. This cannot be put into words, the Holy Spirit is ineffable, but I know the bliss of the age to come and I know the fulfillment of the promises... Lord, give me strength to walk in Your ways, teach me to do Thy will! [cf. Ps. 143:10].[28]

11/24.VI.1924

Since evening there has lain on my soul a dark cloud—the thought of my miserable, increasingly godless, suffering homeland heading towards a new trial of famine;[29] dark and heavy were my thoughts about my homeland. But today in prayer I entrusted myself and my homeland to the will of God, and then there was calm and peace. Accomplish Thy will, O Lord! You direct our paths, You know them; have mercy, have mercy on my brothers, have mercy on Your Church.

Like waves in the sea do all these feelings in my soul constantly displace each other: inspirations and then dejections. How surprising is the life of this sea! If only this present depth would remain forever, if only the sea of my soul would not prove the plaything of every wind [cf. Eph. 4:14].

13 / 26.VI.1924

Lord, your world is a miracle, and every day and hour of life that You give to Your creation is a miracle of Your grace. We all wait for and seek miracles, without noticing that we live in one unceasingly accomplished miracle. And what is this daily miracle? Prayer. I, the most sinful of sinners, the most worthless of the worthless, dare to lift up my unworthy prayers to Your throne, and when I pray from the heart, I know—even in this moment I know—that my prayer is heard. For even here the Lord is near [Phil. 4:5], He sees and hearkens; it is only we who do not see and hearken to His presence. But with Him and in Him are all His gifts, all His mercy, His whole garment [cf. Matt. 9:20], all His miracles...

15 / 28.VI.1924

Lord! What a miracle love is! Miraculous are Your worlds, miraculous is Your creation, but there is no miracle more miraculous than the love that burns in the heart of Your creatures. The one who loves possesses everything he loves, he rejoices at and in everything that he loves, he is blessed by everything that he loves. Love is the Holy Spirit. The revelation of the Spirit is the revelation of love, God-Love... O, set me as a seal upon Your heart and as a seal upon Your arm [Song of Sol. 8:6]; I grow faint from love.

23.VI / 6.VII.1924

Conscience is the voice of God in the human heart. How subtle it is, how it denounces falsehood and sin, tears off masks, strikes at vices. It cannot be bought, and it cannot be fooled. But when there is confusion in the soul, and when the soul itself lacks the strength to sort itself out in a sea of contradictions, then ask the Lord to pour His light into the darkness of ignorance and to show the right path.

Blessed art Thou, O Lord: *teach* me Thy statutes [Ps. 119:12],[30] in things both great and small. And let not man proudly imagine that he knows his path and that this path is good, for only by the work of prayer does the Lord grant knowledge of our paths. Teach me then, Lord!

3 / 16.VII.1924

"Knock and ye shall find..." [Matt. 7:7] At times there is despondency, anxiety, darkness in the heart, every kind of human hopelessness. And in that moment there is prayer: it is somehow unbelievable to the natural man that anything can be done. But we should not, we may not, think like this: God is all-powerful, and prayer is all-powerful. It makes the impossible possible, it resolves the unresolvable in an unexpected, at times completely nonhuman, way. The Lord was not lying when he said: knock and ye shall find. And to the work of prayer we must also add *courage* in prayer, confidence in the *feasibility* and in the fulfillment of every prayer that is consequential and worthy.

The fact that prayer is heard—this is always verified in the heart. The one praying somehow *knows* this, and a prayer that is heard is always fulfilled in one way or another; it is only necessary to entrust its fulfillment to the Lord. And it is evident that the fulfilling of prayer is an unceasing miracle of God's mercy, and then all of life becomes a miracle...

1 / 14.VIII.1924[31]

Lord, Lord, my soul grows faint from love for You and thanksgiving to You, for this entire marvelous world that surrounds me and that I insult with my sin, my ignorance, my disregard; for all these people whom You grant me both to know and to love and who, for some reason, love me, wretched and unworthy as I am; for this life, this day, each breath of life, for the time that You, in Your authority, have allotted for me to live: all of this is a gift, Your gift, which I should at no time ever flee from or fail to give thanks for.

My heart burns, my soul grows faint, God, my sweet, good, great God. I must thank you for everything [cf. 1 Thess. 5:18]: for joy and for grief, for life and for death, for bliss and for trials, for people's love and hatred. But at times my poor heart is confounded: how can I thank You for famine, for spiritual captivity, for slavery and woe, for the ruin of those nearest to me, for the ruin of my nation, for the desecration of my homeland? Would this not be a lie and hypocrisy, an abomination before the Lord? I stand speechless in the face of these disasters, in the face of these droughts and famines that the Lord has sent to innocent people, to infants.

Once again, millions of Russian people are doomed to die from famine: how can we fathom this? Oh, even this could be fathomed, if I gave myself over to these people, gave everything that is mine, completely, if I gave myself over to God, who has given me everything. But we do not do this; remaining on the shore, we look upon the one drowning, and then trepidation and horror take us. Yes, not everything is comprehensible for man, and it cannot become comprehensible, for beginnings and endings are all lost in obscurity and infinity, and forever the destiny of people remains a mystery.

But in this lies the sweetness of faith, the feat of faith: the Lord, whom my soul never tires of thanking for His great gifts, He is always and in everything true to Himself. And we must pray to God for His mercies, but we must also thank His all-powerful and loving right hand for everything! Lord, teach me to thank You, grant me strength to give You thanks!

3 / 16.VIII.1924

Lord, my Lord! How long will the anger of Your fury against Your land last? [Ps. 80:4]. Spare the land, have mercy, save it through Your angels[32] from the cruel demons tormenting it, have mercy on these souls who are defiled from birth, deprived of holy baptism, corrupted in thought and feeling. Cast out the one now unbound, who, sensing that his days are numbered, torments Your people [Rev. 12:12]. We do not ask for our former prosperity, of which we were unworthy; we ask only that You free Your holy Church, that you reveal her in Your glory. When you pray for Russia—it's so difficult that, at first, the prayer falls into the void, as if silently ricocheting off a brick wall. It is unanswered. But later the heart hears some sort of answer: that we do not know what is occurring, that the Mother of God is preserving the Russian land, that Russia is saved, and that we must only not despair, but we must believe and hope, we must stir up in ourselves this love and faith.

5/18.VIII.1924

What a scourge has befallen the Russian land, what depravity! The mind grows faint from trying to comprehend what is taking place; Satan, unbound, rages [Rev. 12:12]. But Lord, my Lord, You are just and just are Your ways [Rev. 15:3]. You know that they are not guilty, those who are imbibing along with their mother's milk an education in sin, just as there is no merit in those who have lived in other, more Christian times. But just as You once answered the prophet Elijah, saying that You kept for Yourself those who did not bow the knee to Baal [Rom. 11:4], and just as in Sodom You reserved ten righteous ones [Gen. 18:32], so even now You are keeping from among the Russian people these elect and You are preparing them for the hour of Your glory. You guide them through all temptations and steel them against all assaults. They abide with You in the assaults against You, and they will be revealed in Your glory. At that time they will plead before You for their brothers. And this means that even now there is a path for Your elect, that it is not closed off for man. Reveal it to us, then; strengthen our will and our faithfulness. For Thou hast said: Fear not, elect flock, for it is My Father's good pleasure to give you the kingdom! [cf. Luke 12:32].

7/20.VIII.1924

If only we were submissive to God's will! If only the heart would not waver from lack of faith, from despondency, from fear in the face of what is happening in the world, in our homeland, in the face of all the difficulties and complexities we face in our lives. If these are not due to our choices and not due to our sin but nonetheless given to us, sent down from above as our fate, accept it as the will of God for yourself, as a riddle for the time being, and as a task for the present. Unknown, inscrutable is the path, the end, God's purpose, but in our heart we experience confirmation just by hearing that God *is*, that His holy will is at work in everything.

Therefore learn to humble yourself, to reconcile yourself with reality, with the will of God for you, but do not reconcile yourself with any sinful fact within yourself. Fight this and you will find God's help. But as concerns external destinies—for the world or for humanity—you should ask yourself only what is required of you, what form of action is worthy of Christian faith. Both think and feel as if the destinies of the world depend on you—on your activity or inactivity, however small or insignificant in its sphere—no less than they depend on all these grandiose but illusory events taking place on the stage of history. But do not think of averting your eyes, of drawing back, of pronouncing the real as nonexistent, of *fleeing* from your duty.

Cursed be the lazy and wicked servant! [Matt. 25:26]. Be especially faithful to the human heart whose love and destiny the Lord entrusts to you. Attend to it as the most important thing, as the duty in your life for which you are most accountable, which holds significance for the entire world. Love, take risks, sacrifice, and the rest will be granted to you [Matt. 6:33].

8 / 21.VIII.1924

What is impossible for man is possible for God [Matt. 19:26]—in all things, and in human hearts most especially. If you have difficulty, O man, in your affairs, in relation to those close to you, in love and in lack of love, pray about it; pray also for yourself that the Lord may send strength and understanding.

Pray, entrust yourself to Him, and be at peace, hearkening only to your heart. The Lord sends people. He disposes meetings, He indicates paths. There is nothing accidental in relationships between people; people were created for each other. Pray for those who love you and for your friends, pray for those who hate you [Matt. 5:44], pray for those who do not pray for themselves, the burdened and blinded. For all people need your prayer...

10 / 23.VIII.1924

Sometimes someone near and dear is ill, and we always pray for his salvation and healing. The Church blesses and calls us to this prayer, and it does not know and does not allow any prayer requesting death, except for prayer for the separation of the soul from the body, if the process be especially onerous and protracted.

But it is permitted, and for those who can cope with it, it is even expected, to pray for the end of the world and for the second coming, as the [early] Christians prayed: "Even so, come Lord Jesus!" [Rev. 22:20]. But that just *is* our death, as the apostle testified: my desire is to die and to be with Christ [Phil. 1:23]. Yet sometimes, in response to the human effort to hold on at all costs—even if the Lord's will is obvious to any bystander or if the fullness of life has already been reached—in response to this a voice rises in the soul: "Do not hold on. Now is the time to fulfill all righteousness" [Matt. 3:15]. This feeling occurs when the ear of corn has already matured and is awaiting its scythe. Of course, it is never granted to us to know this hour with certainty [cf. Matt. 24:36], but we can foresee when, for example, death approaches in old age...

12/25.VIII.1924

Lord, teach us to pray as Jesus taught His disciples! It was Divine Wisdom who uttered the Lord's prayer. But now I must bear this unbearable burden: they are asking me to compose a prayer for our suffering homeland! And I cannot but heed this call. Yet what shall I say? Lord, You see my weakness and my sins. You know that I am unworthy of lifting my eyes to heaven and of being called Your son [cf. Luke 18:13; 15:19]. But if You require this, take me, take my hand, and let it write not what my own pitiful mind would say but what You put into it. These days are the holy days of the God-bearer,[33] and the Mother of God Herself has saved the Russian land in the past.[34] May She save it even now and may She aid me in the work of salvation through the prayer of the sons of the Russian land. Mother of God, to You I entrust my sinful hand. Bless and direct me to write what is pleasing to You!

16/29.VIII.1924

Most Holy Theotokos, save us! Pray, O man, to the most pure Mother of God, to the Queen of Heaven and the Mother of the human race; pray with love, with faith, with hope, pray unfailingly and believe that She will hear your prayer! There is no one closer to man, more kindred to the human being than the Mother of God in the heavens. She covers the world [with her mantle],[35] intercedes for it, She is with all creation, over all of nature, She is over the waters and the dry lands, the fields and the forests, over humans and creation. She embraces all things in Herself, unites all things—She is a merciful heart to all. After praying to the Lord and while praying to the Lord, pray also to His Mother, the Bearer of the Holy Spirit. Believe that the Mother of God will have mercy and will send you the gift of the Holy Spirit, and you will behold the Son of God living within you. Oh, who will disclose the mysteries of the Mother of God, who can comprehend them? Most Holy Theotokos, save us!

17/30.VIII.1924

Do not think. Do not think, O man, of your affairs—how they will turn out, how your relationships with people will work out, how to resolve your difficulties. Take no thought for the morrow [Matt. 6:34]. You know neither the course of your life nor all those circumstances that change along with you. This confusion and anxiety that descends upon you, all this is like the rich man who wanted to secure a future for himself when God took his soul from him [cf. Luke 12:16–21]. We must know, and firmly know, how to act today: God provides us this day, full of ever new, unknown, mysterious possibilities. Each day is a new mystery from God, it is the mystery of our life. God would not give days if they were not an unfolding mystery. And we must seek for ourselves a place among these possibilities, we must walk before Him, making sure that our steps are as near to Him as possible.

Be, then, free of concerns, with that holy, evangelical lack of concern, like children. Sinful are your many cares, sinful is your desire to so mull over and to manage your life in hopes of securing it from all of life's chance circumstances. Throw all this away. Over you an angel keeps watch, a guardian of our souls and bodies,[36] as do all the saints and the Mother of God; but you, simply watch over and preserve your heart, give it over and offer it to God, fill it with the chrism of love and rejoicing.

20.VIII/2.IX.1924

While I live will I praise the Lord: I will sing praises unto my God while I have being [Ps. 146:2].[37] Every day that God gives, sanctify by prayer: praise God, love Him, bow down before His greatness!

How boundless is the mercy and grace of God that He hearkens to our prayer, gives us prayer and listens to it, and comes to the one praying and abides in prayer. For the Lord is not in the immeasurable heavens, but He is here, near, in His holy Name, called upon with faith and awe [Deut. 30:12]. And we know His nearness, that He listens. And that is why prayer washes us clean, refreshes us, fills us with strength, calms our souls; that is why after sincere and fervent prayer you return to the world and to life like Moses from the heights of Sinai, bearing on his face the radiance of the face of God [cf. Exod. 34:29–35].

23.VIII/5.IX.1924

Waves always furrow the human soul, and winds darken its surface. Sleeping and waking, we experience at times unexpected and incomprehensible bewilderment. This kind of bewilderment overcame me last night in my bed, and I dreamt that our patriarch had died and that they were burying him.[38] And I arose, bewildered—what will become of the Church without him? But through prayer my soul was calmed: the pilgrimage of His Holiness, who is now suffering for our Russian land, is a great mercy of God, for precious in the sight of the Lord is the death of His saints [Ps. 116:15].[39] But shall we worry ourselves over the Church's fate in his absence when we do not know what will happen tomorrow? [cf. James 4:14].

And then with a new solidity did the word of the Lord resound for me: "Take no thought for the morrow" [Matt. 6:34]—cast your care upon the Lord [Ps 55:22; 1 Pet. 5:7]. Only pray, pray fervently, sincerely, until you become certain of this by the igniting of your heart, by the warmth of your heart. And then with a cleansed soul will you go to your work.

Lord, what miracles of Your mercy, unceasing and daily, do You give to us in prayer! Teach us, then, to pray, ignite the spirit of prayer, undo the laziness of our hearts.

24.VIII/6.IX.1924

Once again the Lord gives a day of life, once again He gives the day's creativity, participation in the destinies of people, of the world, the opportunity to build up one's own soul: *This is the day which the Lord hath made* [Ps. 118:24]...

How little we consider and attend to the fact that the Lord truly creates each day and each hour of our lives, and that He creates it from nothing. From emptiness, from incompleteness, existence swims out: life. And by God's will time stops and again everything is submerged in the emptiness of death. Lord, Giver of Life, thine is the day and thine is the night [Ps 74:15 Douay-Rheims]. Oh, if only we could always bid farewell to and meet every day and hour of our life with this consciousness, then life would appear to us as so many precious stones, and how we would *walk* before the Lord [cf. Mic. 6:8]. Let us stir up this thought and this knowledge in our hearts, let us set the Lord always before us [Ps. 16:8]...

6/19.IX.1924

Yesterday in Zbraslav,[40] on the day of the holy prophet Zechariah and the righteous Elizabeth, at the liturgy, after holy communion and at the time of prayer for the salvation of Russia, I, wretched man that I am [Rom. 7:24], was counted worthy of an otherworldly vision. Before me at the altar stood the icon of the Mother of God of Kazan, a quite good icon of the Stroganov school, belonging to the Old Believer Solodovnikov.[41] It seemed to me that the face of the Most Pure Virgin grew whiter, and afterwards I clearly and without a doubt saw tears in the eyes of the Most Pure Virgin: she wept. And this happened not once, not twice; it continued on, whether for a long or a short time I do not know [cf. 2 Cor. 12:3]. These were not tears that could be seen with the eye, although it would have added nothing for me in terms of credibility if they had flowed and rolled down her Most Pure face. But this was an indubitable sign: the Mother of God wept. And in my heart there was revealed the sweet and inexplicable mystery that the Mother of God loves the world and that She weeps for it. In these tears was one sole, pure, merciful love, one sole suffering for sin and over sin, without any judgment, condemnation, or anger. The heart of the Mother of God is wounded by and weeps over every evil deed, word, and sinful provocation, for She is love.

Words are powerless to express this thought and this feeling, but for me it was clear that if and when *such* a love is revealed, then through it, through this love, *every* soul will be conquered and saved; the ice will melt, the heart will burst in response to this love, this purity, compassion, suffering. The salvation of the world and the revelation of the Holy Spirit will be the revelation of this merciful love that judges not but only shows compassion. The Lord has committed all judgment to the Son [John 5:22], for He is the Son of Man, but the Holy Spirit who lives in the Mother of God does not judge but only shows mercy. At the Dread Judgment, the Son judges, but the Most Pure One will show mercy to and pray for the world. At the Dread Judgment, She is mercy, forgiveness, compassion, not justice-love but mercy-love. And therefore the Mother of God always shows mercy, intercedes, prays, prays for the world and weeps over it, and we, unworthy ones, cause the Mother of God to weep on account of our sins.

She is in heaven, the glorified Queen of Heaven, but She is also a creature, undivided from the world: She lives its life and is wounded by it and grieves for it and will heal the world in the fullness of time. Here is the mystery of the age to come and of salvation. Most Pure Mother, You manifested Your love for the world to my hardened heart; give me the strength to manifest this love to others. Most Holy Theotokos, save humanity.

7/20.IX.1924

When griefs and difficulties surround you on all sides and the human eye cannot see a solution or a way out, cast your care upon the Lord [Ps. 55:22; 1 Pet 5:7], pray and be lighthearted and untroubled. The Lord who hears your prayer will take away your care, He will direct your footsteps. If you see misfortune approaching, looming and unavoidable, try to believe that if it is from God, then it is not misfortune: we simply do not know and cannot understand what is happening. Pray then: not my will, but Yours be done [Matt. 26:39]. But examine your conscience, seek in it whether you are the one at fault—because of your sins, your lack of love, your lack of prayer—in the misfortune of those near and dear to you... And pray, pray...

10/23.IX.1924

Just before the Feast of the Nativity of the Virgin,[42] on the train, I was counted worthy of a vision of the Lord. I was looking through the window at a blushing field, reddening foliage, and a blueing sky, and my soul was beside itself in the sweet languor of love for the Lord and for His world. And suddenly in my soul there arose that tempestuous joy which awaits us, which I came to know for the first time. And this joy was death. For the first time in my life I came to know by experience that death is the greatest joy awaiting man, for the Mother of God awaits him, as does her love. Angels too await us, and saints, and those who were near and dear to us . . . and the Lord as well. This is immense trepidation and horror, but it is also joy, limitless joy . . . "My desire is to die and to be with Christ" [Phil. 1:23]—for the first time these words of the Apostle became a living truth. So it is, yes, so it is. And, at the same time, in that very moment, it dawned on me that one must suffer to attain this joy, that the fear and agony of death is the path to the joy of joys, and that one must bear this, and bear everything, take in everything.

And suddenly the entirety of this doddering old life of mine appeared to me in a different light: it had been gloomily trudging along to its dark, inevitable end, with everything growing ever darker and more pathetic, and then suddenly everything, *everything* changed: everything is headed to joy, to great, limitless, all-transfiguring joy.

O love of God, O love of the Mother of God, all-transfiguring love! How can we become worthy of our destiny, how can we live up to it? There is no fear of death (although, of course, in the weakness of our nature there remains the natural fear and natural attachment to life), no despondency, but there is *joy*, the joy of death. And the meaning of this word of God flashed in my heart: "Love is as strong as death" [Song of Sol. 8:6]. What does this comparison mean when it testifies that love is death? That love bears in itself a deathly self-inanition, but also that death is love. But in this moment suddenly the truth of these words was revealed to me: yes, death is a love that no earthly heart could possibly contain, that rips open our heart . . . But therefore death is also joy, for love is the highest joy, the sole joy on earth. Yes, love is as strong as death, love is death, death is love . . . There is no greater power on earth than death, for everything bows before it, but there is an equal and similarly all-conquering power: love. But death is already destroyed, whereas love abides forever [1 Cor. 13:13].

13 / 26.IX.1924

Once again, during liturgy at St. Nicholas Cathedral,[43] I saw both sorrow and tears on the Face of the Most Pure One, and again I had a feeling that was impossible to bear—it was impossible to see the sorrow of the Most Pure One, my soul was beside itself from this sorrow... Great is the sorrow coming from our homeland, sorrow unparalleled since the foundation of the world, and whether there will be another like it, we know not [cf. Matt. 24:21]. The earth has been desecrated, the heart of the people has been defiled, confessors of the faith languish in captivity and exile. And our conscience relentlessly denounces us: do we really love our homeland? Do we really pray for her? The Lord, perhaps, has even permitted this grief, has allowed Satan to afflict Job, in order to allow us to manifest love, to implore, to beg for and to attain salvation through our prayers.

What is needed is mourning from the heart, what is needed are tears upon my bed [cf. Ps. 6:6], true lament—not for those elect of God who are languishing for the Name of Christ, but for those victims of deception who blaspheme His Name, knowing not what they do [Luke 23:34], who have become merely flesh, like antediluvian humanity [Gen. 6:3]; for these children and youths corrupted by godlessness, deprived of the holy things: of the temple, of faith, of joy, of purity, of chastity; for all these innumerable victims whose bodies remain intact but whose souls have been killed [cf. Matt. 10:28].

Just as the prophet of God, Daniel,[44] sorrowed and cried and did not eat bread [cf. Dan. 10:2–3], and in response received a prophetic vision, so too should we be covered in the sackcloth of the heart, so too should we eat our bread in tears [cf. Ps. 80:5]. What is needed is the *struggle of prayer* in the closet of our hearts [Matt. 6:6], what is needed is unceasing anguish and tears, which the Lord hears and sees. Such deeply sincere prayer is all-powerful: only by such prayerful love and repentance, the repentance of each over himself and for himself, can we *save* Russia, can we, by the power of God, obtain from God the salvation of Russia through our prayers. Otherwise it is we, *we* who are responsible for her perdition and suffering. Lord, set my heart aflame, grant me tears of love and of prayer. Most Pure One, You have revealed to me your tears for the world; grant me, wretched as I am [Rom. 7:24], to draw near to Your weeping for the Russian land.

16/29.IX.1924

The holy cross is the thrice-blessed wood of salvation, and it is the mystery of our personal fate.[45] It is to the degree that we take up our cross that we also have within us the power of life for eternity. The cross is the sign of victory that has conquered the world, but it is also a weapon of battle, as well as the battleground itself, just like the cross's own two axes: they oppose one another and yet are bound together.

"If You are the Son of God, come down from the cross" [Matt. 27:40]; thus they spoke to Him, and likewise the world cannot help but say the same to each of us. "Make peace with the world, put down the cross with its angles that divide so sharply, and you will be saved." But this is deception, because these axes always cross in one's personal destiny. The cross is *given* to each of us: we can only take it or not take it, we can only take action through the cross of Christ or not take action.

Oh, how the heart shrinks at this thought, for even the Son of God prayed: "Let this cup pass from me" [Matt. 26:39], and He had to prove victorious in the deadly struggle: "Thy will be done!" [Matt. 26:42]. Therefore do not fear this exhaustion, O man, do not stumble at the thought of the agony of the cross, because this will pass and there will remain only the sign of victory... Collapse, fall, but get back up and follow after Him until the victorious end...

20.IX/3.X.1924

If storm clouds surround you, O man, if human injustice or ignorance threatens what seems to you necessary, just, and good—humble yourself, and do not stumble on account of these people. Say to yourself: they are simply instruments in the hands of God. This means that what you think is necessary is not, it means that your mind has made an error and that your eye is shortsighted. For you know neither your own destiny nor the destiny of humanity. Take a look at the life of the Lord: misunderstanding, suspicion, and malice surrounded him, and it seemed incomprehensible that Annas and Caiaphas wanted to stand in the way of God's work, of Christ's work [cf. John 18]. Yet they proved to be mere instruments in *accomplishing* the destiny appointed by God's designs.

Our knowledge of ourselves is exceedingly fragmentary—we know neither our past nor our future well enough to make judgments about them. Unless you surrender to the will of God, completely and above all things, from your whole soul and heart, and acquire calm and equanimity in this surrender, you will be confounded by and will stumble at the world's opposition to your noble endeavors (or so they seem to you). And near at hand you will find the temptation of despondency, murmuring, despair. But we must believe in God and in His providential care for us, and we must subject our reason and give it over to the will of God, even in our most obvious and indisputable decisions. And for this we need a glimmer in our hearts (like a lamp shining, even if the flame be weak and vacillating): the remembrance of God and the thought of Him, so that in our heart, like a weak little candle, prayer may be emitted to guard us from evil. For in this way—and only in this way—can you be free: no one can take this from you and impede you, and this is always [the one thing] "needful" [Luke 10:42].

Stand firm, then, in this fortress for your soul. The greater the threats and the unrest, the stronger your prayer should be. Pray for everything out of love for the Lord, pray that He grant you His love, and pray for what you seek, what Your soul wishes would come to pass, and *never* claim that your desires are infallible or settled. Humble yourself before the will of God.

23.IX/6.X.1924

Everything that happens to us in life, every word and meeting, is a certain divine call and questioning to which we must attend with vigilant ears. We cannot receive it all, we cannot even receive much of it, but the little that does reach us we must accept with our hearts. Of all this boundless sea of sufferings and sin, which could only be fully encompassed and accepted by the Only Sinless One,[46] it is granted to our weakness to hear only one tiny piece; but we must listen to it dutifully.

When you find yourself at rest, satisfied, you therefore imagine that you stand in purity and strength, not knowing that if this were taken away from you, your imaginary strength would be taken away too: always remember those to whom this was not granted, by no fault of their own. How then are you better than they, or they worse than you? The human tongue has no answer to this; the will of God in the diverse destinies of people remains inscrutable to us, but with awe we must perceive that this will is at work in all affairs and circumstances, lest we fall into despondency, bewilderment, and murmuring.

To man this will is inscrutable, but it is necessary to cultivate in oneself an acceptance of *whatever* the will of God may be. And this is the feat of faith, of sweating blood [Luke 22:44]. The Son of God accepted through his humanity the inscrutable will of the Father as a law *external* to him: "Not as I will, but as Thou wilt" [Matt. 26:39 Douay-Rheims]. And He, as a man, wanted for Himself something other than what was necessary according to God's will. And life is *always* like this. These tragedies, misfortunes, temptations, sins, corruptions, falls, the victory of evil, the decimation of good, the ocean of sin and malice that horrifies us—these exist by God's allowance. And what we don't need is that enervation which gratefully accepts the will of God only when it is pleasing to us and eagerly desired; no, we must work on ourselves so that we may accept it when it is severe, inscrutable, and cruel, for what could be more cruel and inscrutable than to send the Son to the Cross, to give Him up to agony?

Do not slacken, O man, when you prosper, lest you fall into despondency at the hour of trial. Remember that always, now, at this moment, your brothers are undergoing trials; be ready therefore to give everything to God: your will, your mind, your desires, so that despite everything, and in the face of everything, you may say, "Thy will be done." Only this, and nothing less, does love for God require.

24.IX/7.X.1924

Lord, You are my refuge, You are my strength [Ps. 46:1], You are my joy! What joy it is to love the Lord, what joy to pray to Him, what joy to attend to Him in one's heart. What joy to pray to the Joy of Joys, the Mother of God, what bliss to look upon Her Most Pure Image, what tenderness to call upon Her Most Pure Name!

O people, people, you seek earthly consolations and joys; if only you knew that God always gives us this fountain of joy in prayer to Him, but you do not wish to drink [cf. Isa. 55:1; John 7:37]. In truth the Spirit of God descends upon the one who prays, his heart expands, and his soul overflows its banks and bursts free from the body towards boundless eternity. And blazing with love for God, with a burning love it loves those near and dear, be they many or just one friend—all those whom God has given us so that together we might love Him. My soul rejoices in the Lord, He hath clothed us in the garments of salvation [Isa. 61:10].[47]

26.IX/9.X.1924

Joy of Joys, Mother of God! You are light and delight and comfort. You are the salvation of the world, You are the soothing of the groaning creation [Rom 8:22], You are the Bearer of the Holy Spirit. You are the Holy Spirit Himself manifested as a human being.[48] You are the Mother of our God and of the entire human race. You are the Unwedded Bride,[49] wedded to the Heavenly Bridegroom and united to every Christian soul. It is by Your Love for Christ, Your Son, that every Christian soul loves: like a mother, it loves Christ like a son of its own bearing, and like a bride, it loves by rushing towards her bridegroom. The King's Daughter is all glorious within [Ps. 45:13]:[50] Your whole power creates the inner man [Eph. 3:16], You live with the world [*mir*], You are our peace [*mir*], You who abide in the heavens. It is by Your love that we are spared the just anger of God, and by Your prayers at the Dread Judgment of Your Son we are freed from just condemnation. You are a most radiant sun[51] to the world, You are the Woman clothed with the sun [Rev. 12:1]. On Your account all speech falters, exhausting itself in loving You. At the hour of death You comfort us, You stand at the bedside of the dying. You give delight to Your elect, and by Your joyful countenance You bring joy. Even to us, sinful as we are, You have revealed Your countenance in Your holy icons and have helped us to honor You. You overshadow heaven and earth. You fill forest and field, water and dry land, and you prepare a new earth [cf. Rev. 21:1]. You grant comfort to all existence: for You flowers give off their sweet scent, for You the hues of this world become resplendent. Sounds of sweetness serenade you, mountains and lands praise You, All-Good Queen, the Most Holy Mistress of heaven and earth. Joy of Joys, our only Joy, our complete Joy.

27.IX/10.X.1924

O Joy of Joys, Queen of Heaven! What a joy Your icon is! Spontaneously the soul cries out before Your holy countenance. And whence is this to me, that the Mother of my Lord should come to me! [Luke 1:43]. Yes, the Mother of the Lord comes, and comes to live in Her honorable icon in our homes and dwellings, and brings us joy and has mercy on us, O Joy of Joys, O Joy of Joys, our Lady! And the soul sings, "my soul magnifies the Lord" [Luke 1:46]: it sings with Her, in Her own words! When you see Her Most Pure Face, then on account of joy the soul breaks free from the body; it strains to fly to the heavens, into the endless expanse. And then it becomes clear how and why the Mother of God meets us at the threshold of death. At Her light demons tremble and disperse, at Her light the darkness of our mortal path becomes radiant, at Her light death itself becomes a joyful celebration, a desired meeting, the joy of joys, because at its threshold there awaits us the Joy of Joys. Yes, this is so, unless we surround ourselves with a dark cloud of sins, with earthly attachments and lowly passions (into which demons can insert themselves at will and hide in order to torment and frighten us), unless we blind our spiritual eyes so as not to see this light.

O Christian, love the Most Pure Virgin, pray to Her always, and She will save you at the hour of death and lead you to bow down before our God and King, the Lord Jesus Christ.[52] O Joy of Joys, Most Pure One, All-Immaculate One!

28.IX/11.X.1924

Be ready to give to God, if He should require it, what is most dear, what you love most in life. We must love God more than we love man, and we must not hold back anything for ourselves, against God's will, we must not even wish to do this. This is the cross, the heaviest cross, which man takes up for God; whoever will not hate mother and father, wife and children for My sake [Luke 14:26], is not worthy of Me [Matt. 10:37], and whoever does not wish and does not know how to renounce these for God is not worthy of God. But in this renunciation one acquires the highest love and bliss, as the Teacher truthfully promised: whoever has renounced mother and wife and property, that one, even here, in this age, in the midst of persecutions, has more than he renounced [Mark 10:30]. He has, in God and with God, whatever he has renounced [cf. 1 Cor. 3:22–23].

God puts us on the path of renunciation and awaits our will, He waits for us to give ourselves over so that He can comfort us in our grief [2 Cor. 1:4]. Lord, give strength. If it be possible, let this cup pass from me, yet not as I will, but as Thou wilt [Matt. 26:39 Douay-Rheims].

30.IX/13.X.1924

Marvelous are thy works [Ps. 139:14], O Lord; no words can utter the works of Your hands![53] When you see your life in its crises and turning points, then you behold the hand of God guiding you. The future is closed to us, but it is full, full of opportunities unknown to us yet known to God. And this is the marvelous book of God's miracles, the book of our life, that we read in the course of our life and that we, with astonishment, perceive when before us a new page is revealed. But isn't this true of the future as well? And isn't it also true of life's final threshold, which at present we can neither see nor catch a glimpse of, but which is also the place where the Wisdom of God has prepared for us new life and new lives? Only believe, only rely on the strong hand of God guiding you.

3/16.X.1924

Lord, if it be possible, let this cup pass from me, nevertheless let Thy will be done! [Matt. 26:39]. If the waves of life overwhelm you, if you are experiencing hopelessness, pray that the Lord might reveal to you His will, that He might reveal it however He pleases: by a sign, by revelation, by encounters, by an event. Take heed to yourself—lest the Lord's visitation pass you by [cf. 1 Pet. 2:12]—that you hearken to the voice of God. But if you do come to comprehend His will, fear to oppose it, for it is a fearful thing to fall into the hands of the living God [Heb. 10:31]. If the Lord sends you a cross, take it up [Matt. 16:24]. Do not fear its weight, for the Lord who gives it to you knows what is within your power. At times, a man faces situations or periods in his life when only a vivisection of the heart can save either him or those with whom his life is bound up. The Lord too grew faint and fell under the weight of the cross, and yet there is no other path for the Christian. Believe; the Lord will grant strength, he will grant peace and comfort in your grief [2 Cor. 1:4].

4/17.X.1924

Only pray, only believe, O man! There are circumstances in life we cannot escape, there are knots in relationships that no human strength can untie.[54] A person falls into sin, gets tangled up, languishes in hopelessness. There are times when human hearts suffer such that they can neither part nor be united, and then one of the mysteries of life, a mystery of the age to come, comes to pass in the present. Pray more passionately and more fervently, pray to Christ and to the Mother of God, and from prayer you will receive peace, and calm, and clarity, as well as the strength to carry on to the next day of life, forward from day to day, as if the future did not exist, without seeing into the future. For sufficient unto the day is the evil thereof [Matt. 6:34], and cast thy care upon the Lord, and He shall sustain you [Ps. 55:22 Douay-Rheims]. But walk always before the Lord, be ready to give an answer to him in the purity of your every word and thought. Remember that nothing is hidden from Him: no movement of the heart, no word or wicked thought. But the Lord said: I desire mercy, and not sacrifice [Hos. 6:6; Matt. 9:13], and He is merciful towards our weakness. For He Himself was pleased to create us, He has given us a heart that loves and pines. Cast your care upon the Lord [Ps. 55:22; 1 Pet. 5:7].

7/20.X.1924

Before me lies an unfortunate woman, writhing in spasms, in such terrible pain; she has lost her husband and is now left alone in a foreign land, no longer young, already withering away. What can I say to her with my merely human mind and human strength? O Lord, grant me the mind, grant me the words, grant me the strength to comfort her, to encourage her to accept Your will. We were created for eternity, we were not called to live here, and this becomes evident when in this world everything dear to us departs from us; but the one who loves these things remains here, in this world. How to save love from impotence, how to save the soul from despair? Only through God and in God, only through prayer. The wings of prayer reach that other world, they provide an invisible connection with the one we love, they will carry us closer and closer to that one until the hour of our summoning, when we too shall have the light in our eyes extinguished. I made the sign of the cross over her, I blessed her, I embraced her, I took pity on her, and in my own heart I myself called upon the Lord who alone is able to help and to comfort. He gives, He takes away, but He also comforts [Job 1:21].

8/21.X.1924

Lord, here I begin a new day of your grace, a new page of life. Help me so that the day may not remain barren on account of my laziness, as has been true of most days of my life, and that it may not be covered over by my vile sins, both voluntary and involuntary, committed in knowledge and in ignorance,[55] but grant that this day may be marked by even the smallest bit of service to You. Guard me and my dear friends through your holy angels on this day, shield them from every evil, grant it to all of them this day to fulfill Your will so that You may not repent, all-blessed Lord, that You gave us, unworthy as we are, this day of our life [cf. Gen. 6:6]. In the name of the Father, and of the Son, and of the Holy Spirit.

11/24.X.1924

The cross of Christ is the power of love for Christ; without the cross there is no love for Him. And sacrifice is the power of love, and without the agony of the cross there is no Love. We must deny ourselves [Matt. 16:24], we must decrease [John 3:30] and despise ourselves, hide ourselves and trample ourselves so that there may be good for another, for one we love; and then from the earth of our souls the Lord will grow the white flowers of paradise, the anemones of suffering.[56] The heart bleeds, it grows faint, but somewhere above the song of paradise rings, the song we will hear on the other side of time. Love your cross, do not groan, do not complain. But thank the Lord if He has granted you the kindness of a *voluntary* cross, of a voluntary sacrifice to offer in the name of love. Your heart is intincted in the blood of the cross, and its wound scabs over; this life passes away, but a new life mystically begins to be born within [cf. 2 Cor. 4:16]. Lord, make me worthy of Your cross, grant me to love not for my own sake, but for all those whom You love; send Your love, the love of the cross.

12/25.X.1924

Lord, my Lord! You are Love and You give love. How can I thank You for the joy of Love, for the fact that You allow me to love. On my bed my soul trembles and pines away from love for You, my God, and for Your Most Pure Mother, and for Your marvelous creation: the human being. Before my eyes the miracle of Your creation is revealed: how You rule the soul that is pure and by Your fingers make it Your instrument. O miracle of the soul revealed in God, O miracle of creation in God and for God! The banks of the soul cannot contain this burning love; it seeks to overflow—but to where, to where? Into You, the ocean of divine love and mercy. There are no words, no thoughts, no feelings—only Your scorching love burns and thunders in the soul. I am a coal in Your flame, and when I burn I become one with all my loved ones and with all Your creation. I want to burn—ignite me with love. You have spoken, O Gracious One: Whoever is near Me is near the fire…[57]

14/27.X.1924

Be not despondent, for there is no weakness or sin more deadly. Consider: the all-wise and all-marvelous God has, from the ages, elected you to exist. He has given you life, he has determined your destiny from your first day to your last. He elected for you a time, a land, a people, those near to you, family, friends. He has endowed you with the gifts you need and those you can handle, and He desires only one thing from you: to love Him, to trust Him like a son does a Father. But you, fearful and despairing, see not a Father but only an evil torturer in the heavens. You are ungrateful because you do not see and do not want to see blessings. You do not want to recognize that there is no blessing greater than life, the gift of the Giver of Life.[58] You are blindsided by trials, sins, calamities, you grow faint from your filth and the limitations you constantly rediscover in yourself. But consider that God, more clearly than you do, sees your destiny, and He knows not only this instant, in which you are growing faint, but also the ages of ages. Renounce fear, which is the offspring of the devil, for the one who fears is not perfected in love [1 John 4:18]; cast away despondency, that death of the soul before death. Repent for your sins, but do not fear them, for boundless is the mercy of God. Fear the justice of God, but do not despair, for the scales of His justice also weigh all your creaturely weakness. Do not make peace with this sinful world, but know that it is upheld by God's hand, just as you are. Without this very moment the world would not exist, and the world—despite all its sins—is upheld by the all-knowing and all-forgiving love of God. So how could you, how dare you, be despondent?

15/28.X.1924

O, dreadful hour of death and dreadful judgment of God! How will I stand before Your face? How I will grieve over my life lost in laziness, in idleness, wasted away in self-love—what a total mistake, what a sin, what a failure it will seem! How far away will stand everyone near and known to me, and then my conscience alone and none other will unroll its impartial list! How meaningless will appear then what now appears so important and necessary, how fleeting all these earthly disturbances, but over them all and in them all there will be pronounced only one dreadful verdict: God gave you a long life, gave you strength and health, gave you friends and people close to you—how and for whom did you spend this life, what mark will it leave in the world? And there is no answer besides one final, impotent regret, the eternal torment of the good that was left undone.

The end is near: you see its face at times, but you don't bring it into your life as a constant check, as a constant *correction* to your everyday life; you have no remembrance of the hour of death. But it approaches unexpectedly and in a totally *simple* fashion, just like every simple moment of life. In whatever work the Lord catches you, in that will He judge you; and in just what will the Lord catch *you*, pitiful soul of mine? There is no need to be intimidated by eternal torments—this is unworthy of the Christian soul, although without a doubt there will indeed be such torments. But what is needed is constant seriousness and rectitude in life, what is needed is a remembrance of God that is loving, solicitous, filial: how can we avoid grieving our Father? How can we avoid losing ourselves, our eternal countenance, in this stream of evil and vanity? *By never forgetting*: never forget what it is you love, never forget what it is you serve, and above all never forget Your God for whom you labor. And if you will remember *this*, then you will thereby remember the hour of death as well, because nothing new will be revealed in this hour beyond what you are always bearing within your soul. The very *ordinariness* of each day: this is what makes up the content of our lives, and it should be transparent, serious, worthy, and majestic.

17/30.X.1924

Blessed are the *meek*, for they shall inherit the earth [Matt. 5:5]. The Lord blesses *meekness*, to it has He promised that conquering strength granted neither to intelligence, nor to riches, nor to common resourcefulness: meekness shall inherit the earth. How dear is meekness, how wise is meekness, how strong is meekness! If you are tempted to violence, if you have been treated unjustly, if within you anger and resentment arise and conquer you, then you are the one who is captive to your abusers, and your spirit is unfree. But only try to be meek and lowly of heart [Matt. 11:29], and you will become free, bright, and calm, your mind will calmly show you the way, and you will come out the victor of a difficult situation. The main thing is—guard yourself, guard your soul. Do not allow yourself to take offense, to become embittered, to give into passion, for then you stumble into captivity, then you no longer stand on solid ground. But if you keep your bearings, you will be unshakeable.

And how joyful it is to yield, to give up, not to cling to one's own—and how victorious it is! We must not strive for victory solely for victory's sake, for then your meekness will be nothing more than hostile craftiness and hypocrisy, a lie; only meekness can conquer. And how easy it is to commit sins against meekness in particular, how often we ourselves injure tender, loving hearts with our lack of meekness, how often we provoke precious tears. Meekness is love and the power of love; the one who is not meek does not love, and sins against meekness are sins against love.

18/31.X.1924

Again the sun has risen, the worlds are set in motion, once again the good God gives us life, gives us the day. How it would shine, how joyful would our life be, if we could acquire within ourselves the strength to give thanks—for what is more blessed, more joyful, than gratitude? Gratitude is love, it provides us not only with the gift, but also with what is immeasurably greater: the giver himself. My words fail, my thoughts fail, O Lord, when it comes to gratitude. How could I possibly take in all Your blessings, known and unknown? You give me this world that I sully with my sin and negligence, You allow me to love and You give me love, and how could I possibly thank You for love? When you consider this or that gift, while in a state of love, then you thank the Giver of the gift, but when you give thanks for *love*, then your soul burns with love for both the Giver and the Gift, and it faints from love.

But You, Lord, grant us the strength and the mind to love You and to thank You and to know Your blessings. You grant strength and intelligence to love those You have given us, for it is through You that we love: You are love and You are present in every breath of love, every time the callous human heart goes forth out of itself. O Lord, for everything, for everything I thank You, but still more do I praise You for the love that You give.

21.X/3.XI.1924

Lead us not into temptation [Matt. 6:13]. The Lord taught us to pray for this because we live in the midst of temptations, we are unceasingly subject to their dangers. It may happen—and according to the testimony of those who are wise in God, it happens quite often—that temptations strike us with their unexpected arrival; they come immediately after graced epiphanies and a special softening of the heart. And suddenly there rushes in some kind of demonic vortex that blows everything away, and the person languishing in temptation impotently asks: what is happening to me? And—so the fathers teach—if you have a special joy and grace, *expect* temptation. The enemy of the human race does not slumber: with envy he looks upon spiritual fruit born in the soul and seeks to pluck and to trample on the seed, to spit on and to taint the beautiful fruit of the soul. And always he thirsts for evil, but a guardian angel keeps him at bay and does not allow him to reach a person.

But sometimes this defense is removed, and then woe to you, impotent and defenseless man. Like he did to Job, he will strike with leprosy not only your body but also your soul, and in bewilderment you will cry out from the dung heap [Job 2:7–8]. Whence, and why all this? We do not know the mysteries of God's providence, but we can know the secret meaning of temptations by their fruits. If there must be temptations [cf. 1 Cor. 11:19]—for the one who is not tempted remains untried, unwise—then they must take place when a man is more prepared, when he is equipped with gifts to receive them. That is the very reason why the gifts of God so often precede temptation. Furthermore, temptations admonish and humble us: how easily, how imperceptibly the heart gives itself over to spiritual self-flattery; it takes the gift of God's mercy and grace for its own power, as its own entitlement;

it turns fortifying grace into gratification, it falls into spiritual sensuality, with pride lurking just below the surface. But when the heart sees itself in a ditch of sin, in the vomit of temptations, it sees and feels both its nothingness and its sinfulness, as well as the immeasurable mercy of God and the right hand of God that guides us. And then with new joy and new gratitude it returns to life and receives its gifts.

Only learn, O man, from temptations, for every *recurring* temptation leaves ever new scars on the heart, shriveling and diminishing it...

24.X/6.XI.1924

Every temptation experienced—despite the sin—brings us closer to God and softens our heart towards others, it leads us out of the undue equilibrium for which self-satisfied and pharisaical pride lies in wait. We must acquire a peaceful spirit, but a peaceful spirit is different from equilibrium, which is merely the absence of misfortune and temptations. The question always remains: why is it that the Lord allowed near Him harlots and sinners, publicans and even demoniacs? Not on account of their licentiousness or their filthy acquisitiveness or the fact that they were possessed. Rather, all these people had fallen precipitously from their former station. They had lost themselves and experienced the agony of shame, the agony of something like death. And if they had despaired and fallen into despondency or if they had grown embittered and become mired in their sin, they would have perished. But they rose up and with wounded and broken hearts they came to the Source of grace. Then they no longer looked down on others from above, but rather from below, and in their hearts arose a natural condescension and mercifulness. Sin, the experience of fallenness, and repentance all softened their heart, made it merciful... O the depth of the riches of the wisdom and knowledge of God! [Rom. 11:33]. God hath concluded all in disobedience that He might have mercy on all [Rom. 11:32]. Only from the heights of spiritual accomplishment can a just man see himself as the greatest of sinners, and only then will his heart not grow cruel from haughtiness.

To the priest-confessor is given the grace not to be scandalized by the sins revealed to him; he sees and knows people as sick and weak, as captive beings, and this makes him only more merciful towards them. In them he sees his own sinful soul as well, and he grieves over it. A priest must be uncompromising, like the law of God's justice, and condescending and merciful, like the One who allowed publicans and sinners to gather around Him. But woe to the priest who excuses sins, for he will have to answer for them, but even greater woe to him if he stamps out, hardens, or torments the human heart.

Temptations surround man: some come from his sinful being, and some by God's allowance, as Satan was allowed to tempt the righteous Job. There is one most difficult and dangerous temptation: temptation in love. Sin in love and against love directed at a neighbor, at a friend—due to pride, due to a hidden egoism and self-love—covers the heart in pretense and wounds it. But if you fall into this temptation, bring forth the fruit of repentance [Matt. 3:8], learn anew, with new strength, to love, to love *love*, to love the beloved, to stand in awe before the mystery of love...

25.X/7.XI.1924

Holy Father Sergius, pray to God for us![59] This God-pleaser guides and preserves his people, and his conquering power lives within us. What is this power? An impoverished son of a boyar, an unknown hermit, with no glory or fame to speak of. This power is a love for Christ that is selfless, a self-renouncing love for His cross, an unstoppable power of the spirit to which we cannot ascend even in thought, like the snow-white peak of Mt. Kazbek. This power overcame all things, not only all human foibles and weakness but also, it seems, nature itself. Who could even come close to comprehending this forest, abandoned for two centuries and overgrown, this living death uniting in itself all forms of the cross: death from solitude, death from weakness, from beasts, from freezing cold, from hunger? Who is able? But the silent answer to what occurred there was a church in the name of the Life-giving Trinity. There, in the desert place, Saint Sergius saw the mystery of the Most Holy Trinity, of God-Love. And he also learned the mystery of the Mother of God, of the Holy Spirit. She was revealed to him together with the two first apostles, Peter and John.[60] In the hour of need, God raised up a man for Himself.

And now he is with us, helping, guiding, teaching us patience and confidence, teaching us to discern in the desert the future lavra[61] of the Life-giving Trinity. How marvelous is this mystery of love for God, of love in God, how omnipotent it is! Saint Sergius has appeared again today for the work of saving his homeland from the Tatar dark ages;[62] with us he cuts down and carries the heavy lumber, with us he personally builds the temple of Sophia, the Wisdom of God.

26.X/8.XI.1924

The greatest and most difficult victory to accomplish over oneself is to *forgive* offense and unjust treatment, not when it is directed towards us—that is still easy—but especially when it is directed towards someone we love and revere. *Blessed are the meek* [Matt. 5:5]: offense weighs down the heart like lead, it clouds our spiritual eyes, it obstructs prayer, it makes the air heavy and thick. *Endure,* endure, O man, the hour of temptation, cover your head with the koukoulion[63] and abide in solitary tears and prayer in the closet of your heart [Matt. 6:6], in the cell of your soul, until the merciful Lord send you the bliss of meekness and until the joy of forgiveness and reconciliation raise you up.

In patience possess your souls [Luke 21:9]. The Lord sends trials of patience. This stone on the road that has caused your weary legs to stumble you wish to dig up and to cast aside, and yet you need it, for your legs are capable of walking only on smooth ground, but it is the "stubborn way" that you must walk [Judg. 2:19]. Struggle and pray, do not allow your heart to be ruled by petty, base, unkind feelings. Cast your eyes on the image of the Patient and Longsuffering Christ the Savior, and from Him learn patience-love. For indeed love is patience [1 Cor. 13:4], and there is no love without patience, just as there is no (true) patience without love. Patience is the trial of love, the measure of patience is the measure of love, the one who is impatient loves little. And through patience you will educate even the one who causes you offense—perhaps with good but misguided intentions—and you will help him, you will save him. But through impatience, through offense, you will lead both yourself and him into the pit of perdition [cf. Luke 6:39]. Struggle, do not let yourself be overcome by base feelings, call unto your Lord for help...

28.X/10.XI.1924

After we pray, the Lord places, by means of our guardian angel, His word in our heart, and the more fervent and humble our prayer, the more authoritatively and clearly does this inner word resound. We seek miracles and signs and yet we cannot see that hourly miracle which is unceasingly being accomplished in the secret place of the heart. This voice of our guardian angel, if we attend to it worthily, provides an answer both to our difficulties and to our questionings while also forewarning us of those temptations and tasks that await us in the day ahead. And now the Lord says to me once again: blessed are the meek, for they shall inherit the earth [Matt. 5:5].

O holy Lady Meekness, wisdom of wisdoms and victory of victories! How distant you are from the sinful heart and how great is its need to find rest in you. In truth there is no rest without meekness, for in meekness there is no offense, no bitterness, no vindictiveness. Meekness conquers all and shall inherit the earth. The Lord, meek and lowly of heart [Matt. 11:29], stood in the midst of his tormentors who were breathing forth satanic malice, and yet His meekness was in no wise conquered—not one unmeek word escaped His Most Pure mouth. And it is precisely in this that His victory over His enemies consists, and through this that the prince of this world was conquered [cf. John 16:11], he who approached the Lord with new temptations and, after he failed to entice Him with his illusory gifts, attempted to conquer Him through trials. This is why the meek shall inherit the earth: this earth belongs to them and to their strength, it belongs to the humbleness of mind of the sons of God who have put on the good yoke of the Son of God [Matt. 11:29].

And yet how difficult it is for the bitter and sinful heart to receive this gift. It is possible to be in control of one's conduct and words and yet have a heart lacking meekness, a raging and angry heart. Nesting within our sinful hearts are the snakes of self-love and pride, vanity and self-admiration. But don't concede this to your heart: cut off the provocation, compel it mercilessly, and the Lord who is merciful, seeing your effort and your tears, will grant you the grace of His meekness. Beg meekness of God.

29.X/11.XI.1924

We pray and appeal to our guardian angel. He is our friend, given to us by God, yet how faintly and weakly does our heart sense this friend, how little it gives thanks and how little it loves! If only our eyes could be opened, then we would constantly see him, the "guardian of our souls and bodies."[64] We would comprehend that, in those situations when—by some sort of confluence of circumstances—we were unexpectedly saved from deadly troubles or misfortunes, it was he who saved us, our luminous guardian. And when some good word or thought came into our hearts, it was he, our friend, who implanted this thought in us. Our entire life would appear to us not so lonely and gloomy as we see it, but as a life of two, a life with a loving, solicitous friend. Yes, our guardian angel has been appointed to us by God, but he is no superintendent; rather, he is a friend, he *loves* us, we are loved by him. And this is why, according to the Church's pious belief, our angel "weeps" when we sin or perish, and he fights for us and with us (but only in the spiritual world) against the spirits who tempt us.[65]

Take your concept of this marvelous friend from our human feelings and relationships: why do we unconsciously call our most beloved, our most true friend, our wife, brother or sister our "guardian angel," in order to express our love for them and their love for us? Because here shines through, *breaks* through, this heavenly love and heavenly friendship. It is revealed to us both at the hour of death and beyond its threshold. This will be one of those great and unexpected spiritual joys that await us beyond the threshold of this world, but it will also be a source of new and unbearable griefs and of belated repentance if we discover, to our grief, this friend fleeing from us...

How can we open our hearts to our guardian angel, how can we come closer to him? By praying to him, thinking about him, reaching for him, by attending inwardly to that barely audible whisper that resounds in our hearts at the time of prayer and after it, in those blessed hours when prayer envelops us. For he is our "kind guide,"[66] he guides us with open eyes while we walk blindly, for we do not know the world of spiritual beings that surrounds us, we do not know the beginning and the end of the path. Be attentive then and hearken to the secret whisper of your soul, for that is the voice of your guardian angel.

31.X/13.XI.1924

"That the whole day may be perfect, holy, peaceful, and sinless, let us ask of the Lord."[67] Thus does the holy Church insistently and unceasingly pray, to sanctify and to bless this new day of life. The new day is revealed to us as emptiness, as possibility, as hope, and as danger—as the unknown. On this day a decisive pivot in our lives could come to pass; on any day this could occur. Not to mention that on this day our very life could be cut short, we could lose those near and dear to us; we could also accomplish something, or leave it unfinished; we could profoundly and sinfully fall. And what we should desire for this day, just now beginning, is not that it be happy, cheerful, and pleasant, but that it be peaceful, that the peace of the Lord not leave our hearts, and that everything in our ambit be at peace with the Lord.

That the day be sinless—oh, but our every breath is sinful, and we cannot even imagine complete sinlessness, yet there are grievously deadly sins that murder our souls, and it is from these that we ask to be preserved on this day, for every day we have lived without committing such sins is a petal on the flower of our life. That this day be holy: we cannot consider ourselves holy, but we should desire nothing besides holiness. And for each day this is all we can desire, that it be holy. The words of this prayer resound for all people, in all situations. They resound abstractly as long as you do not wish to bring them into your heart and to attend to the fact that they are speaking to *you*. You know what robs your spirit of its peace and what constitutes a temptation to your calm: conquer in yourself this provocation, ward it off, and then this will mean that your prayer has resounded in your heart and not only in your mouth, and that you genuinely desire what you are praying for. You know which temptation to sin most torments you now. And if your sin becomes something vile to you, if you ward it off in your will, that means that your prayer has reached your heart. I can accomplish nothing with my sinful flesh, but I can do all things through the One who strengthens me: the Lord Jesus [Phil. 4:13].

1/14.XI.1924

Bear ye one another's burdens [Gal. 6:2]. How often it happens that, seeing the error or weakness of your brother, you count yourself better than him, you condemn him, while you mourn in your heart his lack of wisdom. Meanwhile, if you do in fact see truly, then you must lay this onto your own conscience as well. The visible iniquity of your neighbor is also your own iniquity if you are not preoccupied with conquering it, and it will be required of you at the Final Judgment, as if it were your own iniquity [cf. Luke 12:48]. We must have a merciful heart, we must hurt for and not judge the other. Why are all our attempts at forming brotherhoods so weak?[68] Why is it that we disgrace holy Orthodoxy with our dissensions? Because we do not have a merciful heart. Do not be cold towards error and lies, be fervent and courageous in truth, but learn to love those overcome by the former. What then—must we love even the evildoers who are tearing apart our homeland? We must not love their evil deeds, but we must pity the evildoers. Commit them to the judgment of God, but keep your heart from hatred, for through hatred we are conquered by our enemy. Or do you not think that God could send legions of angels against them and annihilate them? [Matt. 26:53]. But if the Lord is long-suffering, so must you be [Exod. 34:6]. This doesn't mean that you need not fight evil by every means available to you, but you must fight it first of all in your own heart. The Lord is long-suffering; you be also, as your Father in heaven is [Matt. 5:48].

2 / 15.XI.1924

How long, O Lord, how long will your anger burn against the Russian land? [cf. Ps. 80:4]. Wherefore have You abandoned it to desecration and corruption? Why do you endure the satanic rule of the atheists? You know the weakness of our nature, You know that human patience has its limits. Why then do You allow us to be tempted beyond our measure [cf. 1 Cor. 10:13], why do You permit this to the point of an inevitable fall? The entire nation, all its children are deprived of faith, their souls are defiled from a tender age, they are becoming little beasts. But can they really be considered guilty? This is death, death within life, which is a thousand times worse than actual death. For You are omnipotent, at the wave of Your hand the wicked are crushed, and yet You abide them. Nebuchadnezzar was the iron rod that broke a stiff-necked people, and we, the fathers, were the ones who received the iron rod; but this is a kingdom of death into which *children* are being born, sent by You into... hell on earth.

O Lord, Lord, forgive these cries of my heart. I know what You desire *from me*: You desire true repentance, genuine tears, and grief for the homeland that we criminally forget. You desire genuine, tearful prayer for the salvation of Russia, and prayers are always heard; but until we have offered this prayer, all our questionings remain vain, insincere, cold. You are good and omnipotent, do Thy will.

4/17.XI.1924

For the peace from above...[69] Lord, send us Your peace from above. There is nothing greater or more needful than peace from above, but how difficult it is to find it. "Acquire a peaceful spirit, and thousands around you will be saved," said St. Seraphim [of Sarov],[70] but this is acquired only through a lifetime of spiritual struggle. Our soul is ever vexed, ever surrounded by anxieties, questionings, preoccupations. Always our soul is blinded by some worry, held captive by it, unfree. But the soul should be free, like a bird, it should belong only to God and to no one on earth; everything should belong to *it*, and it ought to love everything, but the soul itself must be turned only towards God. Peace from above is from Him and through Him. This is not insensitivity towards the world and people, this is not coldness, it is a kind of balance, a measured spirit in all things, even in love itself; this is freedom from every *idée fixe* that constantly possesses us. And when this freedom exists, when the soul turns towards God without any obfuscation, then it finds quiet, peace, light.

But when it is ruled by any kind of independent force—a thought, feeling, even love for a person—then the soul is captive and vexed, it loses itself and at the same time also loses the one it loves. For to love another without sin is given to us only in God and with God, so that nothing created might eclipse Divinity for us. And if there is no peace in your soul, then something is not right. Examine yourself, examine your relationships with people, and you will discover whether passion, or some petty feeling, rules over you. But whatever it is, it *rules* your soul, which only the Lord ought to rule, to whom alone your soul should belong. And when a person is not at peace, nothing within him is right, nothing is normal, everything is ruled by passion. Then no one—neither others nor he himself—will be able to believe any testimony or counsel that he gives. And if your soul lacks peace, then gather all the powers of your soul and put yourself on trial, as it were, before the omnipotent and omniscient God. Look upon yourself from the window of eternity, try not to see yourself from your perspective, try to know yourself impartially. And the Lord will help you and will send you His peace from above for which your soul thirsts. Lord, send Your peace!

7/20.XI.1924

Cast your care upon the Lord! [Ps. 55:22; 1 Pet. 5:7]. If a hopeless situation should arise in your life, if an implacable fate leads you against your will and unawares—leading you both from within and from without—then I implore you, brother, and I implore myself, wretched man that I am [Rom. 7:24], not to tear yourself from the Lord, to hold on tightly to His hand. Believe that He never abandons and never will abandon you, and that this apparent hopelessness is for your enlightenment, that it is a trial. With God and for God there are no hopeless situations, and everything is the work of His blessing and love. Arm yourself with patience, readiness, and the desire to endure from the Lord and for the Lord any agony it may please Him to send you. Hearken to yourself. Try to distinguish what in your present difficulty comes from you and from your sin (try to root it out, to wash it clean through repentance) as opposed to what does not come from your will, what is instead your fate: God's will for you.

The most important thing in our lives is encounters with people, human hearts that burn with love, and not by their own will and power. This is the divine destiny of man, whom God has allowed both to love and to be loved on earth and to suffer for the sake of love. Suffering can vary: sickness, loss, parting, instability; but love, which grants the highest, most unique joys, always redeems suffering. And do not murmur at this suffering. If possible, love it as your own love, for only through suffering can you acquire the right to a love that is not self-seeking, not self-indulgent, but instead truly sacrificial. The Mother of God herself unites the human hearts of Her elect. She guards them and covers them with Her mantle. Look to Her. What was *Her* love like towards Her Son? Was the purest and highest love the love of joy and pleasure? This is why cowardice, murmuring, and despondency is a sin against love, why it constitutes a rejection of the example of Mother of God.

"Take no thought for the morrow" on the day of your apparent hopelessness [Matt. 6:34]. The Lord miraculously removes the burden from your heart, He provides solutions, He shows mercy and He saves. Give thanks to the Lord for His gifts, but still more for the great gift of love He has given us in His creation, for without this gift our entire life would be empty and dead, in view of the difficulties and burdens under which we at times groan and lament. And if anyone is truly worthy of our sympathy and pity, it is the one who is poor in love, who has no one to love, who loves little. O Lord, tri-hypostatic God, unity in Trinity, God-Love! You created us in Your image, and the power and heart of this image is in the gift of love, in the image of Your tri-hypostatic love! That is Your image and that is Your likeness. Teach us *worthy* love, pure love, sacrificial love without any self-interest, blazing love. Ignite our hearts with Your fire!

8/21.XI.1924

The day of Michael the archangel and the other bodiless powers. The holy angels keep watch over the human race, they fight for its sake, the war goes on not only on earth but also in heaven [cf. Rev. 12:7–12]. And yet we play the coward, we are despondent, we go about in perplexity, we come to despair over our own impotence—all while having heavenly help at hand! An angel appeared to the Son of Man to wipe His brow of bloody sweat in Gethsemane, and now the angels invisibly do the same for suffering humanity [Luke 22:44]. The motherland languishes, it is dying spiritually, it stinks like Lazarus four days in the tomb [John 11:39]. But do you really think that God could not find a legion of angels to destroy the wicked? [Matt. 26:53]. Or even by natural reasoning, could not a confluence of circumstances lead to the collapse of this atheist rule? And yet despite all this, this rule endures and even seems to grow in strength, so that the nations marvel: who will conquer this beast? [Rev. 13:4]. This means that God has allowed it, that this is an instrument of God's anger and a means to accomplish God's paths. If this is dreadful, monstrous, incomprehensible to you, then ask yourself whether it is more comprehensible that on earth the Lord was surrounded by demoniacs—in whom demons made their homes, convulsing their hosts—and that He healed *some* of these; but nowhere is it said that He healed them all. And is the demon possession of one man really more comprehensible than that of an entire nation?

But when you lose heart—and it is inevitable that we will, due to our sinful human weakness—remember that there are heavenly hosts aiding us, remember that the "Lord of hosts" possesses hosts, and that the evil confounding us is permitted for purposes unknown to us. Ask of God faith and patience. Ask of God a guardian angel for our souls and bodies.[71] Know that without his help and protection we would be torn to pieces in body and soul by demons: the insanity of demoniacs and of Soviet rule is only a partial example of what demons wish to do to us due to their hatred of God, their hatred of God's creation, their hatred of man. Before us would be revealed a world of dark powers (which we in our frivolity at times recklessly try to catch a glimpse of), all possible ailments would assault us, we would not last even one hour if we did not have an angel of peace, a faithful guide, a guardian of our souls and bodies. For the Apostle says that the devil, like a roaring beast, seeks whom he may devour [1 Pet. 5:8]. And can we really stand before him on our own strength without the constant protection of our guardian angel?

11/24.XI.1924

When you learn of the troubles and difficulties that those close to you find themselves in, think of everything for which you will have to answer before God and think of how unworthy You are of His mercies. How little your heart loves, how little you care about those close to you. And yet in an instant your fate could change and become no better than theirs, and it is only through the inexplicable mercy of Providence that you have been saved from misfortunes. Be with them, do not close off your heart from unceasing remembrance of them, and then you will inevitably lend a helping hand. Faced with these elect who are now being crucified on Russia's cross, how it confounds your soul that you are not with them! But you should not be confounded, if what is happening is God's will. It is not given to us to choose our lot, and we must accept all things with gratitude. Only remember, only remember that they are suffering while you prosper, and do everything for them that is in your power. And entrust the rest to the Lord. Do you really think the Lord lacks the power to drive out atheist rule in one day and to save His servants who cry out to Him day and night? But just as a legion of angels was not sent to Gethsemane to defend the Son of Man, and He remained defenseless against torments, so too now the Lord is long-suffering—out of *love* for the world and for humanity. But we do not know God's paths and we do not know the paths of this love. Did the scattered and despairing apostles know that the salvation of the world was being accomplished before their eyes? And now, although the meaning of Russia's devastation is also inscrutable to us, we nonetheless believe that God's love is permitting this for our common salvation. Only let not your heart be frozen over, only fall not asleep before the advent of the Bridegroom [Matt. 25:5]. Watch and pray, that ye enter not into temptation [Matt. 26:41]. And remember, remember those suffering for you, pray for them unceasingly, look after them as you are able.

12/25.XI.1924

Out of the depths have I cried unto thee, O Lord! [Ps. 130:1]. How temptation swoops in! Like a tornado on a clear day, in the peace and clarity of the heart, suddenly a wicked spirit works up a storm of temptation, everything loses its taste, everything seems dead and horrifying! It is as if a demon has obscured everything and the world has darkened, as before a storm. Fly far from this storm and this darkness—through humility, patience, prayer, and tears. Endure through love, forgiveness, and compassion. But do not give into the woeful premonition coming over you, for everything happens in accord with God's will, and you should have only one premonition: that the will of God is being accomplished for you and for those close to you. Remember the recent hours of light and joy that the Lord has sent to you, and in everything and for everything give thanks.

16/29.XI.1924

I will love thee O Lord, my fortress. The Lord is my refuge and my strength! [Ps. 18:1–2]. What power and what strength lie in these words, in these thoughts and feelings—provided they reach the outer limit of the heart and bring this power into it! They are a fortress in the face of oppressive weakness, against my weary impotence, a refuge amidst the hopelessness and endless inconstancy of my soul, as well as a confirmation amidst my vacillation. The Lord is near [Phil. 4:5]. He is in your mouth, which pronounces with fear and awe the Name of God [Deut. 30:12; Rom. 10:8]. You yourself are God's temple [1 Cor. 3:16], your heart is His throne, your breast His altar, just as it was for the martyr Lucian when he celebrated the Eucharist.[72] And so everything is close, everything is within—only arise, stretch out your hand [Matt. 12:13], turn your face.

But always a feeling of heaviness oppresses you, a feeling of impotence, of distance from God. It seems then that it is not you who are far from God, but God who is far from the world, and unbelief imperceptibly steals into the soul and fills it with its cold, icy solitude. A cold and icy heart is far from the Sun. So turn to Him, hold fast the edge of His garment with your hand [Matt. 9:21]; grow faint, but desire to love Him more than yourself, more than your life, more than what is dearest to you, be ready to give up everything, everything for the sake of love for God [Matt. 10:37]. And in your heart a fire will ignite in response, the ice will melt, your eyes will be moistened with tears; the heart will ignite and tremble, it will catch the scent of the nearness of heaven. And once again you will find all your dearly beloved ones, and the world will light up in its beauty, and the darkness of your soul will become the light of joy, and your whole soul will fall, in blissful exhaustion, into the hands of the Lord. O Most Sweet Jesus, Bridegroom of my soul, joy eternal, come into the chamber of my soul, be with me, sup with me [Rev. 3:20], do not leave me. I call to You, I love you, I pray to You, Jesus, my Lord!

16/29.XI.1924 (SAME DAY)

Lord, guard us from pestilence and the noonday devil [Ps. 91:6]. How dreadful is the disease of madness and how incomprehensible to our mind, how inaccessible to our eye is that door through which evil spirits enter the soul and then possess it, torment it, corrupt it, so that the soul as it were dies before death, its powers in the hands of demons. How does the soul—one, undivided, eternal—become divided in itself? How does the image of God become the seat of satanic powers? Not by merit or the lack thereof but for reasons hidden from us: who sinned, this man or his parents? [John 9:2]. And every person asks himself: is it I, Lord? [Matt. 26:22]. Timidly he shrinks away, fearing that an impartial voice will answer: yes, you! And so it is I, an unworthy priest, who these days ask my Lord: is it I, a great sinner, willingly or unwillingly, who is the reason that my spiritual daughter is suffering in Russia, my daughter who is like a candle burning before the Lord and who comforts me simply by her very existence?[73] Does her ascetic soul grow cloudy and murky?

In situations like these, ignorance need not attempt to understand by straining its proud intellect, for the intellect is powerless. It is with a broken and humble heart, with patience and prayer, that we must penetrate the meaning of the destinies given by the Lord; will not the Lord reveal His will? And we must pray, pray with faith... Lord, you cast out demons and healed the suffering when You lived with them on earth; have mercy even now on Your suffering servant. You can do all things, if you wish; therefore, Thy will be done! [Matt. 26:42]. And grant me, a sinner, the most sincere repentance and prayer for my spiritual daughter. Let none of us boast [1 Cor. 13:4] but instead let each know that he could always become the victim of demonic violence, and that only his guardian angel with his shield protects him from this.

18.XI/1.XII.1924

Acquire a peaceful spirit, and thousands around you will be saved.[74] Thus spoke the blessed *starets* Seraphim. And truly it is so: futile are intellect, learning, strength, if you do not have an abiding peace in your soul, if its surface is unceasingly furrowed by the waves of passions and turmoil, if your soul is unceasingly fatigued by these and languishes in them. He will renew thy youth like the eagle's [Ps. 103:5 Douay-Rheims]. And indeed our soul is renewed, but only when we taste peace. "Youth" is not simply the early years of life, for those years are always disturbed by passions and agitations, and this kind of youth, like an onerous legacy, can follow us even into our later years. The people of this age are even capable of rejoicing in this kind of youth and seeking after it, but we must be freed from this false youth for the sake of true youth, for the sake of tasting peace. Peace is what the Lord sent to His disciples, and alongside the Holy Spirit, He left His peace as the highest gift for His disciples [John 14:27].

But if you are not at peace, if there is unrest in your soul, that means that you are not with Him, that "legion" has overtaken you

[Mark 5:9]. The loss of peace always seems justifiable enough: either some person or another has done something against you, or some sort of event has disturbed your soul. Yet you know that it ought not be disturbed, that this is a grave sin on your part that has distanced you from the Savior. There is a stone weighing down your heart, a dark hand constricts it, you are running about day and night, and a demon keeps whispering and repeating angry words of resentment and annoyance, and you are *in captivity*: you do not want this and yet you can't be freed from it. Oh, how unhappy is the one possessed by a demon! However right you may be in your petty justice, nonetheless this possession, this malice, exposes you. You have rejected, you have lost the peace of Christ: it is Christ you have rejected. Set about acquiring peace through struggle with yourself, through repentance, through tears of the heart. Ask forgiveness of God, of the one against whom you have borne malice, and of your guardian angel. As long as you have no peace, then you yourself are perishing and you are dragging others with you into perdition.

19.XI / 2.XII.1924

The miracle of Saint Sergius! Just as when the brothers were suffering from hunger and had no bread, when they were despondent, and then some pious layman—by the prayers of the saint who had kept his faith strong and his hope unchanging—brought a cart full of bread,[75] so too in our days, when it seemed that a good undertaking was falling apart due to lack of funds, someone appeared and offered help.[76] The difference in time, place, and object is completely inconsequential: the first [miracle] was in a remote northern forest, the latter in Paris; the first was for the sustaining of the body, the latter for education; but it is the same Saint Sergius and his same help and prayer. O marvelous God-pleaser, you are ever the same, and you keep vigil over our nation and over all who love your name.

And if in our nation today we see disasters and assaults against those who bear and honor your name, this too you know, and you prayerfully preserve them, and you guide them, both young and old, priests and lay people, to the prize of the high calling [Phil. 3:14]. How our faith increases at the sight of this manifest miracle, how we ought to hearken to the Holy Church's teaching that the saints are always with us, that they assist and guard us. If only we knew how to preserve in our hearts this seed so that it might sprout and not be trampled upon. Alas! We rush along senselessly, chasing after new impressions, never taking in what surrounds us or even stopping. No: bend the knee of your heart, reflect on what has taken place, on what sort of sign this is for our nation, for you (and the darkness of your life), and for all your friends and loved ones. You have not been abandoned, and neither have they. Guardian angels are keeping vigil, God-pleasers are keeping vigil; only let *your* heart too keep vigil with prayer, love, and faith.

22.XI/5.XII.1924

The Most Holy Virgin's entry into the temple was Her consecration,[77] the greatest consecration possible for man, for the High Priest took Her into the place where only he could enter, into the Holy of Holies. In this way did the Most Holy Virgin receive the power and honor proper to the high priesthood of the Old Testament, and afterwards, in Her heavenly glory, she received the New Testament high priesthood as well, though in a different, non-institutional sense, just as did her Son, the High Priest forever after the order of Melchizedek [Heb. 7:17]. And yet She also wears the omophorion with which She covers Her people, according to the vision of Blessed Andrew of the Mantle of the Mother of God.[78] But for Her, who already at that time was three years of age, this consecration was—as it always is and always should be—a death for the soul, a self-immolation for God. She was already separated from her family, torn from her parents' embrace, and Her ascent of the steps of the Jerusalem temple led immediately and without interruption, through sorrows and ascetic feats, to Golgotha, to standing at the foot of the cross, to the sword in Her heart [Luke 2:35], to a life consisting of an unending series of sacrifices. And all those who follow Her path She calls to this consecration.

Our life is and must be an unceasing consecration, in which solemn, formal acts of consecration are simply its external identifying marks. Life must be an unceasing dying and withering away for the Lord. We notice how we lose our taste for this or that worldly good, yet at the same time, we want to lose it for the Lord's sake. And we notice how even our life constitutes, or rather should constitute, a series of lesser or greater sacrifices for the Lord, and only in this does it have meaning and justification and does it become a source of inner peace.

Should we pity—as we do with our merely human feelings—those whom the Lord has sent a life of ascetic struggles, sorrows, and trials, especially when we compare their situation with our relative prosperity? Or, on the contrary, is it that they are God's elect, and that the Lord sends to the one He loves this way of the cross? [cf. Heb. 12:6]. We grieve and cannot but grieve the martyrs in Russia, but were they not chosen by the Lord and made near to Him? And is not the voice that speaks in our hearts actually the fear that our comfort will be disturbed and not genuine zeal for the Lord? We must stir up in our hearts a willingness for the highest consecration, a readiness for sacrifice, for dying for the Lord, but this will not happen while our heart is sluggish, timid, and cold. Whoever is near Me is near the fire,[79] and perfect love casts out fear [1 John 4:18]...

23.XI/6.XII.1924

In wisdom Thou hast made them all [Ps. 104:24]. Lovely is Your world, Lord, and everything is lovely within it. And—strange for me to say it—lovely too is my own bodily nature, lovely because You created it. How often we lose heart on account of our sinfulness, which obscures from our very selves our true image! Satan is a slanderer, and he slanders both us and—to do us harm—God's creation as well; he implants confusion and faintheartedness within us, and as a result faintheartedness and laziness grow in our souls. We lose ourselves, we refuse to wage battle against ourselves for the sake of our very selves; but God, who created all things in wisdom, by the same wisdom created each of us as well. God's Wisdom was an artist before His face [Prov. 8:30], and she artistically formed our image as well, which we, like spiritual artists, must also form. Do not turn away from the work that is yours, for everything is from the Lord: your gift comes from the Lord, and your work is for Him. Fulfill your responsibilities to the gift of your life, to the gift of this world. Do not let God's world become a temptation for you on the pretext of the world's sinful state. If you disrobe yourself of your life now, then you will stand naked in the age to come as well. Therefore cursed be he that doeth the work of the Lord neglectfully [Jer. 48:10]. But the work of our life is God's work, and the Lord has entrusted to each his own talent, and from each will He demand its harvest [Matt. 25:14–30].

25.XI/8.XII.1924

When there awaits us a change of place, a journey, the soul experiences some kind of special excitement, as if having a foretaste or recollection of something.[80] Every relocation is a symbol of our status as pilgrims in this world, and it also reminds us of that final unclothing, of the final journey awaiting us all. And then the soul is filled with unutterable agitation, anxious but at the same time sweet. The Lord says of Himself: "I am the Way" [John 14:6]. This means, of course, a way of life, but still it is a *way*. He Himself is the Way. In Him and with Him there is no immobility but instead eternal ascent, unclothing and being clothed [cf. 2 Cor. 5:4]. Having become human, He Himself traversed the way and thus became the Way, He crossed the gates of birth and the gates of death. There, beyond the gates of death, the way—to our eye—comes to an end; but only to our eye, for in that place there is life, in that place we ascend from glory to glory [2 Cor. 3:18], and in that place is found the way to eternal life. The Lord alone is the Way, yet for Him there is no way, for eternal is He. But in His humanity, indivisibly and unconfusedly united with His Divinity, He raised humanity to the eternal way of endless ascent and immersion in the ocean of eternal life.

There is no standstill, no immobility in creaturely life; the path to eternity is endless. And this path is joy and bliss and comfort, it is the power of the age to come. But in this age it is ascetic struggle and the power of this struggle. Apostleship has no stable place: in life the apostle must go from city to city, and this is the ministry that is most near to Christ. The Lord Himself spent his whole life going from city to city—He lacked not simply a home but even a hole, as the foxes have [Matt. 8:20]. Yet how difficult and painful it is for our weakness to tear itself from a place, and how easily and willingly do we attach ourselves to a place and wall ourselves in. And is it not then a special mercy of God's when He grants us a sense of [the entirety of] God's earth and of God's world by tearing us out of our shells, by tearing us from our familiar surroundings and scattering us to the wind? Precious and lovely is the promised land, our homeland, but the whole world is God's earth, the homeland of the sons of God. Do not attach yourself to one place, for any one place is too small for you; every place is yours, and the power of the way is within you. Your Lord is the Way, the Truth, and the Life...

26.XI/9.XII.1924

But the very hairs of your head are all numbered [Matt. 10:30]. Believe this firmly and without wavering, believe it not only about yourself but also about those near and dear to you, those whose life and whose good are more precious (or at least seem more precious) to you than your own. Upon leaving them, when you part with them, entrust them and yourself to the Lord, who holds all creation in His hand, in whom we live and move and have our being [Acts 17:28]. What resolution and what joy there is in the thought that each day of life, each one of its smiles and each one of its tears, is sent to us by Him, and that He Himself keeps watch over and upholds His creation. You love those who are dear to you, you wish to guard them and to shield them with the mantle of your love and prayer, and your love keeps vigil over them; but consider that God's love watches over them and preserves them before you do, and more than you do, and more wisely than you do. And if you love God, if you love your loved ones with God and in God, then you already know this in your heart. Your every breath is filled with joy in God, and then that which should make your heart ache with sadness and dismay becomes merely a new feast in celebration of God's love. Separation from loved ones is distressing and agonizing, but in God there is no such thing as separation. In God everything is eternal, and love is eternal, inseverable and unseparated,[81] and the short moments of love's sufferings drown in the ocean, in the "ages of ages" of triumphant love.

When the Lord said farewell to His disciples at the Mystical Supper, He told them incomprehensible words about how He would both leave them soon and soon come to them [cf. John 14]. And they did not know that these words describe every earthly parting in God. If there is a rushing of the Comforter, the Spirit of God, then He comforts and assures that every human parting is drowned in the eternity of love and that every dark cloud overshadowing the human heart vanishes and dissipates in its flame. Who can separate us from the love of God!!! [Rom. 8:35].

20.XII.1924 / 2.I.1925[82]

O Lord, my Lord! How I thank You! In the paths of my life I have seen Your hand, I have known Your mercy, in amazement I have looked upon You. O Lord, my Lord! How I thank you! You have had mercy and preserved me, You have granted me thought and bravery, You have brought me to Your people, who are accomplishing Your will. O Lord, my Lord! How I thank You! In all my paths You have watched over my loved ones for me, You have given me the joy of union with them, You preserve them. Preserve my soul for You, O Lord, my Lord, grant it the fiery power of Your love, grant it to labor in prayer for Your glory, grant it the pleasure of Your most sweet Name, grant it the tears of Your love, grant that it may forget this entire world for the sake of Your love, grant it freedom from the fear and anxiety of this world. Grant it to see Thy face evermore [cf. Ps 104:4], grant it to kiss the hem of Your garment [cf. Luke 7:38; Matt. 9:21], grant it to stand at Your holy table, grant it to hear the heavenly hosts and their doxology to You, grant that it may be joined with the choir of Your saints who ever glorify You, grant it to die in Your love, grant it to undo itself and to be lost forever in the ocean of Your majesty, grant it to look upon Thy glory, grant it to know Thy majesty, grant it to be held in Your hand, grant it to kiss the feet of Thy Son and to drench them with tears for its wretchedness and to wipe them away with its hair [Luke 7:38], grant it the Holy Spirit, the Comforter, the all-filling, all-enlightening, all-cheering, all-enkindling, all-gladdening One, grant me to behold and to kiss the feet of the Most Pure Mother of God and Ever Virgin Mary, the Joy of Joys. Save, preserve, have mercy on all my brethren and lead them to Your faith and glory. Glory, glory, glory to God in the highest… [Luke 2:14].

21.XII.1924 / 3.I.1925

And unless those days were shortened, no flesh would be saved (Matt. 24:22 NKJV). The Lord Himself testifies that there may—and indeed will be—such great suffering, such great temptation, that all will become powerless and…will fall. It will be like the night of the Mystical Supper, when the Lord proclaimed: "one of you will betray Me," and then *all* began to ask: "Is it I, Lord?" [Matt. 26:21–22]. Even the self-assured fervor of Peter left him at that moment, and each one trembled for himself. And just as on the night of Gethsemane all abandoned Him, with one betraying and another denying Him, similarly in the days of affliction there will be no human strength to *endure* the entire trial. So great is human *weakness*, and the knowledge of one's weakness and of the common weakness of humanity is given in this terrible crucible of trials permitted by God. The world becomes subject to Satan,[83] and Satan conquers human weakness. And then a terrible, tempting question cannot but arise in the soul: are they not correct who scoff at the faith, who reject the spiritual life and recognize only the animal life of man? Are they not correct in disbelieving a faith that cannot endure tribulations, which has no strength—either its own or from heaven above—to stand against all? Are they not correct to say that faith is merely the seasoning sprinkled on a content and satisfied life, and if the latter is taken away, then faith too will die out?

Such are the temptations the devil brings to people on this Gethsemane night of horror and distress. The one who passes through this crucible of temptations knows that this temptation is *beyond* his power or anyone else's. For such a person, human self-assuredness and pride has burnt up forever, he sees through the small-mindedness and blindness of those who, not having suffered, imagine otherwise. To him comes both disenchantment and the sad sort of wisdom it brings. He will learn that faith is a gift from God—but the possibility of faith is just as much a mercy from God: it can be taken away, and "no flesh" can withstand its absence. It is possible to withstand—without flinching—martyrdom, fasting, solitude in the desert, but not, from day to day, this unending and limitless sacrilege against all that is holy... The soul grows cold and wastes away. This is the *ultimate* tribulation. It teaches either disillusionment or ultimate humility.

Man is certainly in the captivity of sin, he is certainly powerless. So no one should judge another [Matt. 7:1]; all judgment belongs to the Lord God [cf. John 5:22]. In fact, are our former children who were nurtured by the church any better than today's Russian children who are being raised as the offspring of hell? Can anyone in this circumstance truly be *personally* guilty? And if so, then everyone is guilty, both ancestors and descendants, in this Satanification descending on the country like a dark cloud.

The Lord is no respecter of persons [Acts 10:34]. He will judge all people together: those who are now demon possessed will find themselves justified in His sight while their pious ancestors will be condemned. O the depth of the riches and wisdom and knowledge of God! [Rom. 11:33]. But truly, of ourselves we possess only weakness; everything else, *everything*, is from the Lord.

22.XII.1924 / 5.I.1925

When the Lord said, "One of you will betray Me," the disciples in bewilderment began asking one another, "Is it I, Lord?" [Matt. 26:21–22]. They were frightened, and every one of them was unsure whether he might be capable of such a fall, and even Peter in that moment forgot his self-assuredness and fervor and did not begin making his typical pledges. On that dreadful night everyone scattered—overwhelming fear filled every one of them. All their love for Him, all the miracles and signs they had seen, all the mighty works they had performed: all of that proved insufficient to conquer human weakness when God did not provide strength. But here, on that night of Gethsemane, they were left to their own human strength.

One must know this weakness of humanity so as not to be scandalized by it on this *new* Gethsemane night now descending upon our motherland. Nor is there any reason for disillusionment with people or for despondency in faith. Only by experience have we now come to learn that everything in ourselves that we thought was the product of our own virtue, anything we called *ours*, and even our very faith in God, even our very love for Him—all of this is in fact the *mercy* of God. It is *humility*—a profound and definitive humility—and not disillusionment that our present experience is teaching us. Having lived through it, we now look with new eyes upon human greatness, pride, and strength, like those returning from the land of the dead look upon earthly life and its futile hopes. Seeing the imprint of death on every face, these look upon the living with the illumination granted by the next life; likewise do we survey this life, knowing in advance what it could have been had it not been plunged into a crucible of tribulations.

Why and for what reason were the apostles plunged into this temptation, which the Lord, calling them to prayer, warned them about (pray that ye enter not into temptation [Matt. 26:41])? The Lord wished to make manifest the *weakness* even of those whom He elected out of all people to do His work, those who by God's grace found in themselves the strength to serve Him. Here every kind of Luciferian pride in man is exposed. *There is not and cannot be* a person who could remain invincible against temptations and tribulations, against the power of sin. And holiness is a special gift, a mercy of God; it is from God. How great a mystery is human destiny! The Lord enclosed all in disobedience in order to have mercy upon all! Oh, the depth and the riches of the wisdom and knowledge of God, how unsearchable His ways! [cf. Rom. 11:32–33].

28.XII.1924 / 10.I.1925

We bow down and worship Your Nativity, O Christ![84] How silent and sure, amidst the daily noise of life, does this sacred feast come down into the soul and reign over it! How joyful it is to love and to rejoice together on this feast! How unfortunate for those who do not enter into this love but remain in the dim and grim working day world! The ear hears the inward singing of angels, and this echoes in the heart. To hear it, we need no marvels, no manifestations of the angels who have already once appeared. For this, it is enough to attend to your heart and to its bright, festal silence. In this clear, transparent light of the heart, angelic wings flutter and the angelic song can be heard. The mind is astonished and the heart grows mute before the mystery of God's condescension and of God's love for the world.

And it becomes clear how shot through the world is by Divinity: how nothing can add to this Divinity, nothing can impede it, nothing can obscure it. The Lord took for Himself a manger and a cave from this world, and through them He showed that all the riches of the world are nothing to Him, that He has no need of them. The Lord came to earth under the cover of anonymity for the sake of the world, in order to accomplish in it His cosmic work. Even the most concentrated villainy of the world, in the person of Herod, proved powerless to impede His work—much less to encroach upon the Lord Himself. And the sword of Herod, coming down upon the children of Bethlehem, impotently missed its [intended] victim, whose time had not yet come to be offered up.

What freshness, youthfulness, and cheerfulness does this great feast pour into the soul! It is as if you realize anew and become convinced that evil is illusory and impotent with its Herod-like machinations, that here, in the vanity of the world, *God is with us and we are with God.*[85] And all that is being done by today's Herods is similarly ludicrous, pathetic, and powerless against the star of Bethlehem, shining on high. This star is *untouchable* in heaven and in the heart. Or is the human heart itself heaven? Yes, heaven, for in it the stars shine. Yes, heaven, for in it is born the Christ Child: yes, heaven, for in it angels soar and the angelic hymn rings out: "Christ is born!"...[86]

30.XII.1924 / 12.I.1925

"*For I walk through many snares...*"[87] Invisibly the soul is wounded and made to stumble: a word overheard, an impression, lies on the heart like a heavy stone, crushing it with some kind of fright, exhausting the weak heart. This is the action of Satan, and seldom does a person ever suspect whose instrument he has become. Then God's light seems dark and joy is extinguished. Then there creeps into the heart unclean fear and the night of despondency. That which you have always known suddenly appears as if dead to you. This is a temptation that one must bravely endure and not surrender to. You must say to your heart: you are a liar if you forget the God who saves [Ps. 68:20]. Through prayer, you must warm up the frozen parts of your soul until this dark cloud dissipates. Now is the time of the antichrist. The antichrist sows his seeds everywhere, in defenseless souls, and calls them to revolt against God. But even more fearful than this coldness is indifference and sloth of heart: deadness of heart.

O Lord! Grant me power and authority to awaken the dead, You who were raised from the dead. Before you my heart is aching. Teach me how to gather Your people, how to shepherd them before You. This scattered flock languishes, they imbibe the sands of exile and swallow the little that remains to them of the moisture of life. And I understand their lot and the lot that has fallen to all [of us Russian exiles], and with my human understanding I look upon this hopeless dead end. But in You and with You there are no dead ends: You are the Way and the Truth [John 14:6]. So summon your flock to Your Way, grant me a fiery power, break loose the fetters of my soul. I know You and I hear You, I love You. Allow me to ignite with the flame of Your love these cooled and darkened hearts. You know the affliction of Russia, You know the stream of this godlessness that has flooded our land. Thou knowest all things [John 21:16], You are guiding us, You know the way. I am Yours, I do not desire my own will. But ignite, ignite my heart on this cold, Gethsemane night of the world.

31.XII.1924 / 13.I.1925

Another year has passed, another page in the book of my life, burdened with new sins and temptations, has been turned; it belongs now to eternity and will appear before me, wretch that I am, at the Dread Judgment of Christ. O Lord, my Lord, how long have I angered You, tested Your longsuffering? I see my infirmity, my sin, I languish in it and remain in it. But I praise Your miracles, O Lord, which You revealed to me in this world. All of life is a miracle, Your gifts are miracles: my loved ones, my family, my friends, all my joys. It is a miracle to labor for You, for Your work on earth with which You have honored me, unworthy as I am. Miraculous are Your mercies with which You have crowned me [Ps. 103:4]. You ask for an answer and justification for every year of life that is given to us, and what shall I say? Yet, I see how wonderful and blessed this past year was, how much has been given to me by God, how many hopes and possibilities were planted in it. I commit myself to Your will: whatever pleases You, let it be done—not my will, nor my desires [Matt. 26:42]. Cause me to know the way wherein I should walk [Ps. 143:8].

2 / 15.I.1925 FEAST OF ST. SERAPHIM

Holy father Seraphim, pray to God for us! Pray to God for the Russian land, which is beloved by you, illuminated by you, glorified by you. Like a titan you stand, filling half the heavens with the greatness of your form: our great *starets*, the protector of the Russian land and her intercessor. Your heart is a burning coal, your lips—the most sweet Name of Jesus [Isa. 6:6], your eyes—the radiance of the Theotokos. You foreknew all that was destined for us, you already mourned over it, but you also promised that after great afflictions our land would be glorified and made radiant with you, O great and marvelous *Starets*.[88] The feet of the Theotokos have tread upon the Russian land, toward you and because of you, our father, the elect kin of the Most Pure One, and these footprints remain indelible upon the land of the Theotokos.[89] O marvelous one, how clouded our skies would be, how impoverished our hearts, if you had not been with us, if your great ascetical feat had not acquired for us your protection. In you is contained the mystery of Russia, the seraphic mystery, in the burning coal that is your heart, O saintly father of ours. You sanctified the earth on which you lived through your works and through your sweat, you sanctified the rock through your prayer, you sanctified the forest by residing in it, you sanctified the beasts through communing with them.[90]

O Spirit-bearing *Starets*, to us you were the herald of the Holy Spirit and the beloved one of the Spirit-bearing Virgin. You discovered in Her the joy of joys, and this joy was in the Holy Spirit. You came to know the shining joy of life. You looked upon every human being through the illumination of the Holy Spirit, and you acquired the joy of love, you addressed each person as, "My joy!" Truth, peace, and joy in the Holy Spirit lived in you, our father. You came to know the fragrance of the Resurrection, you tasted the gladness of the divine vintage, and it was always Pascha for you, Your lips ever greeting people with the joyful tidings, "Christ is risen!"[91]

Our Elder, in you the Unfading Light shone forth to us, in you the holy Divine Sophia, the Wisdom of God, became manifest to us. In you, a Seraphim from God's altar came down to earth in a human, monastic form, and that earth was the Russian land. In you and through you was accomplished the election of this holy land. And this election is irrevocable [cf. Rom. 11:29], whatever may happen in and to this land. On this day dedicated to your memory, all these present troubles of ours appear to the eyes of faith as nothing more than an insubstantial specter, and there is nothing but Sarov, Diveevo, Seraphim's orphans, their mills, the moat, the footsteps of the Mother of God,[92] and the marvelous elder himself—hunched over, leaning on his staff, with azure eyes that radiate the joy of joys—saying to us: "Christ is risen!"

4/17.I.1925

O Lord, here am I [cf. Isa. 6:8], your servant, prostrate before you, tell me Your will... My soul has been weighed down by good fortune, by self-love, by calm. It clings to them, powerless, it does not wish to and knows not how to "go up to Jerusalem" for crucifixion [Matt. 20:17–18]. But You lead, You call Your elect to crucifixion with You. This Jerusalem is our woeful homeland that kills the prophets and the saints [Matt. 23:37], and there is no end to the brutality of its Herods as they take new sacrifices for themselves. But we look on from a distance, as if this did not concern us, as if the Lord will not ask us on the day of the Dread Judgment to answer for our homeland—once given to us and then lost because of our sins. O Lord, conquer my forgetfulness and spiritual slumber, ignite my heart with the love of Your Cross.

7/20.I.1925

Angel in the flesh, the cornerstone of the prophets,[93] O Forerunner of the Lord! You beheld and recognized and baptized the Lamb of God, the one which taketh away the sin of the world [John 1:29]. You stood fast, not running away in bewilderment, when the sea looked and fled and the Jordan turned back [Ps. 114:3].[94] Your silent feat is the feat of faith, bravery, and self-renunciation. Just as your kinswoman Mary in her hour uttered what had been pre-established from the ages: "behold the handmaiden of the Lord," and thereby brought to pass the salvation of the world (on the human side), so too, you, sent as an angel of God from among men to meet the Messiah, revealed yourself as the Forerunner: you remained in your place to accomplish this awesome task—to baptize Christ, to be a witness to the Theophany, Christ's own Pentecost. Yet what human powers today could face this fear and trembling? Thus did the Lord proclaim: there is none greater among them that are born of women [Matt. 11:11], for who else was able to see, face to face, God in the flesh and in the manifestation of the Most Holy Trinity? The Forerunner *recognized Him*, he recognized *everything*. His eyes were not shut with the ignorance that allowed the apostles to endure the vision of Him.[95] But *he saw*—and he stood fast. In his person the world's meeting with its Lamb was accomplished. It could not but be accomplished. Having become human, God needed to be met and received by humanity; in no other way could *free* salvation be accomplished. If John had become afraid or fallen into the dreadful temptation of competing [with the Lord], the world would have been knocked down from its foundations, for it would not have recognized its hour, and

Christ would have remained unrecognized and unreceived. O Holy Forerunner of Christ, gather us to your synaxis.

10/23.I.1925

How ought we to pray for our own needs? We ask God to fulfill our request if it is not obviously sinful, but we cannot make our human wishes and fantasies become God's will. To every one of our human petitions we should add, in our hearts: "Nevertheless not as I will, but as Thou wilt" [Mt 26:39 Douay-Rheims]. We must strive to make this prayer of ours resound in our heart sincerely—otherwise we pray like the heathens in their vain repetitions [Matt. 6:7]. The fewer of our particular needs we pray for and the less we express our particular wishes, the better; better simply to ask God to help and save us and our loved ones. For our Lord knows our needs before we ask and He comes to meet them [Matt 6:8]. But at the same time, try not to start any task or take any step in life without the consecration of prayer; try thus to train yourself so that anything else would be impossible for you! Pray at all times and for all people, and the Lord of peace will be with you! [cf. Phil 4:9].

10/23.I.1925 (SAME DAY)

If you, O Lord, should mark iniquities, O Lord, who could stand? [Ps. 130:3].[96]

The soul grows weary from its sin and impotence. The world wounds it, and in its impotence the soul weeps and sees its own sin and infirmity. The death of the soul arrives: out of the depths have I cried unto Thee [Ps. 130:1], but my voice does not ascend and I myself do not hear it... Days of lethargy, days of trial, days of tears... O Lord, I cannot, I do not want to behold my own nothingness; allow me to behold You alone, to think only of You, to love only You, to serve only You. Serve the Lord in fear and rejoice in Him with trembling [Ps. 2:11].[97] Grant me tears, but tears of prayer, tears of tenderness. I am Yours, Lord, I do not wish to be my own or another's—take me, receive me...

11/24.1.1925

Lord! Send Your peace into my heart! What is sweeter than Your peace, sweeter than the tears You send, sweeter than to stand before You in prayer when You grant us prayer! Lord! I love You,

I want to be set ablaze in Your love, I want to love those whom You give me to love—not for my sake, as my sinful nature desires, but for their sake and for their sake alone, as You love Your creation. Grant me this love, teach me to love—to love not myself in others, but others in myself. O Lord, my Fortress, my refuge and my strength, I will love Thee evermore! [Ps. 18:1–2].

13/26.I.1925

Lord, my soul grows faint from giving You thanks. You have given me life, You have given me the world, You have given me a family and loved ones, You have sent me friends at all stages of life, You give me now a grace-bestowing friend, a support, and a comfort. Preserve him, Lord, by Your grace; teach me, help me, enlighten me to know how to preserve the shrine that is this friendship, how to guide and to save the soul You have elected for me, and how to be saved by it and along with it. I know, Lord, that my heart is unclean before You, I know that my life is sinful, that I am not worthy of this friend and that I am unqualified to lead and to guide him. But I believe that You, O Lord, sent him. I know that Your Most Pure One Herself, Your Mother, overshadows him and us with Her Mantle of Protection, and I hope that through my unclean and dumb mouth, through my dark soul, You might send Your light and reveal Your path—as the sun shines through dark clouds, as a dirty lamp nonetheless gives forth light, lit by You. Help, O Lord, preserve, sanctify!

16/29.I.1925

"And I have wasted my life in slothfulness."[98] My days are winding down, and all the more clearly and mercilessly I hear the coming verdict: slothful and wicked servant! [Matt. 25:26]. And I see my whole life, mired in narcissism, idleness, and laziness, laziness... If only I could devote myself to some work, *any* work, to the point of sweating blood [Luke 22:44], if only I could escape self-pity at least for a *moment* for the sake of the Lord and His work! But at all times and in everything: only self-will and idleness. And you see the long life God has given you as an empty, uncultivated field, overgrown with weeds, nothing but unfulfilled and missed opportunities. O Lord, grant me to make a beginning of good:[99] thus prays the soul, while never seeing this beginning. But, O

Lord of mine, I know that these complaints to You invite Your anger toward me. This is grave despondency, which is greater than all sins. This is the loss of hope in Your mercy that conquers all—even my laziness. Your saving grace irrigates the dry, unfruitful field of my soul. Your power supports and vivifies it. I am Your servant, accomplish in me what You wish, lead me where You wish, command what Your servant should do. O Lord, teach me to do Thy will!

17/30.I.1925

At the end of the day, I see its sins, sins of impotence, sins of weakness, sins of incontinence, and sins of laziness. And who will help me out of this sin? And upon rising in the morning, I see before me the same sins that like a dead weight press on my conscience. O Lord, forgive, heal the wounds of my soul. You give me more and more life, you give these months and years, and I, wretched man that I am [Rom. 7:24], incinerate them in the fires of my sins. But You, O Lord, are my hope, my refuge, my shield, my comfort. To You I give up my sinful soul.

18/31.I.1925

Holy guardian angel, pray to God for us! What joy, what cheer, what comfort it is to know that we have a guardian angel, a true and buoyant and good friend, and that we may call upon him in prayer. Immediately after praying the canon to one's guardian angel,[100] there is such a freshness and clarity in the soul, as if he—a true guide and friend—had brushed me with his wing, as if my soul had drunk from the cup of celestial beings. And somehow, my soul joyfully knows and believes that it is he, yes, *he*, that is with me and with all of us. What immeasurable joy there will be when our eyes are opened and we see the entirety of our life, and, through it all, our faithful companion, preserving us and our sweet loved ones from plunder, from being torn apart, from evil demons and from those who serve them; what immeasurable joy there will be when we discover this love for us (which we have done absolutely nothing—besides being neglectful—to merit) and discover this prayer that is uttered for us, together with the angelic doxology, before the throne of the Most High.

20.I/2.II.1925

O Lord, I thank You for the trials, for the difficulties, for the sorrows that You send me. I know how tough and callous and dry my soul is without Your admonitions, how it falls asleep, how it hardens. I glorify and kiss Your guiding right hand.

23.I/5.II.1925

There was an amazing and touching scene of a young woman's departure to God. The Lord brought me to her deathbed not long before she passed away. Christ visited her and communicated His Body and Blood by my sinful hands. Like a bird in the azure of the heavens, her soul soared to the Bridegroom, and then in that room of grief, we were in heaven, the Lord was near, a miracle of God's mercy took place. And then she lay peaceful, calm, and dignified, having learned everything that we here below do not know. All around us the atmosphere was prayerful and solemn. How blessed is priestly service: the Lord grants to a sinful man, drawing near to His mysteries, to be present when the Lord passes by. As Moses saw the back parts of God [Ex. 33:19–23], so also the priest sees them, and upon him falls the reflection of this Glory, as it did upon Moses [Exod. 33:18–23]. O marvelous and dreadful service! How can I give thanks to God for such mercy!

24.I./6.II.1925

Lord! Sometimes my shoulders grow weak and then seem to collapse completely. Hold me up by Your power. You fell and collapsed from exhaustion when carrying Your cross, You fell and collapsed from exhaustion under the burden of my sins, for You carried upon Yourself my cross as well, You have already borne it and brought it to the place of Golgotha. And yet *I* am weary!... How great is this sin of weakness and cowardice! But You have permitted us to grow weary, and You have blessed exhaustion, for You fell under the weight of the cross and carried it. And so likewise, Lord, admonish and teach your servant to love his cross and not to become exhausted by it on the soul's path, even when strength fails. Help me, O Lord; You are with me, my arm leans upon You. You lead all people, O Lord, down the path of sorrowful and onerous repentance, of seeing our sins, of testing our conscience. Before Your cross I bow down in worship, O Master; teach me to love my cross.[101]

25.I/7.II.1925

Deliver us from all ignorance and forgetfulness and *hard-hearted insensitivity*. When this malady visits the sinful soul, it grows dark in the miserable soul, and the world darkens along with it. The words of prayer fall into silence, unable to echo in the vacuum of space. The lips pray, but the soul does not. Thoughts rush by like scattered clouds.[102] All of life becomes some boring ritual, and there is no enchantment in it. A cold hand crushes the heart, and there is no love in it—not for God, not for humanity, not for God's world. Like some roaming shadow, the human being becomes a phantom in a world of phantoms, and Satan laughs, celebrating his slanderous victory. Begone, slanderer! Let God arise and let His enemies be scattered! [Ps. 68:1].[103] The merciful God sees my need, sees my grief and my infirmity. The merciful God goes out to meet the prodigal son, He embraces him and feeds him until he is satisfied [Luke 15]. This is a concession to my sin, to my wretchedness in asserting my own capacities. The Lord is near and will quickly help those who call upon Him [Ps. 145:18]. Lord, ignite this weak heart, grant me to love You with my whole soul, with all my heart, and with all my mind [Matt. 22:37].

27.I/9.II.1925

Lord, teach me the humility of the publican [Luke 18:9–14], grant it to me to come to hate myself in my filth, but preserve me from despondency and terror. O Lord, I am just as You were pleased to make me. You gave me life, you gave me love, you gave me all Your gifts. But I, wretched man that I am [Rom. 7:24], became prideful, did not give thanks, complained, grew weary and lazed about endlessly, spent my whole life in laziness. And now, in my decline, I see how I have spent my whole life in laziness and have not put Your gifts to good use, have not labored for You, for I have indulged in self-pity to no end. I have learned nothing, I have accomplished nothing, I have understood nothing and I have helped no one. I am leaving the world as if I had never been in it—not counting the innumerable victims of my sloth and parasitism. Before me lies a small remainder of my days, which You continue to give to me; grant me the will to repent. It is too late to accomplish anything in life, I cannot return to my past, to that which was lost in laziness. Grant me at least to weep sincere tears over my past and to thank You for all Your gifts. Give me the voice of the publican: O God, be merciful to me, a sinner.

28.I/10.II.1925

Holy guardian angel, pray to God for us. What comfort and strength we find in prayer to our guardian angel, to our friend who is always close and who belongs to us. We must at least once in our life see our guardian-friend, we must find him in prayer so that we may carry in our hearts the joy and hope he brings. What fear, but also what great joy, await us when we will come to know him face to face, to see him after we cross the threshold of this earthly life, when we depart from the flesh. How great a teacher and guide in this life we have in him, who knows our life, who has *lived* all of it with us, who has wept over our falling and rejoiced in our rising again. He knows *how* to teach us the first lessons we need for the new life that awaits us after the grave. Oh, we shall not be alone there, we shall not be abandoned. For no human friendship—not even the loftiest and most tender—can compare with this spiritual friendship: disinterested, not disdainful of our foulness and stubbornness, but conquering all things through love. Even here he is with us, he stands behind us, covering us with his wings. Holy angel, our guardian appointed by the Lord, pray to God for us!

30.I/12.II.1925

Thine is the day, and thine is the night [Ps. 74:16 Douay-Rheims]. You have established the times and the seasons [cf. Acts 1:7]. You have established each person's life and his work. You have given me a long life and have revealed Yourself in all of its seasons. You preserved me as a child and allowed me to taste of the paradise of childhood's sweetness. And You granted me to carry away and to keep, throughout my whole life, the fruits of this paradisal tree that I tasted back then. You sanctified my inward parts and dedicated me to the temple [cf. Ps. 139:13]. As a child and adolescent I loved the sweetness of Your house, the sweetness of its life. You touched my heart with compassion for the people, and even as a child my eyes knew the tears of repentance. You brought me into this world under the shelter of St. Sergius Church, and if it pleases You, in death You will receive my sinful soul there too.[104]

And I, like the prodigal son, took my wealth and went away into a far country to squander my estate, living first sinfully and prodigally, and then meagerly and shabbily. This is how things were until I heard the call in my heart and began the journey—with difficulty, with hesitation, timidly, faltering, glancing about—and came to the house of my Father. The road was long, but my Father met me, embraced me, and brought me inside, and granted me the feast of faith. Thus began my life with my Father, but, O merciful God, what an affront I was to this house! I brought in and kept all the bad habits of my prodigal life, all the ambitious pride, all my untamed fantasies and passions. And I once again began to embellish myself, began to puff up with pride, and the voice of true repentance was reduced in my heart to a lull. Then you admonished me with trials, with grief. I woke up once again, and stumbling, I plodded onward, and thus, in a battle with the prodigal habits of my sinful and turbulent youth, I lived out my adult life. The Lord surrounded me with friends and loved ones, showered me with His gifts; I received it all as something owed to me, and my heart was cold. But the Lord ignited in me a new love for His house, the church bells of my childhood began to ring triumphantly, our shared troubles [in Russia] began, and the Lord once more met me along the road and brought me into His house, to the order of the priesthood.[105] And thus began my old age, bringing my life to a close in weakness, yet crowning it with strength and glory. You brought me through trials and miraculously preserved me, but I remained deaf and hard of heart. Then you poured out a new and great mercy, you sent me a true friend in prayer and in life, a guardian angel, and You have granted to me to live life's twilight alongside this angel.[106] You surround me with love, O Lord! How can I repay You [Ps. 116:12], how can I become worthy of You? But I *want* to give back to You my entire life, which You have been pleased to give me; I want to completely dedicate to You this paltry remainder of my energies, which You, if you wish, can multiply [cf. Matt. 14:13–21]. I want to live in You and for You, and I desire nothing else. Help me, O You who can do all things, who can fortify my nothingness!

31.I/13.II.1925

Lord, I thank You for love. There is nothing higher than love, more blessed than love, or more wonderful. You grant me to love and to be loved: me, a stiff-necked, unworthy, and callous man. You, through Your grace, kindle in me a love that makes my heart boil over and my insides burn up. You grant me to despise myself and to love my neighbor through Your grace, through the communion of Your Body and Blood. O, how marvelous and fearful is this sacrament! How it saves and gives life to those who partake of it! How blessed is the lot of the priest who possesses this fearsome authority, and how we must strive more often to teach the faithful about the holy mysteries. As priests, the nature of our essence changes, that which is unnatural to us becomes natural, another's joy becomes our joy, another's pain becomes our pain. In the heart there is a jubilant joy for every person, for every one of God's creations, as well as for those who have gone astray and are perishing, who do not know their Creator. And with heavenly, paradisal joy, from the bells of the heavenly Jerusalem, there rings out joy over those who love and over those who are loved, who are gifts from God. Glory to You!

1/14.II.1925

Jesus Christ, Son of God, have mercy on me, wretch that I am! Jesus Christ, through Your most sweet Name, you calm the tempest in my heart occasioned by these brutal circumstances. You appear in the troubled waters of my soul and extend a helping hand to me, and I hear Your most sweet voice: "Why did you doubt, thou of little faith?" [Matt. 14:31], and I go, I go to You across the stormy sea. The clouds have melted away—clouds of grief, of doubt, of despondency, and all is clear and bright in my soul, and in the sky stands my Sun: Your Name. Lord, I love You, my Fortress, You are my refuge and strength [cf. Ps. 18:1–2]. Give me love, give me desire, reason, give me a mind for You, for You alone.

3/16.II.1925

"But when the Son of Man comes, will he find faith on the earth?" [Luke 8:18]. Grievous is the malice, grievous is the blasphemy, grievous is the animosity of the enemies of the cross of Christ, but all the more grievous and deadly is the indifference that is

spreading like a toxic cloud over the world and over the Russian land and filling our lungs with its fumes. At times one suffocates in this affliction of coldness, of unbelief, of spiritual re-barbarization. *For they are flesh* [Gen. 6:3]: God's verdict against antediluvian humanity is being fulfilled in our day as well. But how to live in this affliction? Should we condemn these wretches, be outraged, boil over with resentment, desire to help the Lord by human means and to bring down fire from heaven? [Luke 9:54]. Is this not to poison oneself with the very same poison? Or should we rather quietly mourn, weeping, begging God for both help and forgiveness, without condemnation and yet also with sadness, enduring and crying out to God? The Christian is not alone, for Christ is with him. Nothing can separate us from Him—not life, not death, not the depths [Rom. 8:38–39]. Seek in Him your support and comfort, and be thus victorious. Remember that you do not know and cannot expect the time of the general apostasy [2 Thess. 2:3], remember that the Lord foretold it, that He has permitted it in the course of times and fulfillments. These have some kind of meaning, unknown to us, for the triumph of the good, for the victory of Christ in the world. Wail, lament, weep, but fight back in Christ, be His true servant, and may He and He alone be your fortress and strength [cf. Ps. 18:1–2].

4/17.II.1925

I pray to the saints of God, I look upon their faces in their icons and call them each by name, I converse with them, I pray to them for my needs and together with them I pray to the Lord of glory. The saints in their icons surround my home altar and serve with me, praying along with me. Wondrous is God in His saints [Ps. 67:36 Douay-Rheims], and blessed is the man who is with God's saints. This is God's rainbow, this is the angelic-human choir that, together with us sinners and together with me, a wretch, prays to God. They do not abhor my wretchedness, and I do not grow ashamed, but instead I call upon them. Our love for the saints becomes ever warmer, more palpable, more vital, the more we pray to them, and their love for us in return becomes even more ardent—if this "more" is even possible for them. And yet the saints of God are people, and for them there exists an eternal *more*, and they grow richer in God by love for us through our prayers to them. This is the circle of human *interconnectedness*, linking heaven with earth, sinful humans and the saints of God; this is the palpability of the church visible and invisible, this is the rainbow, the bridge of our ascension from earth to heaven. And all the saints respond to our prayers, each saint to every prayer, regarding whatever we ask of them, and they speak in their own tongue to their own people: St Nicholas to his, St. Sergius to his, St. Seraphim to his, the Greatmartyr Panteleimon to his, Mary Magdalene, the Greatmartyr Barbara... Wondrous is God in His saints, the God of Israel!

7/20.II.1925

Death! A wondrous and great mystery that we are constantly encountering but that we pass by in a hurry, distracted by the little things of life. O stillness, O silence, O voice of this age, audible, audible silence! How near is death—like prayer, like God in prayer. No need to go out, no need to search, it is always here, and near; so also is death always here, and near—there is no distance at all. And yet, it is an abyss, and in this abyss lies the meaning of life, its justification, its solution. If only we could measure life by death, from the beyond, as the Church teaches us, calling to continuous remembrance of the hour of death, summoning us to stir up within ourselves eternal memory and the memory of eternity! [cf. 2 Tim. 1:6]. Excruciating are the hours of death and fearful is its arrival, and yet this is but a transient moment, and after that, liberation and then... the result: sad, terrifying, unvarnished.

From the perspective of youth it can seem that death is something abnormal, but then it becomes ever clearer that life *is* death, just as death is life. In youth it can seem that death is so far away that, practically, it does not exist at all. And then it becomes clearer and clearer (as it does now for me, wretched man that I am [Rom. 7:24]) that I have long outlived the typical lifespan (a time marked by all those deadly dangers from which God preserved me) and that I am already in that unmerited, extra period of life, a special gift of mercy and longsuffering from God, a gift of God's generosity. And for every day and hour of this undeserved life one must thank the Lord in a special way, must in a special way rejoice in each of its hours, and must take special responsibility for it before God. The Lord revealed to you that your life had exhausted itself long ago, and in the depth of the soul you know this yourself. But He in His mercy gives more and more periods for repentance, and He watches and waits to see how you will make use of this extension of time: will you spend it just as lazily and selfishly as you did all the other days of your life you spent in laziness, or instead by bringing forth the fruit of repentance? [Matt. 3:8]. Every death is a summons and a reproach and an unmasking—every death. Lord, grant me remembrance of death and a soft heart!

10/23.II.1925

If you endure injustice, do not bear malice and do not gloat, and do not lose heart in the face of evil, but accept it as a trial, as a mercy from God, rejoicing and thanking God for allowing you to undergo vilification. And *pray* for those who have wronged you: place yourself before God and, praying for them, forgive them within your heart in the presence of the all-knowing God, and sigh for them, take pity on them. Let it not be the sighing of the Pharisee: Lord, I am not as other men are [Luke 18:11]—you must see or at least seek the truth within their falsehood, their zealotry; you must place yourself in their position and ask yourself, if it were you, how would you behave? Wouldn't you do the same thing? For every individual is limited and one-sided and biased. And then you shall ever see your sin and your guilt and know that their judgment, while unjust in the particulars, is what you deserve. Always seek out your guilt and confess it before God, beg forgiveness of God for scandalizing your neighbors and leading them into temptation. But above all, do not bear malice, do not vaunt yourself, and do not despair. Remember that every man is a liar [Ps. 116:11], and so you too are unjust and have yourself committed injustice. Try to defeat evil with good [Rom. 12:21]. It is your sin and your weakness if you cannot turn the heart of your enemy who is against you on account of his ignorance. Be patient. Endure. In your patience save your souls [Luke 21:19]. He who endures to the end will be saved [Matt. 24:13]. Patience produces meekness, meekness forgiveness, and forgiveness love. Love your enemies [Matt. 5:44]—what is more blessed than to love your enemy! Lord, help me to love and to forgive and to pity and not to condemn my brothers, who are zealous for You!

12 / 25.II.1925

Lord, send Your peace to Your people! How the unpeaceful soul thirsts for peace, what a grace-filled treasury Your peace is! Our whole life changes when we have Your peace: our every inclination, our every thought. All of man's power, his entire salvation, is found in the preservation of peace. Only one who is peaceful in his heart can love, can rejoice, can help his neighbors, only the peaceful can distinguish good from evil, the important from the unimportant, the necessary from the unnecessary. Only the peaceful one is in possession of himself and rules himself in wisdom. But the unpeaceful one yearns for a peace lost and unobtained, and he even rages because in his heart he is not at peace with his lack of peace and so thirsts for peace. And the provocations of wickedness always deprive us of peace before all else.

Suddenly, it seems to you that someone has wronged you, that someone has offended you, that you are in danger, and then a storm of passions begins in the soul, petty and evil feelings. You feel ashamed of these feelings, you do not want them, you fight them, you are defeated by them. Pray, then, pray; ask God for peace, pray above all for those who are a stumbling block for you; pray unceasingly, pray to the point of blood for your peace [cf. Luke 22:44], and the Lord will send you His peace.

13 / 26.II.1925

Humble yourself before the will of God. If you see that things are working out decisively and conclusively, yet not how you wanted in your most sincere, fervent, and pure desires, submit yourself to this, the will of God; humble yourself. Force yourself to love the right hand of God that is leading you; force yourself to desire not what you want but what God wants for you, even if your heart should ache and grow weary. In this lies a higher wisdom and a higher obedience. It may happen—not right away, but sooner or later—that the truth of God and the love of God that are guiding you will be revealed to you, and you yourself will understand all the narrowness of your present desires and will give thanks to the Lord. So let not your heart be distraught if things are not working out your way. If you have done all that you can and that you consider to be useful and necessary, then expect trials from the Lord and submit yourself to Him. Don't torment your heart with excessive worry over the future; you do not know what or how the future will be for you. You darken the heart with sadness, which is always sinful, and do not rejoice in the joy given to you now. Cast your care upon the Lord, and He shall sustain thee [Ps. 55:22]. Calm your troubled heart.

14/27.II.1925

Our companions in life depart to that world, and each one calls to us: come this way! And, summoning us like a clanging bell, each one speaks of the approaching and imminent hour of death. The death of sinners is grim, and dreadful is the hour of death for every sinner and for me, wretch that I am. But I place my hope in the mercy of Your loving kindness. My soul has long heard and known this call, not as something unfamiliar and foreign, but rather as a summons both native and familiar. Death is both dreadful and not, for death itself decays and dies the nearer we draw to it. And after the terrible and distressing event of the grave and of corruption, a new life is ignited, a new youth. For thy youth shall be renewed like the eagle's [Ps. 103:5]. We need not wrap ourselves up in a Stoic toga of dispassion and indifference—because that is pride and hypocrisy—but we must humbly give ourselves up to the loving hand of the Lord. It is as if, little by little, the leaden gates of death become ever more transparent, a light shines through them, the singing on the other side reaches us, we become aware of the souls who dwell there. The soul is sprouting its wings, it's like teething—there is still a long way to go, yet there is already a beginning, already life proceeds with the feeling of the break of dawn, and the soul basks in the morning air... We must live with complete fullness: with all love, with total effort, but we must bear in ourselves this knowledge that everything is *for a time,* that everything is not only going to end but *must* end, *must* receive... the new.

24.II/9.III.1925

The holy days of Great Lent! How invigorating is the clean air, how brightly the sun shines, how vividly these days in their succession cleanse the soul... God has established the seasons [cf. Acts 1:7], and to every season He has granted its own rank and its own power; out of all other days, He has chosen and honored these days that store up and progressively amass the power of the Great Day of Christ's Resurrection. In the soul the buds of a new day swell. But for this to occur, old branches must be cut off, and how agonizing and onerous is this removal, when you see yourself, your whole life, in the light of the Dread Judgment of Christ, in the light of His truth. Where is our greatness, ever imaginary, where is our pride, which amuses itself with shadows? What a heavy thing this is—*to see oneself*. Truly, a man cannot bear this for long, he seeks to forget, to turn his back to himself; only ascetics, men of strength, have endured this unremitting vision of their sins, this unremitting repentance. But for us, small and weak as we are, the Lord shortens the time for weeping over our personal sins by granting us forgiveness, granting us indulgence, granting us a feast. And in humility let us accept this indulgence, as we are incapable of anything beyond this... In the monastery, while the monk is engaged in continual ascetic struggle, another visits to pray for just a short time—but let not the second one lose hope. Truly, it is *terrifying* to see oneself, and one must be neither frightened nor poisoned by fear, sinking into despondency and despair over oneself. This would be merely a new, inverse pride; one must *be patient* with oneself also, one must acquire a spirit of *patience*.

25.II / 10.III.1925

Lord, have mercy and help Your sorrowful and embittered servant! Your plans are accomplished by human hands, by the forces of nature, and by that which people call blind chance. Our heart exhausts itself in the face of what cannot be changed; powerless, it knows not how to cast its care upon God [Ps. 55:22], it cannot see here the right hand of God at work at all times and in all things. Our eyes are shrouded... they cannot raise themselves to see this, but arduous striving is required. Just as, after deep prayer, an imperturbable serenity reigns in the soul, so also, after sorrow, tranquility reigns. Let Thy will be done!

27.II / 12.III.1925

O Lord! What a miracle Your icons and those of Your saints are, how miraculous is Your presence in others, how miraculous is Your nearness and theirs to our sinful world. Beholding an icon of Your Forerunner, traced by a hand wise in God, I, in trembling and with my soul abashed, felt that he himself had touched my soul, that he had left his heavenly abode in order to illumine the darkness of this world, in order to once again call us to repentance, in order to once again announce to us the coming of the Lord. One senses that this marvelous icon does not simply trace but also marks in reality the nearness of the times and seasons, marks the nearness of Your witnesses and luminaries, those who make ready the way of the Lord [Matt. 3:3]. It was not this timid and delicate hand that traced this icon, but rather the very hand of the Forerunner himself, having touched heaven and earth [when he poured water] over the bowed head of Christ. One can drink up fountains of consolation, of tears, of joy, and of grace before the icon, one can pray before it, one can rise up to that world above.

The icon is not [yet] consecrated[107]—it is here with us, it has been relayed to us, human beings, it is a revelation for humans, it is the Lord on earth, who grants us to see Him, to hear Him, to receive Him, to clasp His knees, to wash His feet and to wipe them with our hair [cf. Luke 7:44]. But a consecrated icon is already departing from us; it is sinful to try to embrace it the way Mary wished to clasp the Savior's feet [John 20:17]. It is the Ascended Christ, Christ in the Resurrected Body: we are not able to look upon it; we should only pray toward it, and immodest glances are sinful by definition. Unless you are praying, you may not look upon icons that are already consecrated, and we commit a certain undue transgression (yet, according to human weakness, it is perhaps something involuntary and unavoidable, which, however, should be cleansed through repentance) when we *scrutinize* an icon, when we feast our eyes upon it. But an as yet unconsecrated but reverently traced icon is already the one who is depicted, it is *his* presence, his face. Into this home has entered the Baptizer of the Savior, John.

28.II / 13.III.1925

O Holy Spirit, heart of the Father, Love of Love, Love of the Holy Trinity! You breathe where you wish [John 3:8], Thou art everywhere, Thou fillest all things: fill me also, so that I, as one of humble birth who is unworthy, may sing Your glory to the lyre of my mind, may herald Your love, may sing forth Your presence and Your coming and Your nearness. Words fail in the attempt to describe You, for You are not the Word; for You every heart trembles, because You are the trembling of the Father's heart. In You all creation rejoices,[108] for You are the Joy of Joy, perfect Joy. In You, every grief is comforted, every infirmity made whole, for You are the Comforter. In You, all twilight is made bright, for You are light unending. In You, every human dream is fulfilled, for You are the fulfillment of all things. In You, we are divinized—hay in the fire [1 Cor. 3:12–13], for You are the divine fire, divinizing us. In You, every hope is realized, for You announce what is to come. In You, every heart is ignited by love, for Thou art love and You ignite it with love. The new commandment of Christ: "Love one another" [John 13:34] is also the promise of the Comforter, the promise of You, O Love. The teaching of the apostle to the Gentiles concerning the "more excellent way" of love is a teaching about You [1 Cor. 12:31]. Through You we rejoice, in You we pray, in You we draw breath, through You we love, through You we are deified, O Holy Spirit, the True Light, the Joy of Joys, the Comfort of the world.

1/14.III.1925

O Holy Spirit, Love of God, enlightening, delighting, gladdening! No one knows Your coming and Your going, but the faithful heart knows, when it suddenly rejoices with trembling, thawing and going out of itself, but then just as suddenly, when left on its own, it abides in desolation, empty and enchained. When You come, life blossoms, earth and heaven rejoice, people are ignited with love, and the scent of joy wafts from all Your creation, and especially from humanity. How blessed life would be if we could hold on to this, how bright God's world would be, earth and heaven, if it were always illuminated with *this* light, how miraculous would human relationships be in the Spirit of God, when people become for one another not gloom but joy. But no one knows the time of Your departing. And then we are left victims of our very selves, of dissatisfaction, of ulceration and emptiness, the emptiness of the coldness of disconnection. The heart thirsts for comfort, all creation thirsts for the Comforter. O Comforter, Spirit of Truth, come and abide in us![109]

3 / 16.III.1925

The human soul is more precious than the world. What a treasury is the living human soul, what gems may lie hidden in its depths, jewels that a person himself, as well as those around him, do not suspect, but to which, with astonishment and thanksgiving to God, God's priest bears witness when he hears a confession. What a frightening responsibility it is for us—to crack the surface of that field of treasure within souls, to break the soil of souls loose for the grace of God, to irrigate them with the rain of the word of prayer! [cf. Matt. 13:44–46]. The Lord knows His creation better than we, who in our limitation see only the earth's crust and sands, while He knows the paths of salvation for each. How precious and how good is a person in his repentance, in his love for God, in his striving for Him, how wonderful is the one who repents. He never sees and cannot and should not see this in his own repentance, but God sees it, the holy angels see it, the priest receiving the confession sees it. Along with the grace of the priesthood the Lord grants the grace to receive the sins of others and the grace to sincerely not condemn but rather to forgive; to the priest is granted a benevolent heart. He sees the penitent not in his sin, but in his beauty as God's creation: in him shines the image of the Lord that is inscribed within him...

4 / 17.III.1925

Lord, every day You give Your food to the soul and the body, You give us work, You give us life. Every day the soul, cleansed by prayer, once again breathes Your air and hearkens to You, the living God, until You issue your command and a new day arrives, with its new sustenance. The human person faces forward in hope, but it is with fear that we look backwards, for there we see an endless succession of days spent in laziness, wasted, lost, and with each new day, as we grow older by the hour, we hope to begin a new life. Is this hope a fatal self-deception born of our own weakness, or is it rather the saving mercy of God? God does not take away hope even when man takes it away, and God does not put to shame those who place their hope in Him [cf. Psalm 2:12]. And so, my soul, what is it that prevents you? Begin this day a new life, and conduct it as the Lord commands... Seek out what you need, where you should begin. What lies in your power, what can you—and thus, *must* you—immediately correct, uproot, or accomplish? Is it cultivating a prayerful will or keeping vigil, is it fasting or trusting in God, is it loving concern for your neighbors? Keep watch, O soul, and give to God the fruit of your new day, even if it is not much. The Lord Himself will multiply your bread, but give it to Him yourself [cf. Matt. 14:16].

6/19.III.1925

The power of love is sacrifice, and the highest love is sacrificial. The Lord wants and gives such love, as well as its power, to His elect. Their entire life is ascetical struggle, sacrifice, and self-abnegation, with no alleviation, no pleasure. Of such a kind was the love of the Mother of God, which in its entirety was one single sacrifice. Her entire life, along with Her Son's, was dedicated to the struggle of sacrificial love, and the sword always and unceasingly pierced Her heart [Luke 2:35]. As the handmaid of the Lord [Luke 1:38], She served Him through the sacrificial love of Her maternal heart, and to this day She, though glorified in the heavens, offers this sacrifice, for she weeps and intercedes for the race of sinful humanity.

And such too was John the Forerunner, Her kinsman. To him it was granted likewise to taste of sacrificial love and of nothing else, to be not the bridegroom but the friend of the Bridegroom, not to increase but to decrease [John 3:29–30]. He willingly offered the sacrifice of himself and his mission when he met the Lamb of God, but he did not taste of the joy of participating in the wedding, of being present at the wedding feast. He did not join His disciples, he did not walk with Him, he did not have the pleasure of hearing Him and seeing His face; he, who is the greatest of those born of women [Matt. 11:11], was of all people the most worthy of this, but he remained *alone* with his own disciples, continuing to baptize with the baptism of repentance [Luke 3:3], to prepare others for meeting Christ. He remained alone in the expectation of his death by the sword of Herod, and no relief, no pleasure, no human joy (except the most spiritual) did he have on his path, which was lonely, filled with holy awe, and dreadful. His love was sacrifice and sacrifice alone, as was the love of the Mother of God; and this sacrifice was accepted by God... And the seal of the spirit of the Forerunner lies upon those elect who travel the "stubborn way" [cf. Judg. 2:19] of strain, sacrifice, ascetic struggle, and yet do not stop. *Never rest*—thus their soul speaks within them—and they walk, ascending from glory to glory [2 Cor. 3:18] along the path of the Forerunner toward the hosts of the Queen of heaven and earth, who on earth appears as the Disconsolate Mother.

7/20.III.1925

How lovely are Your tabernacles, O Lord of hosts! My soul longeth and fainteth for the courts of the Lord [Ps. 84:2–3 Douay-Rheims].[110] The lot of the priest—how joyful, how elect, for the sparrow has found herself a nest [Ps. 84:4]. Though not all are priests, still the Lord allows those who are not to reach out and to touch the sanctuary and to rejoice in it. I behold women, old and young, making clerical vestments and veils for the holy mysteries of Christ, and my heart expands as I rejoice in their love, in the miracle of God's mercy. Unceasingly created and continually traversed is the grace-bestowing ladder between earth and heaven [John 1:51]. This ladder is brought into being even now by timid and obedient fingers. For whatever is intended for the sanctuary is already holy by virtue of its purpose, it is holy in its consecration, and, after entering through the curtain of fire, is taken out of human hands to remain in consecrated hands alone, for in truth consecrated hands are no longer human (no matter how sinful or wretched my right hand may be, O Lord). And that which is sewn and woven in our daily, mundane life is already regenerated and sanctified in [priestly] hands and becomes a thing of another world, of the new heaven and new earth.

The Lord has elected the most skilled and endowed them with the gifts of the Holy Spirit for the completion of their work for the tabernacle [cf. Ex. 31:1–6]. But this gift, having once come down for the elect, remains and is passed down even now in the Church. It rests even now on those who worthily and prayerfully complete this work. And these deaconesses [*diakonissy*] of Christ are admitted to the outer court (so to speak) of the sanctuary, and they are invested with the priesthood in their own order among those not ordained. Through them, a bridge is created between the sanctuary and the outer courts, a link by which angels ascend and descend from heaven to earth and back. And the woman who offers the Lord her love and her work is like the woman who bought the alabaster jar of expensive oil and poured it on the feet of the Savior and filled that home with fragrance; and the Lord said of this blessed woman that she hath wrought a good work.... Yes, may there also be a blessing for those women who do a good work today by offering a vial of the precious oil of love from their hearts [cf. Matt. 26:6–10].

8 / 21.III.1925

Glory, O Lord, to Your precious Cross.[111] I look upon the glory of the Cross in its endless forms. I behold it in a person being crucified today. He stands on his cross of willing love for the Lord with lips compressed, with members tense, with arid eyes, with the pain of fatigue, and he looks out on a world that, although familiar to him, nonetheless provides him no answers; he dies in love and from love for that which is greater than the world and higher than the world. How wonderful he is, how bright his gaze, how quiet as I bow to him and kiss the edge of his garment [cf. Matt. 9:20], as I take in his air and take in the trembling of his flaming heart. This burning bush is aflame, it burns and yet is not consumed [Exod. 3:2], and in this fire the gold of his heart is refined.

Our weakness fears the sight of crucifixion and self-crucifixion, yet at the same time, what can we offer to God if not our very self, in order to love Him with the love by which He overcame the world? It is a natural impulse to say to our loved ones who are being crucified: "come down from the cross, don't torment yourself" [Matt. 27:40], but do we have the authority to give voice to this impulse? Do we not thereby become blasphemers of the cross of the Lord? Is it not better to co-crucify oneself with the one we love and, suffering for him, to touch his cross, to love it? O people, if only we had within us the strength to love each other's cross, so that they all might merge together into one, common, great cross of humankind, for this is the Cross of Christ, His light and sweet burden! [Matt. 11:30]. The Most Pure One stood at the cross of the Beloved Son, a sword pierced Her heart [Luke 2:35], and the world has known no greater suffering—yet She never once uttered, either with Her lips or in Her heart: "come down from the cross, free yourself from torture." She was co-crucified, She who is His Mother and the Mother of the entire human race. Grant us too the strength not to speak in our heart this sinful thought, grant us to kiss with our lips and our soul the all-precious Cross of the Lord and the cross of humanity that bores into the precious shoulders of those we love. Grant that we, bowing down beneath it, may carry it together, may grow weary under its weight together with our beloved...

10/23.III.1925

Humble yourself, submit, learn to make your peace—beat, force, and wear yourself down in order to receive what has been sent to you, to recognize in it not some chance occurrence, not some mere whim, but instead God's will and God's plan. If it seems to you that people have treated you unjustly, let not this splinter remain in your heart: recognize in this God's admonition, God's punishment for your sins, for your secrets, which God sees. Preserve the peace of your soul, fight for this peace, reach for it like the greatest hidden treasure. And if your spirit is not at peace, it is an ominous sign that your spirit is sick with sin or is in battle with temptation. Overcome with love those who fight you, try to place yourself in their position, in their situation, try to understand and to accept them, and then there will be no need to forgive, for there will be nothing to forgive. Seek imperturbability and equanimity not in human pride but in the peace of God. The unpeaceful person is unwise, unjust, shortsighted, but every victory over the self confirms a person. Thus the apostle writes, "your feet shod with readiness to proclaim the gospel of peace" [Eph. 6:15].

11/24.III.1925

O most sweet Name of Jesus, wisdom and power! You fill my heart, You strengthen my feet, You give me the courage to begin this day before the Lord. O miracle of prayer, O miracle of Divine omnipresence! I call upon You, and You are already with me in Your Name; I seek You, and You are already in my heart and on my lips [Rom. 10:8]; I thirst for You, and You already quench me. O miracle of miracles, it is more miraculous than the miracles of the world, it is more miraculous than the sun and the stars, than the earth and that which is under the earth! The love of God, the love of Christ that is manifest to us, is imprinted upon

His Name and in the power of His cross that overshadows me and the whole world. With this weapon in hand, I go out into the world undeterred, and if I become afraid, I once again feel around for it, making sure that it is with me, and I continue on further. The Name, the Cross, the power of Christ. Clothe me, cover me, preserve my heart from wicked imaginations, lock out impure thoughts from my heart, engrave my heart with Your ring of betrothal, O Bridegroom, O Word of God, O Lord Jesus Christ, Son of God, have mercy on me, wretch that I am!

13 / 26.III.1925

The manifestation of angels! We are unworthy and too weak to bear the vision of the angelic world that surrounds us. The angels pray with us, they co-serve at the altar with us. But by the will of God, the eyes of our soul open up, and with the heart the soul hears the angels' flight, it sees the angels' wings. And then it soars up with them! For the soul, the world below grows smaller—an unbearable bliss. In the hour of death the blessed end of the righteous is accomplished through this unbearable ecstasy. Pure souls have this knowledge of the angels, they imprint it on the icon with needle and brush, they show us visions at which our soul trembles. How merciful is the Lord, that He sends here, to this world, heralds of another world, that He does not allow us to be locked up and to lose ourselves in this world, but instead He breaks our heart open and grants us a foretaste of unearthly blessings. The cherubim continuously encircle the altar, they majestically escort the chalice of Christ, and this is indicated by the depiction of the cherubim on the veils [of the paten and chalice].[112] But how rarely we recognize this, how scant is our knowledge of it, and we are surprised with great joy and astonishment when heaven is opened to us and suddenly, for an instant, we actually feel the nearness of the angels. By one candle is another lit, from one heart does another heart love, by one soul is another soul enlightened. So that thousands might be warmed and enlightened, a flame must first be lit somewhere. How precious that flame is! How we ought to love and to venerate God's elect, whom He sends into the world to proclaim His will and to witness to Him! I am struck with awe and bow down prostrate before the mystery of God's love, wisdom, and mercy.

14/27.III.1925

The seeds of good and evil are sown invisibly, and often we do not notice how we tempt one another, how we dig a sharp thorn into the heart of our neighbor, sometimes by [openly] giving ourselves up to our passions and lusts, at other times simply as a result of our foolishness. As a man is in himself, so is he with others.

Sometimes you wake from sleep with a burden on your heart. The evil one tempts, distracts, obstructs prayer, torments you with unkind feelings. The human struggle of the will to drive away temptation is real, but how weak are these human powers! Yet divine help is also real: force yourself to pray for those who have wounded you; sincerely pray, and, standing before God, this unkind feeling will not remain, it will dissipate like smoke and your heart will become clear. And when the *eye* becomes clear, then everything becomes clear: *the light of the body is the eye; therefore let your eye be bright* [Matt. 6:22–23]. Truly we see the world through different eyes when we pray and when we do not pray, before prayer and after prayer. Humble yourself, beat down your sinful feeling, wish well to the one who hurt you. If your unkind feeling doesn't yield, try to distract yourself and to forget it until it cools down. But do not reduce yourself to petty and base feelings; preserve your dignity, for you are created in the image of God, and you yourself—alas!—stand in need of forgiveness and leniency from all.

And greater than that of all others, more boundless than that of all others, is your guilt, not before those who hate you and who are your enemies, but before those who love you. O frightful and unpaid debt, guilt before love, paucity of love, love of self, mediocrity in love, ingratitude towards love! Direct your gaze toward yourself, lead it away from that which tempts you, and weep, weep for your sins in love against those whom you love, those who love you, an ingrate, even when you do not merit it. And could anyone say of himself that he does not owe a debt to love, that he loves as his conscience tells him to? At the hour of death, at the Dread Judgment seat, we will see this feebleness and coldness of our love, its callousness, we will cry and be horrified, but it will be too late. Ignite, O heart; O God, ignite it, ignite it with Your love, and in the fire, like trash, burn up and consume all the tares of the heart [cf. Matt. 13:24–43], all of its sinful splinters.

17/30.III.1925

Departure and journey grant a sense of detachment from the familiar trappings of our environment that pile up around us, and so they resemble the final path that lies before us.[113] That is why every road affects us: to some it brings distress, to others joy, but it always opens up within the heart a source of new feelings. That is why people of this age are addicted to vacations. But the Truth has said of Himself: "I am the Way" [John 14:6]. In Him and in life with Him there exists this sense of journey, this liberation. O Lord, let my journey be the Way with You...

24.III/6.IV.1925

Blessed are ye when they shall revile you for My sake [Matt. 5:11 Douay-Rheims]. Lord, send me this blessedness. Grant it to me to joyfully accept the trials and adversities that You give to me to endure for Your Name. Grant me a clear conscience and unwavering firmness to walk the true path of service to You. Courage is patience, the readiness to suffer, if necessary—and suffering *will* come. Fear on the other hand is the attempt to come down from the cross and to be free of suffering, under whatever pretext we find plausible. This is so natural to human faintness of heart and self-love that it creeps into the soul imperceptibly. Examine yourself impartially: are you in the faith [2 Cor. 13:5], are you in the truth, are you not now in a state of deception? But if you do not now see this, then work in the meanwhile for your Lord as a true servant nonetheless. Don't judge yourself according to human judgment. Be afraid if all people speak well of you. The most dangerous and suspicious thing is success, and the most enervating and corrupting thing is the thirst for it. What is blameless in youth becomes sinful in old age. Have a fearless and burning heart, and offer it to your God.

29.III/11.IV.1925

The day of destiny, decreed by God! His Holiness Patriarch Tikhon, God's elect, has died.[114] This death has left the Russian Church, and the Russian land, orphaned; they weep inconsolably, but let us submit to the will of God. God's will elected him and placed him on the Church's lampstand [cf. Rev. 2:5], the Mother of God directed him to a great cross, to boundless sorrow, and he has now been recalled from his post. Inscrutable are the destinies decreed by God; we do not know what they mean, in trembling we bow before them. But how grateful we ought to be, how we should love, venerate, and preserve in our hearts the father of the Russian land, one who truly knew its sorrows! He was the glory of his people in this time of endless abjection, he enlightened the whole world with the light of his martyrdom. And for me, wretched man that I am [Rom. 7:24], he proved an instrument of the greatest mercy God has shown me: he blessed me for the priesthood, he extended to me the greatest trust that could be extended, and in tears I kissed my father's right hand of blessing. O Lord, receive and grant rest to his soul in Your holy dwelling places [cf. Ps. 68:35].

17/30.IV.1925

There is nothing more dreadful than sin: it is the death of the soul. Death enters and tears apart the soul, killing it. Just yesterday, on the eve of sin, you were bright and whole and joyful, but sin tore up your soul, with emptiness and loneliness entering in. There is no loneliness except in sin. The sinner is alone, he has been abandoned by, and has himself abandoned, the Lord whom he offended, together with His Most pure Mother, the holy angels and the holy God-pleasers, as well as his loved ones and neighbors. Before all, before everyone has he committed his sin, before everyone is he a wretched criminal. He carries in himself the secret of his sin and its resultant death. Sin is the despair and death of the soul, the second death [Rev. 21:8]. All are rejoicing, yet the sinner is encircled by the ring of his sin, and so this joy torments him; everything is bright, but in him this light is darkness. This is how it will be after the Dread Judgment of God: that very blessedness and joy and light which will be the exultation of the righteous will fetter and execute wretched sinners. One can experience these torments of hell here, in this life, immediately after sin, while still in the captivity of sin. The wretched sinner is judged not by an external judge, not by a dictate from God, but by sin itself, by his very self. The torments of hell—this is the *power* of sin in your own self, this is the shame, the unbearable shame of sin, the shame of deceit, the shame of desecrating what is holy, near, and dear.

Lord, save me, a sinner, from despair, grant repentance, grant weeping. I am unworthy to lift up my eyes to You, to address You, I am unworthy of the sun, of this earth, of this Your creation, which the sinner darkens with his being; I—a deceiver and a thief—am unworthy of my neighbors, of my loved ones, of all people. But You are love, You came to save sinners [cf. 1 Tim. 1:15]. Save, then, this sinner from despair, save, for You can and You Yourself wish to: do not let Your creation perish.

18.IV / 1.V.1925

Sin is death, the second death [Rev. 21:8], eternal death. The sinner bears the stamp of God's rejection. That which is the source of joy and love for the righteous is for the sinner the outer darkness into which he plunges himself [Matt. 8:12], thereby condemning his very self. In sin, a person comes to understand the total power that eternal perdition—inexorable, unconquerable by any human powers—possesses over him. And even these human powers are non-existent. For sin is emptiness, impotence, death. Just a short time ago, a person moved about to and fro, took joy in life, took joy in the strength bubbling up within him, but now he is dead and empty. Such was the horror of the original sin, when all of a sudden people saw themselves go from being beloved children of God to being rejected transgressors, and the Father stood before them as the Righteous Judge, and not being able to bear the gaze of Him whom they had offended with their sin, they hid themselves in the thicket [cf. Gen. 3:8].

And this experience of the original sin is repeated in every human being, when through sin he offends God, the Most Pure Virgin, the holy apostles, human beings—and from among these, those who are the most near and dear, and especially those who love him more than all others and have put their trust in him. Even if no one in the world knows about your sin, still God almighty knows and sees, and at the Dread Judgment, *all people*, everyone, will find out and see your sin [cf. Luke 8:17]. What dreadful disillusionment and woe will come upon them when they see that the one whom they believed and loved is a deceiver and a vile sinner. But in the light of God's face they will be saved from that despair, from the disappointment into which they will inevitably fall, if the sinner will now confess his sin before them. Sin is the mark of Cain, the curse. It robs everything and everyone and is more terrifying than death. There is nothing more terrifying and cruel than sin. And if the Lord in His inexpressible love did not lend a helping hand, did not pour into the soul of the sinner the power of forgiveness, then the sinner would perish in despair.

Weep, weep, O miserable man, cleanse your wounds with tears. Know that no man is more wretched than you, that you make the earth upon which you walk an abomination. The earth was not created for you if you corrupt yourself with your sin. But the yet greater sin is despair. The Lord is merciful. The Lord can *forgive* sin: He cannot be reconciled to it, but He can make the past nonexistent, He can cleanse it by His Blood. He can piece back together the ruined fabric of your soul and resurrect what is dead. It was for this reason that He came into the world, so that He might raise up the fallen. The Lord knew your weakness and your sinfulness and because of it He left His heavenly throne. The Lord suffered on the cross for you and for your filth, in order to save you from despair and death. The Lord hears every sigh and sees every tear. Before the fall you did not know the power of sin within, you were proud in your righteousness, which was merely the absence of temptation. Now you have been humbled, because you have come to know your nothingness. Now you have understood how immeasurable is the sacrifice of the love of God, when you have seen for whose sake it is offered, when you have seen that your sin too was included in His anguish in Gethsemane, unto the sweating of blood, and you have seen yourself in the number of His tormentors and crucifiers. So do not now dishonor the love of God through ingratitude and lack of faith. Place your hope in God's mercy, for God has loved you since before creation. For, says the Lord, I do not desire the death of the sinner [Ezek. 18:23; 33:11].[115]

21.IV/4.V.1925

At the bedside of the dying and the gravely ill you will understand both the vanity of life and its absolute seriousness, when the one suffering—writhing in torment with deathly anguish, fighting between hope and despair—puts to shame and disconcerts by his very person the healthy who will also, sooner or later, meet this hour of anguish and ultimate seriousness, of ultimate accountability. Here there is no longer any wall between time and eternity, between God and humanity, the wall we erect through our thoughtlessness and complacency. Here is a place of prayer, of departure to God, and not of convulsive clinging to the present day and to this moment. The Lord gives the priest the strength and authority to be present at this bedside, to calm this anxiety and to give to the dying the true and final comfort—the absolution of sins along with the Body and Blood of Christ. Beyond this there is nothing one can give, and anything more than this one should not give.

Inscrutable are God's ways [Rom. 11:33]. The Lord loves all equally, both these sick and dying ones as well as the healthy. But inscrutable to us here are God's ways. The one who provides comfort to the sick and dying must undergo a struggle of faith, because otherwise this comfort will be mere pretense, laziness of soul. You must accept in your soul both this sorrow and this suffering. But this has been accomplished only by the Son of God in the garden of Gethsemane, the One who assumed onto Himself every tear and every sorrow. And He has called to action priests made in His image, those summoned to this hour. O Lord, who turned to prayer in the struggle of Gethsemane, grant to us, priests, Your ministers, to participate in this feat of Gethsemane, to suffer along with our suffering children and to give to them not a stone of indifference but the true bread of Christ's comfort and compassion [Matt. 7:9]. Man is too weak to accomplish this feat, but the Lord gives the grace of the priesthood and its gifts.

22.IV/5.V.1925

Out of the depths have I cried unto thee, O Lord [Ps. 130:1]. My heart is in disarray, my soul powerless, my body wasting away; there is no comfort for me in my sins, in my infirmity. Even before death, death enters my soul and body and divides them. And powerless as I am, out of the depths of Hades I cry to You, Lord—help and strengthen, for Thou art the God that doest wonders [Ps. 77:14].[116] I am surrounded by the miracles of Your love, and greater than all miracles is a loving heart. How sought out I have been by human love, by Your love! And yet suddenly I see that I am empty and naked! Liberate me, O Lord, from cowardice, from turmoil, from lack of faith. Grant me to desire to endure everything from You, for You, and for Your sake! I bless Your cross, I kiss Your right hand that guides me, I entrust all to You, I give to You my entire soul, will, and reason. Grant me to die for you, grant that nothing personal or transient should darken the peace of my soul, grant it to me to be worthy of Your love. My sun, my God, my Comfort, my most sweet Jesus, do not abandon Your drowning servant [cf. Matt. 14:22–33], for nothing remains in him save infirmity: my whole being is like a vessel, albeit a filthy one, filled with nothing, thirsting to be filled with Your water. Fill me, pour me out, ignite me, grant me rejoicing, grant me to see You, to know You, to love You, Jesus my most sweet, my most sweet Jesus!

23.IV/6.V.1925

O miracle of God's mercy! Yesterday there was still turmoil, but now—silence and peace from the source of silence and giver of peace, our Lord Jesus Christ. The Lord through His grace fills the soul, floods it with His peace and light and joy, and the soul is brought to rest in the embrace of the Father. How thunderous and staggering is this miracle of God's help, only we rarely notice it, although it is unceasingly accomplished in the sinful soul. Fervent prayer, a graced encounter, the help of a friend, which sometimes, even in the majority of cases, we don't suspect to be an instrument of God's help—yet into the soul a calmness enters, and in the midst of the raging sea of the soul, which overwhelms with its waves, the Lord draws near and says: O thou of little faith, wherefore didst thou doubt? [Matt. 14:31]. And after the sinful turmoil, you find your footing once more on solid ground, you feel a blessed assurance in yourself and an influx of strength, not an insane human self-assuredness, but a new experience and knowledge that the Lord is near. He sees and hears and knows, and one must entrust oneself to His strong hand. There is no need to fear: fear is a sin and perhaps a deadly sin. You need fear neither external difficulties nor even your own weakness and infirmity, which you will discover in all of their implacability in the course of your life, for the Lord is all-powerful—to help, to admonish, to strengthen. God is with us![117] Glory to You, glory to You, glory to You, who save humanity from faintheartedness, trembling, and perplexity. O miracle of God's mercy, of His kindness!

24.IV/7.V.1925

What is impossible for man is possible for God [Luke 18:27]. If an unbearable difficulty weighs upon your soul, if your heart is distressed and your conscience anxious, cast thy care upon the Lord [Ps. 55:22] and await His help in your difficulty. Don't give into fainthearted despondency: there is no power that can overcome the grace of God. And pray fervently, pray wholeheartedly, believe that your prayer will break through the stone wall built up around you—whether by your sin or for other reasons. The Lord is leading you to an unknown and immeasurable good; all the difficulties encountered on your path, excluding sin, are but steps leading up to God, to a joy not of this world. But here, while still in the earthly shell, if you glance backwards [to your past] you can see just how far you have climbed, how much thinner the air is, how much broader the view, but also how terrifying the depths threatened should you fall. Do not succumb to fear, even the fear of hopelessness: at any point you can escape with the wings of faith, with the wings of ascetic struggle and illumination. My Lord, Lord, I love You alone, You alone do I desire to love, to serve: teach me to do Thy will! [Ps. 143:10].

25.IV/8.V.1925

I am the bread of life [John 6:35]. The Lord is life and grants the faithful to partake of Him daily and hourly. Day after day of life is this bread given to us, and we rejoice and live in it. This bread is the Lord, giving Himself in Holy Communion, in prayer, and in His holy Name. All you who pray and who invoke His name with your whole heart, know that you commune in this His holy Name, that you taste the bread of life through the power of this invocation. He abides in you and you in Him [cf. John 15:4]. Not by measure does God give His Spirit [John 3:34], and there exists communion in the Body and Blood, but there is also communion in the Name. For prayer is always a union with Christ, by which the power of Christ enters into us. Oh, how good is the Lord, who has given us prayer, given us the power to invoke His Name, and revealed His Name to people, and this Name is the Lord Jesus Christ, who said of Himself "I have declared unto them Thy Name" [John 17:26]. This Name, introduced for the first time by the angel bearing good news [Matt. 1:21], is the power in which we live and move and have our being [Acts 17:28].

26.IV/9.V.1925

Lord! How I thank You for Your mercies! As I was drowning in sins, You once again called me to life, You grant me to stand before You, to call upon Your Most Sweet Name, to pray to You, to thank You. I have been rejected by You and by others and am fit only for the depths of hell, and yet You have mercifully allowed me into Your court, You do not cast me down into perdition. You grant the hope of salvation and repentance. How can I thank You, Lord, for Your longsuffering toward my wretchedness, for the fact that You gave me this very prayer, in which I have invoked Your Name with my filthy and unclean lips, and yet You fan my heart with the joy of Your presence, with the mercy of Your condescension? My soul faints before Your mercy; what shall I say? Thou knowest all things, Thou knowest my filth, and yet You do not abhor me, You allow me to pray to You, to lift up my heart to You, to call You by name. How can I bear this, what shall I do? Teach me to love You, teach me to immolate myself on the altar of Your love, to burn away my sins in this fire, to burn away the memory of them, so that they may not lie like a black shadow on my path towards You. My soul thirsteth for Thee [Ps. 63:1]. And every day of life is a new miracle of Your mercy, a new revelation, a new wonder, a new fainting from the surprise and the gratitude of my heart. Lord, before You I am but dust and ashes, yet do not cast me away; grant me to live out the rest of my days and to die unseparated from You, grant me to look upon Thy radiant countenance until the very end, cast me not away from Thy face [cf. Ps. 27:9].

28.IV/11.V.1925

Lord, of all Your miracles there is nothing more miraculous than the human heart set ablaze by You, in love with You. You create and recreate worlds with a wave of Your scepter, and they obey You, like clay in the hands of the potter [cf. Rom. 9:21]. They praise You by their being, but not by their will, for only the human heart praises You because it loves You, because it lives through You, because it seeks You, because it desires You. However weak and impotent a person may be, nonetheless he seeks after You, was made for You, is set aflame by You. And by seeing a soul set aflame by You, a person is ignited[118] by another's fire, like one candle lights another. From just one of Your lamps thousands are ignited and saved, O Lord! How shall I thank you for the vision of these lamps that You grant my priestly gaze to behold, how shall I thank You for this penitence, purity, meekness, patience, love, and faith that You show me in the hearts of Your faithful? In the midst of sin, despondency, weakness, and coldness, these flames rise up to You as they illuminate the world and shine over it. However low a person may fall, still in his heart there is nothing he desires but holiness, there is nothing he loves but holiness, nothing he reveres but holiness. And whenever holiness is felt in Your creation, then our heart faints from elation and love. O miracle of God's creation, which is ever being accomplished, which moves, burns, and glimmers with its flames! By this miracle the heart's powers of speech are brought to life and perfected: marvelous is God in His[119] saints, the God of Israel! [Ps. 67:36 Douay-Rheims].[120]

29.IV. / 12.V.1925

Miracles happen all the time, both in the past and today, and every person looking attentively at his life knows the palpable power of God and the works of His saints. It does not matter that these miracles sometimes occur through a confluence of natural circumstances; the heart will still recognize the hand of the Lord, the help of His saints. Though unworthy, how I have been sought out by the miracles of God's mercy! My whole life is but an assemblage of God's miracles. But how difficult it is to be worthy of miracles! How difficult it is to preserve them in one's heart and be saved by them from despondency in days of trials. To each new miracle of God's mercy we are obliged to respond with our freedom: we ought to give thanks to the Lord through some kind of deed, some victory over ourselves, through some attainment. For miracles are but the "signs" of God. They are given to us not merely in order to satisfy some need of ours, but in order that this satisfaction should come from the Lord and not from man, in order that we might be taught to love and to set the Lord always before us [Ps. 16:8]. Above all, our duty is to *believe the miracle.* It comes, it is accepted, and yet we begin to *explain it away* as a natural confluence of circumstances. Our unbelief is such that, even if a dead person rose from the dead [cf. Luke 16:31], this too for us would prove no more than a confluence of circumstances... Such unbelief and ingratitude is a double sin before God. We must stir up in ourselves the faith we need in order to see our entire life as a succession of miracles, as one ongoing miracle [2 Tim. 1:6]. If we could only attend to ourselves, then not only in the satisfaction of our needs ("because ye did eat of the loaves and were filled" [John 6:36]) but also in every movement of our soul, consecrated through love of God and neighbor, we would see the hand of God. Who is so great a God as our God? Thou art the God that doest wonders! [Ps. 77:13–14].[121]

3 / 16.V.1925

Teacher, we are drowning! [cf. Matt. 8:25]. There occur temptations that the soul on the path to God must undergo. The enemy rages in order to confound the soul, to drown it in despondency and despair, to intimidate it. The soul is in tumult and suffers. Where is peace, where is hope, where is prayer? Everywhere you look in the soul you find only gloom, chill, dreariness. The soul loves nothing, wants nothing, can do nothing, hopes for nothing. It is bound by Satan and does not see its fetters. In a fit of its despair it repeats the Slanderer's slander and thereby slanders itself. Repentance and penitential self-reproach is one thing, but despondency and fainthearted alarm at sin is another. And when the latter attitude faces this vortex, it seems there is no strength to fight against it. Yet this is nothing more than the intimidation of the enemy, who has no power against God's creation. He is permitted, for the sake of testing and strengthening, to torment God's beloved creatures, just as he was permitted to torment Job. We must stand on our feet and say to the Slanderer: get behind me, Satan! [Matt. 16:23]. Patience and prayer, hope and faith, meekness of heart—this is the only defense left to one who is losing heart. The tougher and more difficult things are, the closer one is to great light.

The desert-dwelling monastics knew this particular hour when the noonday demon tormented them, when melancholy would visit these ascetics and dryness would eat away at life in general and at their ascetic efforts in particular. In such times—the fathers teach—the monastic must spend the hour in his cell, pulling the koukoulion[122] over his head in order to *pass it in patience and seclusion*, lest he tempt his brother through his own despondency.

For nesting in the heart of each person is the snake of despondency, and each, seeing and recognizing the same frightful beast in another, is disturbed by his brother and succumbs to fear on both counts. And at that point it seems that there is no escape, that you have hit a wall, that you are plunging into darkness. But endure, O brother of mine, cry out relentlessly, even with frozen lips, to your Lord, call to Him for help, so that He might reveal to you the miracle of His mercy. And the Lord will reveal a *miracle*: the darkness of the soul will dissipate as after the rising sun, the wall will crumble, and the dead-ends and ditches set out for you by Satan will be made transparent. O Jesus, Son of God, have mercy on us!

5/18.V.1925

My soul faints from thanking You, my God. You give me a new day of life, a new unopened book of unrealized possibilities, and You command me to write my name inside it. You entrust me to enter indelibly into Your world, into Your creation, You give me the power of prayer, in which my soul is cleansed and clothed with Your Name, and You give me love and my loved ones, the mere thought of whom makes my soul tremble with joy! What shall I say? My soul languishes. It is feeble in everything, feeble even in giving thanks. Perhaps it is all the more out of reach for a sinful person to give thanks; out of the ten only one gave thanks, "and he was a Samaritan" [Luke 17:16]—that is, he gave thanks not from the law, but from grace. We must pray to God for the grace of gratitude, for which the church prays every day in the divine Eucharist.

Oh, how we give thanks to God for that divine gift—the divine Eucharist for every day! Just as we breathe, as we eat food each day, so the earth offers to its God and Creator its daily sacrifice of His own divine Son, immolated for us anew. And every day, every morning the Christian should, if he cannot on that day be present at the Eucharist, thank God for it, for the fact that it is given, that it exists, that it is offered. O blessedness of the life given by the Lord and sanctified by the Name of the Lord, O joy of prayer, O bitterness of the tears of repentance, O love given by the Lord, O life flowing from the source of Life, O Holy, life-creating Spirit! Let us give thanks to the Lord![123]

6/19.V.1925

The mystery of the spiritual life lies in its inexhaustibility and ever new creativeness. We people who are burdened by the cares of this present age do not comprehend the gift of eremitism and desert asceticism, in which a person lives only in the spirit, having renounced the power of outside experiences. An onlooker might think: how poor, empty, and one-sided his life is—it's a miracle that he can bear it. Monastic life too looks the same way to a lay person: burdensome precisely in its lack of experiences. But it can only seem this way as long as, in your own spirit, you stop up the fountain of living water rushing towards eternal life [John 4:14], as long as comforting prayer has not been enkindled, and as long as your soul has not found its treasure by living in God.

Take spiritual friendship as an example. Does its conversation ever really dwindle, its joy and comfort grow thin? It hides but also reveals ever new riches, and, rejoicing, it marvels at this richness. But all human friendship is but a reflection of the one friendship of God with man, whom He has called His friend ("you are My friends" [John 15:15]), and the union of souls is an image of what Christ's Church is. Marriage is union in Christ and in the Church, the union of flesh and spirit, but *every* spiritual union of souls, their fellowship in God, is accomplished in Christ and in the Church, for it is effected by the power of Christ. We do not fully believe Christ's word, that He gives water springing up unto eternal life [cf. John 4:14]. But if we did believe, then we wouldn't marvel at the fact that a person can find all treasures within his spirit, provided he first finds his spirit, and in it—the gift of the Holy Spirit.

8/21.V.1925

Only love gives wisdom, only love gives vision, only love gives forgiveness. The one who loves receives the ability to look upon another as the other sees himself. We are divided one from another by self-love, self-concern, and self-interest. Our gaze is obscured by the partiality of our judgment and vision; we always, when thinking of another, think of ourselves, of our own feelings but not of the other and his feelings. We must feel what the other feels, and then our eyes will be opened. Through the experience of love one receives this experience of wisdom, the knowledge of the other, of one's neighbor, of one's friend. God gives us this miracle of love so that our life may be constantly enriched by it, growing rich in God.

When you feel an aching heaviness and dryness in the heart, when your passions cover up your spiritual eyes, try to come out of yourself, pray, pray with tears to the Lord for love, for the one making your soul ache, for the one who has wounded it. And God will give you in return for your prayer wings for your soul, your burden will melt away, and you will find the joy and blessedness of love. Love seeks not its own [1 Cor. 13:5], it is disinterested; its only interest is the good of its neighbor. If your love is self-interested, then it is not love, for in it your self-love is still strong. Train yourself to love love, endure the work of love, carry the cross of love, and it will become ever easier and more joyful for you. Herein lies the very mystery and power of the cross, the power of Christ's meekness and humility, making the yoke easy and the burden light [Matt. 11:30]. You can detect the sickness of your love by the movement[124] of your heart: if it is light and bright and joyful, full of the joy of love, then it is free from the provocation of self-love, but if it is gloomy, offended, that means it is ill. The loving heart knows no offenses: it not only forgives them, but does not even feel them. Learn to love, labor in love.

10/23.V.1925

The works of the righteous follow after them. After death, their holy relics are made manifest, through these relics they live with us, they perform miracles, they hear prayers and they love, *love*, their heart burns like a blazing fire even beyond the limits of death, and they ascend from glory to glory in eternal life [cf. 2 Cor. 3:18]. But we are wretched sinners, yes, and our putrid works follow after us as well. These works are indelibly written in the book of fates [cf. Rev. 20:12], yet their impact extends beyond the borders of this human life. They enter into the fates of all human beings, into the history of all humanity, and upon each one of us hangs the fate of the entire world. We must pull back neither from participation nor from responsibility, and until the end of human history our works will endure. For this reason the Dread Judgment will occur simultaneously over all humanity, and each has lived the life of all humanity, each of the sons of Adam is that entire, ancient Adam. And not only what we did, good or bad, but also what we did not do, or did not fully complete—upon this too depends the destinies of the entire human race in its history, and we continue to live this life beyond death's border as well. This is why the preliminary judgment at our death judges us individually and together with our immediate circle, but the final judgment is our judgment in all and with all. If only we maintained in every hour of our life the seriousness to comprehend that this very hour belongs to everyone, even though it has been entrusted to us, then we would be unable to waste life's hours as we do, not honoring them and instead spending them in laziness. This is why the hour of the Lord's judgment is so terrible—how the soul cowers, quivering before it, not only because at that hour everything will be revealed to all, but also because to us too will our life be revealed in all its strength and all its weakness, in all its content, and then we shall cry out in lament: O, would that the mountains should fall on us and the stones hide us from our shame and from the righteous wrath of God! [cf. Rev. 6:16]. O God, be merciful to us sinners!

13 / 26.V.1925

"Love seeks not its own" [1 Cor. 13:5]. Yet we are always seeking our own and seeking after ourselves, even in love. And only the grace of love frees us from ourselves. We can offer sacrifices and give up what belongs to us but nevertheless at root still be seeking and desiring our own, however lofty and subtle "our own" may be. But the law of love is this: let him deny himself [cf. Matt. 16:24]. You must desire in the beloved and for the beloved only what is needful for him and not what you wish; you must crucify yourself in love, renounce your will, renounce yourself... This is the cruciform way of love, without which love cannot mature and bring in its fruit. But why does the Lord demand from every person the way of the cross in following Him? Why does He lay such a seemingly unbearable burden upon our shoulders? Because without this trial by fire, love could not be born in us, it could not comprehend its own strength, its own inspiration, its own fearlessness. Perfect love conquers the fear of sacrifice [cf. 1 John 4:18]. Perfect love *is ready for anything* for the sake of love, for it knows itself and knows its eternal nature. But it is a long and difficult path that leads from human love—which commonly appears as an indistinguishable mix of self-love, passion, and provocation together with pure love—to the victory of love in love. For us this path is long and agonizing, but every step along the way, though intrinsically justified, finds its reward. Love is a talent that constantly multiplies, if it be offered for the growth of love and not buried in the ground instead [cf. Matt. 25:14–30]. O God, strengthen my weak heart, overcome my exhaustion. You see our hearts. Thy will be done!

17/30.V.1925

How powerless is the heart to give thanks, and yet how it longs to give thanks, how it needs to give thanks—to give thanks until the end, down to the depths, unto exhaustion! When you see the mercy of God and the gifts of God that have been poured out upon you, you wish your whole soul to become a hymn of praise, but the weakness of your nature, the power of sin, fetters the heart, seals the mouth shut, and praise dies away before it can sound forth. What a joy for one's very self is this thanksgiving, this "setting the Lord always" before me! [Ps. 16:8]. But giving thanks is something we can do only according to the measure of our own strength; as we live, so we give thanks. If we live in the dark, drowsily, if our prayer is cold and lazy, then the soul will lack the wings to give thanks. But upon these wings the soul can most easily and directly fly up to the Lord. In thanksgiving there is joy and love, but wisdom too. There can be no callousness in the heart that gives thanks, no pride and haughtiness, for the gift of God shows the heart its own emptiness and infirmity without that gift. Thanksgiving begets repentance, for you see that you are unworthy of this gift, and it also begets a wisdom born of humbleness of mind, as well as meekness, for you know that the gift, precisely because it is something *given*, can also be taken away, and so you prostrate yourself beneath the merciful right hand of God. O how needful, how vital it is to stir up in yourself the gift of thanksgiving [cf. 2 Tim. 1:6], for by this path we ascend to the love of God, by this path we ascend to unceasing prayer and joy. For the apostle united these two in the commandment: rejoice always, pray without ceasing, in everything give thanks [1 Thess. 5:16–18].

19.V/1.VI.1925

O Lord, you give joy, perfect joy. My heart cannot contain Your joy, it wishes to pour itself out and melt away in it. Heaven is found in man's soul, the stars and the sun trace their course within it, and the Lord abides therein. What breadth, what vastness, what light! The heart grows faint from giving thanks. O Lord, my Lord! What have I done to deserve this, how have I merited that You should reveal to me Your love? I am a creeping worm, nothingness from nothingness, full of stench, sin, and self-love, and still You come to me and grant me to love Your beloved creation! But You, O Lord, always give freely... If Thou shouldest mark iniquities, who could stand! [Ps. 130:3]. Immeasurable is Your mercy and immeasurable is your condescension. And I believe and know that You have not abhorred my nothingness, and instead have revealed to me Your mercy. Help me—not to become worthy, for never will I be worthy of Your mercy—but rather to walk the path of correction, to begin repentance, to fall in love with the ascetic struggle to which You call us, and to hate my flesh. Reveal to me this mercy also, give me a heart ready to labor, for in my life I have been a lover of pleasure. And never, never, in my long life have I undertaken a single, even the smallest, task for Your sake. I know that whatever a person does with his life and whatever he makes of himself, he does this along with others and for others, for everyone, and above all for those whom the Lord has given to him. You have granted me to see heaven within my soul; grant me the heart, grant me the will to labor for Thee[125] and to come to hate myself, in Thy Name.

22.V/4.VI.1925

"Ye are strangers and pilgrims" [cf. 1 Pet. 2:11]. Whenever we must part from a place in which we are settled, we experience sorrow about that place and feel that we are part of it. There is also a good feeling of gratitude, of a living fellowship with everything that surrounds us. But there is simultaneously a captivity with respect to the place; the mercy of God lies in the fact that He does not allow us to become attached to it. One must be a free stranger on the earth in order to love it with a free love. *The Lord was a stranger*, He had no place to lay his head, he had neither a home nor a "fox's hole" [Matt. 8:20]. But in all things

He revealed the form of a perfect life, and in this he likewise showed us the measure and example. The Lord had a homeland and loved it with a human love, he loved Jerusalem as well, and yet He never lingered in one place simply because He loved that place. So too the holy apostles, who parted from their homeland that they loved with a fervent Jewish love and went out to all the ends of the world. Thanks be to God that He grants us to know both the anguish and the sweetness of this separation and this freedom. We would not be citizens of *His* world and *His* land if we remained merely citizens of our own land. We would not feel around us *everywhere* this vast expanse, this Divine vault of the Father's House, open for us all. We would not know that we ourselves, each of us, harbors this possibility—to be simply a human being, a son of God, living among our fellow man—if we always remained surrounded by those of our own tribe. And in the Kingdom of God there will be this great joy for every nation under heaven. O Lord, I thank You for the paths of exile.

23.V/5.VI.1925

There is no "important" or "trivial" in human relationships—everything is significant and can impact the human soul. We are sometimes able to show magnanimity in what we consider to be important, but in trivial matters we are weak: irritable, capricious, fickle. [In monasteries,] the *startzy* test the degree of spiritual growth by producing various annoying trifles, and only the most experienced endure without getting irritated. It is ugly to be petty, and it is disconcerting to see oneself as ugly. Yet what matters is not the ugliness but rather this testimony that exposes the state of our soul. So great is your impatience that your soul cannot and will not withstand a small, trifling trial. This is a weakness in love, and against weakness one must fight to the death, because one must not be weak; it is sinful to be weak when you can be strong, when you can be *strengthened*, which is what the apostle calls us to [cf. Eph. 6:10]. Show yourself no mercy if you have exhibited pettiness, irritability, and impatience, for then you have exhibited your sinful weakness and your complete lack of restraint, you have demonstrated the weakness of your love for God: you were not at peace. But peace is the greatest treasure of the soul; the soul that is not at peace cannot love and praise God.

29.V/11.VI.1925

People live for tomorrow; all they hold dear, all their hopes are transferred onto it, but only the present day exists. Today is already *given* to us by God, as an inexhaustible depth, as the source of all possibilities, in *today* one must find everything, for within it everything lies. People live in the *future*, they cherish this future, dream about it, expect from it what has not been given to them right now. But this is a false feeling: everything is already given, and we need only find it. Every moment of time and every present day contains eternal life, and to the extent that we commune in it, inexhaustible possibilities are revealed, and the mirage and self-deception of the future disappears. We must seek not the future but the eternal present, eternal life. Such is the wisdom of the Church, such is the wisdom of the ascetics. And then everything shifts away from outcomes we can't control and instead towards the *struggle* of our faith, of our life, of our love for God. The one who waits for the future is inattentive to the present, his eyes are always away from that which is given uniquely to us, he becomes a *dreamer* in the negative sense of the word. The point is that he waits for external occurrences and events; meanwhile, man is granted the power of inner becoming and nothing more. Dreaming weakens the strength of moral struggle. The future does not exist, for in both the present and the future there is only the present, but in the present everything is given that is in the future—provided we wish to take it. People say: the future *does* exist, for it is said of the Holy Spirit that "He will shew you things to come" [John 16:13], for the final fate of the world has been promised, as well as the end of the world, and the judgment. Yes, but all this that is coming is already present for us, since all the *fullness* is given to us, all is revealed to us, the path has been shown to all. There cannot be anything coming that is not already in the present—anything else is harmful self-deception. Therefore: pray always, rejoice without ceasing, and give thanks for all things [cf. 1 Thess. 5:16–18].

30.V/12.VI.1925

Rejoice always, says the apostle [1 Thess. 5:16]. He speaks of a graced joy, of joy in the Lord. But, even before this, we must preserve and maintain cheerfulness in ourselves as well as freshness of soul. Man carries within himself the seeds of death and despondency, a fall lies in wait for him with every step of his life. These things are natural for him, although sinful. Against these ailments we must possess cheerfulness in ourselves, we must amass a stockpile of it, we must multiply our vital powers within, not in order to use them for ourselves and for our own pleasure, but to render them back to God. This cheerfulness is a natural vestibule of the joy in the Lord to which we are called, and its absence darkens the window of the soul with the blackness of despondency. This cheerfulness can become a temptation when its supply runs short (Oh, how many people have died spiritually for so many different reasons!), but not for those who have a stockpile's worth; and for the latter, even despondency and lapses are useful, if only in order that they might free themselves from self-satisfaction and seek out what is higher than mere cheerfulness. But just as how, when we are exercising the soul, we should not forsake the body (for we have a duty to work our bodies just as we have a duty to work our souls), so too when ascending to the life of the spirit: we should conquer, humble, and nourish the soul, which should not forever be vacillating between conflicting moods but should be light and cheerful. The soul should be in obedience to the spirit and not sway like the sea. Not Stoic calmness but Christian perseverance is its health.

31.V/13.VI.1925

O Lord, I thank You for prayer, for giving us Your great and terrible Name. Every day, the morning begins with the miracle of prayer: awakening from the land of shadows, we once again present ourselves before the face of God and, coming before Him, we ask God for help and blessing, and we praise and glorify Him.

Our whole life would extinguish and darken without this prayer, death would enter into our being and swallow it. Least of all do we know how to value these gifts without which we cannot live, these breaths, the light of the sun, the land of our birth. And we do not realize, we do not see how our whole being is constituted by prayer and saved by it. Why is our prayer so cold, so hasty, so inattentive? Why do we insult God and our very selves by our coldness and spiritual sloth? Keep striving, do not let up, persevere in prayer, and the act of praying itself will help you, the Most Sweet Name of God will be like honey on your lips. O Lord, teach us to pray, grant us the will to pray, inspire us to love prayer!

2 / 15.VI.1925

At times, anxiety clouds our vision. Alarm about life's troubles takes possession of the soul, and then the soul is left barren, the poor soul no longer belongs to itself but instead becomes an agitated wave. It would seem that we should eliminate the things that disturb us and then everything would fall into place, but in fact what we need is for these things to stop disturbing us, for they should not have power over the soul that knows its walking before God [Mic. 6:8]. Strive to preserve a serene spirit, and then temptations will disappear and dissipate on their own. And this happens only when you *sincerely* and completely give yourself over to the will of God. The ability to give up these agitations is a measure of growth. See how weak and shallow is your sometimes seemingly deep spiritual constitution, your spiritual world, if it can be destroyed by a mere trifle, by an everyday occurrence. How shameful, how sinful to be faint of heart, to offend God by over-burdening oneself with worries, with excessive impressionability, with lack of faith. Everything "important" is made up of trifles; do not allow the enemy to beat you up with the little things, take courage and deflect him with the shield of faith [Eph. 6:16]. Be at peace, and then you will be wise.

3 / 16.VI.1925

Faith without works is dead [James 2:26], and so is love without work and patience. Love is patience, although patience is not yet love. Love is built through patience, which is the sacrifice of love and its work. In this sinful world, differences between people become the opposition from which friction arises. The closer people draw together, the more sensitive they become to mutual friction, and so patience always remains on guard to protect love. Restlessness and impatience weaken and chill love, for they are born of self-love, of self-assertion. Patience teaches us the very power of love, teaches us to put ourselves in the place of another, our own life in the life of this other. Love is married to joy, and in joy there is no patience, no sacrifice, but without love's power there is also no true joy. That is why it is said: through patience will you save your souls [Luke 21:19], and the one who endures to the end will be saved [Matt 24:13]. Patience is a test, a testimony of our love for God, which likewise should not be cheap and freeloading. And God's love for us is slow to anger. The Lord is merciful and gracious, slow to anger, and plenteous in mercy! [Ps. 103:8].

4/17.VI.1925

"And there was a great calm" [Matt. 8:26]. It is necessary that what you read daily from the Gospel be a real event in your life, as if it had taken place in your presence and with your participation. For that is precisely why we are given the holy Gospel, in order that all the faithful, and not simply the elect who were with him in the past, might see His earthly days and take part in them. Therefore, train your eyes to see it not as a story about something that happened once upon a time to *others* but instead as what is taking place this very day with *you*. Scrub your heart clean until you feel the truth of these words. That is exactly why we have the daily Gospel readings, so that from day to day we might live with the Lord. And, if you read the story about the calming of the sea, then understand—not allegorically but directly—that this is happening to you, that you are drowning or losing strength, or that you are being made to stumble and being tempted by the waves of sin or circumstances, and that the words "O thou of little faith" [Matt. 8:26] are directed at you. But this miracle is also happening in you: there was a great calm, the tumult of the heart is quieted, and in the clarity of its waters heaven is reflected. Place yourself before the face of the Lord, pray to Him for help, take His hand outstretched toward you, and you will conquer the tumult of your soul and you will know the joy of meeting the Lord once more. O mercy of God, O miracle, to daily read the Gospel!

6/19.VI.1925

The human soul is more precious than the world. But it is also its own spiritual world, this human soul; the Lord created it according to His image and gave it unending depths and riches. We live in ignorance and carelessness about these riches, but sometimes they are revealed to the gaze of love in all their beauty, and then the soul in ecstasy gives thanks to God, who created this soul. We marvel at the beauties of the world, which proclaim the glory of God [cf. Ps. 19:1], but even more do we marvel at the beauties of the human soul, found in man. And yet, while marveling at the beauties of the world, we remain exactly as we were; we merely behold. But even we, stiff-necked as we are, cannot look upon spiritual beauty with indifference, and our souls are ignited by love, and in this love they become assimilated to this beauty, they shine with its brightness. Just as a candle is lit by a candle, so love makes holiness shine forth in souls. That is why there is nothing more necessary or important for a person than holiness. The saint draws others to himself and ignites, imbues, saves, and summons them to ascetic struggle, as cranes from the heights of heaven call out to us to join them on high and tell us that our souls have wings. We ourselves do not know what we possess from God, and then suddenly a saint—through his own soul—manifests to us our own power and our own beauty in all our infirmity. And then the soul, taking flight, ascends to the heavenly heights and bathes in light and air.

7/20.VI.1925

O God, grant me to humble myself! How often it happens that if something occurs not according to my will, my spirit is troubled and I am full of fury and impatience. Yet what I fail to see is that God is sending me a lesson in humility. Humble yourself, and you will conquer temptation, you will once again stand firm and lucid, free in your soul, but until that point, while you continue to revolt, you are a slave. The monastic fathers used to test the patience of their disciples at times in a manner that seems—from the outside—most scandalizing. You must preserve peace in your soul, and do only that which you can see when you are at peace. While passion or fury rule over you, do not trust the movements of your heart. They deceive you, because you think that you are sincere and not self-interested, when in fact what drives you is a flagrant or subtle self-love. Do not be confounded by the outward appearance and strangeness of the trials that are sent to you: is it reasonable for you to be angry at the rod with which the Lord tests and disciplines you? [cf. Jonah 4:9; Heb. 12:5–6]. This rod is in the hand of the Most High, and both during and after your punishment you will begin to see clearly again and will revere the hand that guides and disciplines you. And especially do not grant pride and self-love any power over you, for they will whisper to you that you do not deserve this humiliation or trial. No, you are always deserving of punishment and are always evil, except that the Lord is merciful to you and longsuffering. Stir up the gift of patience and wisdom [2 Tim. 1:6], and may the patience and peace of God abide in your heart.

9/22.VI.1925

The Lord sent His disciples out to preach and gave them the power of miracles and signs [cf. Luke 9:1–2]. But this same power He gave them also at the Ascension and likewise then sent them out to preach. And the gift of Christ remains in His church. Why have we forgotten this gift, why do we so disbelieve it that we pronounce the Gospel words of the Savior's promise with embarrassed haste? Have these words lost their power, the power of Christ? We do not need to cling to the letter and form [cf. 2 Cor 3:6], namely those miracles and signs that were given to the apostles; God will provide the gift that is needed, but what we must do is to learn to believe always and wholeheartedly in the power of Christ and in the power of prayer to Him. In humility, every Christian should be careful regarding signs, but by prayerful boldness he too becomes a wonderworker by the power of Christ, and he brings down power from above through his prayer.

It is to this that the Lord calls us, this is what He wants from the faithful. How often our prayer is timid and lacking in faith: faithlessness already resounds in the heart even while our mouths are pronouncing the prayer. This faithlessness is either lack of faith in ourselves or in the Lord Himself, and these two often blend together. But there exist on the one hand degrees of prayer, and then there are also powerful feats of prayer—the latter can be reached only through boldness, in the full knowledge of the power of prayer. But it demands of us great exertion, work, and sweat, which we do not give. And so, it is not that the Lord has stepped away from us, but rather it is laziness in our prayer that has distanced us from Him. The hardest path and the hardest work is the work of prayer. O Lord, instill prayer in us, grant us the gift of prayer, give us the will and the work.

14/27.VI.1925

It happens at times that God performs His deeds for people through us, unworthy though we are... This is particularly the case with priests, who have been given authority from God. Our sinful conscience, which knows all our infirmity and uncleanness, confounds us, and we are ready to reject and suspect the very work of God. But this is not right; we must not reject God's gifts. Just as we must have faith in the power of sincere and fervent prayer, which reaches God despite the sins of the one who prays, so too we must not doubt the efficacy of God's power accomplished through prayer. The Christian, even in his sin, remains the temple of the Holy Spirit, having the anointing of the Holy One. He bears in himself a *power* that he himself is afraid to trust, for it imposes a responsibility upon him to make good use of it. And, meeting a person who is in need of such power, he should not keep that power to himself, or else he will face judgment as one who did not provide for his brother in need [cf. Matt. 25:31–46]. This consciousness should maintain in us an unremitting attention and feeling of responsibility. Our laziness will use any pretext for comfort and self-deception, and that's exactly the excuse we use in instances like these—or, more often than not, the excuse is our supposed meekness. Meekness is not the sole or even the highest virtue. All things are good in their place and within their limit; but boldness has its place too, as does the holy insanity of love...

16/29.VI.1925

Above all else, learn humility. It is a difficult science and has many stages. The very first stage is when our eyes are opened to see ourselves and there falls away that self-delusion into which we are indiscernibly plunged from early childhood, when we begin to form an image of ourselves. To every human being God gives an image in which he may mold himself by undertaking ascetic struggle. But our sinful imagination inculcates in us the idea that this image already shines in us, and furthermore, that we alone possess it while other people lack it. Such a conviction of your own uniqueness very subtly and inconspicuously becomes implanted in the heart and rules over it <...> it constricts [the heart], and you must suffer much along the path of humility and repentance in order to really grasp with your whole heart that you are not unique, or rather that you are unique only in your own sins.

The merciful Lord humbles every person, sending life lessons and circumstances, the experience of which reveals to him his infirmity. For people who are gifted and strong, the "rich" [cf. Matt. 19:23–24], it is harder to acquire humility, because they tarry longer in the consciousness of their own power, yet such an epiphany inevitably awaits every person on the path of life. But this is not yet humility: rather, it is merely a negative condition for it that still requires certain positives. In the absence of the latter, this disenchantment with the self poisons the soul with a wicked despondency, with envy, and then a person's "underground" emerges.[126] You must overcome this through the submissive power of humility, which consists in knowledge of your infirmity and the *acceptance* of it as a well-deserved retribution for your sins and as God's will for you. You must stop perceiving your infirmity as infirmity, as something below you, but must see it as your own proper condition, for you could not be otherwise, and neither should you fight it; nor should you imagine yourself in any other way. Everything human is insignificant in the face of God's grace—even if that insignificance, like all else that is human, comes in degrees. This is why human infirmity is inconsequential for eternal salvation. A human being can interfere, through his sins and his pride, with God's impartation of grace, but he cannot add anything to it. Whosoever shall exalt himself shall be abased; and he that shall humble himself shall be exalted [Matt. 23:12]. You need to get away from the whole idea of "my rights" and "what is mine"; you need to keep your eyes fixed above, not below. Then this departure—into humility—will grant you true freedom, a childlike lightness, peace and joy. There is no peace and joy without sincere and deep humility, nor can you achieve impartiality without it. The acquisition of humility is the most important task for a human being, without which he simply cannot embark upon the path of spiritual works. Therefore you must always be attentive to seeing the good in people, and, seeing yourself as derelict, you must reproach yourself and consider yourself unworthy of the mercy of God by which you live.

17/30.VI.1925

Cause me to know the way wherein I should walk; for I lift up my soul unto thee [Ps. 143:8]. Man directs his ways while not knowing where they lead, but the One guiding him does know. Hence there is no need to concern yourself with where the way leads—you need only walk it in accord with the will of the One guiding you. The whole length of our human way concludes at the open casket, it leads there and only there, and yet it also leads from our life here to life eternal.

We must preserve our soul's freedom and look above, not below, and firmly, clearly, and calmly traverse our way on earth, without anxiously watching our step. The Lord said of himself: I am the *way* [John 14:6]. How can He become the *way* for us? He, who is both the life and the truth, not only shows us our way, not only leads us down it, but He Himself is the way for us, for He, through His enhumanization, through His feat on the cross, gave us the way to salvation. He Himself traversed it both here and beyond the grave. And no matter where we may be, we can always find ourselves spiritually on this Way, seeing ourselves with Him and in Him. So do not get lost on your way, do not forget yourself in the midst of its agitations, but firmly know that, as He did with Luke and Cleopas, Christ is walking alongside you [Luke 24:13–32].[127]

16/29.VII.1925 (ON HIS 54TH BIRTHDAY) PARIS

O Lord, I thank You for everything: for life, for destiny, for parents, for family, for friends, for meetings, for acquaintances, for fortune and misfortune, for joys and trials. How to grasp all Your miracles and Your mercies? They are innumerable. But above all I thank You that You have allowed me to love and to know love in return. There is no greater joy and no greater bliss. And I thank the Lord that He, despite all my laziness and sinfulness, has allowed me to serve at the altar, for on earth there is no lot more blessed than this. The Lord determines for every man at his birth the length of his life—some he calls [to Himself] in childhood, others in adolescence, and to others still he grants long life by His inscrutable counsel. With each year, we should consider this new chapter of life as the path to death's threshold, but we should also accept the new tasks that are revealed within it. We must not consider the time we have left as merely "the remaining time of our life" that we must somehow get through, but we must instead live it out worthily, "in peace and repentance."[128]

Approaching or even entering into old age conceals in itself its own precious possibilities: it is, or can be, the crowning of life. He who has reached old age is thereby freed from the passions of the flesh, and though he remains in the body, its passions are now alien to him; through the experience of a long life he has comprehended what was necessary for him in youth, and the closeness to God that is given to the one who stands at death's threshold grants a special freshness to his spirit. Old age in God is humanity's most precious inheritance, its spiritual remainder, a pure distillation. But old age is the crowning of the *entirety* of one's life: as your life was, so shall your old age be. One must earn old age. People fear old age, they don't want it, but one must love old age, must desire it as freedom in God. My youth shall be renewed like the eagle's [Ps. 103:5 Douay-Rheims], and old age is this eternal youth of the spirit being renewed in God…

18.IX/1.X.1925 PARIS

I have wasted my whole life in slothfulness.[129] My days are coming to a close, my days are few, what can I offer to my Lord? What answer will I give for the days of my life that He generously gave to me and continues to give, all while enduring my innumerable trespasses? Embarrassment and fear, and shame, shame intolerable, encompass my soul; I cannot lift up my eyes, I cannot give an answer. I will never get back the days of my life, days squandered in sin, I will never get back those possibilities to love God and my neighbor, opportunities that the merciful Lord showered upon me, I will never get back the past, and I dread to look back upon it. But what of the present? Does not the Lord still grant you "the remaining time of your life"? How are you using it? Do you not end each day by weeping and crying out to the Lord for forgiveness, seeing as you squandered yet another day given to you, despising the mercy of God? When you were young and did not know yourself, and did not see your sin, it <…> to you. But now, when you see and know the limitlessness of your sin, do you at least try to fight it and to repent? The Lord patiently awaits your repentance. Give Him but one day, the *today* that has been given to you; toil for Him at least at the eleventh hour [Matt. 20:1–16], but toil and offer the fruit of repentance [Mt 3:8]. Yet you, lazy and wicked servant [Matt. 25:26], you only complain and sit on your hands, waiting for the abyss to open and to swallow up your fallen soul. Lord Jesus Christ Son of God, have mercy on me.

23.IX/6.X.1925

Your days are coming to a close. There is a silent grief in your heart because you have not completed your work before the Lord and have vainly squandered the life He has given you. But in this sadness of yours there shines the love of God and the forgiveness of the Lord. He has not abhorred us as we are. He came to us prodigal and sinful ones, but we need not fear on account of our unworthiness before Him, for to insult the boundless love of God indicates a lack of faith. At every liturgy this miracle of God's condescension is accomplished: on the diskos the Lamb reposes—He Himself, the Lord, once again sacrificially gives himself over to my wretched and filthy hands.[130] My soul faints from awe before God's condescension, before God's humility towards creation. God gives himself to be sacrificed and to become food for the faithful.[131] I marvel and tremble and rejoice, and then I marvel again, and again my heart is filled by God's condescension, and I pray to Him as He lies, reposes before me on His Holy Table. I pray to Him, gazing upon Him, falling down before Him, face to face, like Moses on Sinai...

And how can I, worm that I am, wriggle about straining to justify this condescension through my own righteousness, imagining that I could become worthy of Him? What utter insanity is this idea, as is the notion that I could justify my own life before Him, a life I have vainly squandered. But I believe, I love, and I hope in boundless mercy. Have mercy on me in my squalor, in my laziness, in my sin and wretchedness, for I believe in the boundlessness of Your love!

27.IX/10.X.1925

There is the fear of God, and then there is the fear that casts out love [cf. 1 John 4:18]. And this (latter) fear fills the sinful human heart when you consider your life and the Dread Judgment of God. It becomes all the more frightening when you see ever more clearly your wretchedness before Him, when you can see that your whole life is nothing more than mistakes, indolence, and the pursuit of base pleasure. It is a dreadful thing to see oneself, and it is *this* fear that drives out love, because love grants faith and nourishes hope. Boundless, boundless is God's love: not according to merit does He save a person, but according to mercy, and that's exactly what we must unceasingly acquire in our heart, lest it die of despondency. The past, alas, we cannot change; we can only lament it. In silent reproach it stands before our conscience and judges us prior to the Dread Judgment. But there is no need to be terrified, for that is merely demonic intimidation. One must abhor the sin but not the sinner in whom the Lord has placed His own—albeit now sinfully profaned—image. We need abhor neither others nor ourselves, for this is just as much a sin when it is directed at one's neighbor as when directed at oneself, for each person is a neighbor to himself, since the all-loving Lord Jesus Christ lives in him.

When life still lies ahead of us, youth is self-confident, but when our entire life—which was a constant failure—is behind us, old age makes us despondent. But we must always be with the Lord and commit ourselves to the Lord: O My Father! [Matt. 26:42]. I see myself, I know that my afflictions and sins age me, they control my weak will, and I no longer hope to change my ways and to walk with You. But this one thing I desire, just one, for one thing do I pray: let me love You more than life, more than myself, more than anything in the world. You know how sincere this prayer is, and You hear it, You forgive this wandering creature of Yours...

REMEMBERING FR. SERGIUS

From the Memoirs of Sr. Joanna Reitlinger

ON THE REMEMBRANCE OF DEATH

Fr. Sergius left Russia when he was 51 years of age. In Constantinople, a doctor diagnosed him with arteriosclerosis. In light of the fact that Fr. Sergius died from a stroke that he suffered while he was "on the job," as they say (at church, while celebrating the liturgy),[1] the *concrete* idea of the closeness of death never left Fr. Sergius after that moment, although, physiologically speaking, this was of course only the very beginning of his illness. Yet it seems that I cannot recall even one liturgy that he did not celebrate as if it was his last—in fact, whenever he would invite me to the liturgy, it was always to "what may be my last." We are all familiar with the practice of remembrance of death, and this invariably enters into the ascesis of the spiritual life, but in this instance it seemed that this remembrance was somehow *sent* to Fr. Bulgakov, and he both received it and preserved it. Perhaps it was this remembrance which lent that particular acuity to his inspection of God's mysteries, to his inquisitive theology. Occasionally it also lent acuity to his conscience, which he meticulously scrutinized. (On this score, he would always repeat the saying, "Let not the sun go down upon your wrath" [Eph. 4:26]. He would say this after all those little quarrels typical of everyday life. In the evenings, Fr. Sergius would always seek full reconciliation: "for this night you may die," he would say to himself.) This granted his entire life a sort of special rhythm: never putting anything off, he was always fully experiencing the *present moment*, as befits a genuine Christian.

COUNTDOWN TO DEATH

Fr. Sergius had a silver watch he had bought as a youth with the first money he ever earned from work (tutoring). He called the watch his "countdown to death" and joked that it had begun to seriously malfunction and then finally stopped working at the very moment when his health received a serious blow. From then on he thought constantly of death.

Sursum corda!

Sursum corda—this was Fr. Sergius' regular exclamation in the last years of his life: "Let us lift up our hearts..."

"ITS OWN UNIQUE COLOR"

All of Fr. Sergius' relationships with people were personal, lively: he always used to say that every relationship should have "its own unique color."

ON FAITH, AND ANSWERING BY NOT ANSWERING

Fr. Sergius' faith was hard-won. Faith grants peace, but little solace. Faith is always seeking, living, moving. It trembles! In Kiev, when Fr. Sergius first started speaking to students about God, they would say, "Why does your voice quiver when you say the word, 'God'?"—as if exposing some doubt in him! But how could one's voice *not* quiver when uttering the Name of the Unfathomable? Throughout his whole life, Fr. Sergius trembled, searched, suffered, *lived.* He never offered illusory and false answers to perplexing, unanswerable questions, "if only just to give an answer." Often this was tormenting not just for him but also for the one asking the question; but he would sooner be tormented than to deceive, than to pretend to cover the abyss with a sheer veil. During the final years of his life, the excruciating worldwide drama, with all its horrors, provoked endless questions in him, as it did in all people. And often Fr. Sergius would answer these questions... by not answering.

ON EUCHARISTIC THANKSGIVING (CHRIST IN THE WORLD)

And yet there is no such thing as a question without an answer... Faith and love will "find it!" [cf. Matt. 7:7–8].

And Fr. Sergius found it within himself, in his inner experience, in the revelation born of suffering, in the sufferings of Christ revealing themselves within him.

Fr. Sergius spoke of this sense that Christ was suffering in the world now, truly participating right now in all human suffering, in the description of his own dying[2] and in a separate study, "Christ in the World."[3]

In those grievous days of the war, in those grievous days of horrors, how many stories could be heard of human suffering, of the endless torment of human beings...

Once, he heard a story from a Russian woman who herself was relating the words of a soldier from the defeated German army. This soldier had been on the Russian front. The scene was a crowd of hungry children: as he was giving them candy, they cried out, "Bread! Bread!" Fr. Sergius thought long about these children... On the next day he celebrated the liturgy.

"...Today during the liturgy I asked myself, 'How can I offer up to God my Eucharistic *thanksgiving*, how can I thank him for these horrors, for these children...'" This is what he related to me in the morning at our (then established) regular Sunday and feast day conversations (in those days Fr. Sergius, having already lost his voice,[4] only celebrated the morning liturgy): "'Can I sincerely offer up to God [my Eucharistic thanksgiving] for this?' And suddenly the answer resounded within me: 'Yes, I can [give thanks]...for Christ, who suffers in them and with them!'"

MIRACLES IN THE LIFE OF FR. SERGIUS

Fr. Sergius' teaching on miracles is well known.[5] The greatest miracle of all according to Fr. Sergius was life itself and its "engine"—love.

Fr. Sergius always offered a correction to the typical view of miracles by laying the stress elsewhere. Often when miracles are explained, too much stress is laid on their material accomplishment, and it is this that is seen as the "supernatural" element. Fr. Sergius corrected this by moving the center of attention to the spiritual cause that occasioned the miracle. For this reason many people got the mistaken impression that Fr. Sergius transferred miracles from the realm of supernatural phenomena to the natural realm.

Fr. Sergius never "performed miracles." Yet his whole life was permeated by miracle, as the life of a person cannot fail to be when he is living or striving to live in God. One such miracle was his "visitation by God" in his "conversion";[6] miraculous too was nearly every encounter he had with people. How often he grew faint at the prospect of some "difficult meeting" that was awaiting him, a difficult conversation. He would ask others to pray that God might help him, and he would completely entrust himself to their prayers... And he would later return, after the conversation—inspired, energized, and somehow renewed. "God helped me," he would say.

ON HOLINESS

Fr. Sergius' writings on holiness are well known. But there are also certain *bon mots* and individual remarks of his that capture well his ideas on holiness. Often he would say, half-joking and half-serious, in response to one of life's many situations, "But of course I'm no saint." Often he would poke fun at those "aping" holiness, that is, those imitating the external forms of its manifestation. He often mused on V. A. Zander's book on St. Seraphim and the Curé d'Ars,[7] and especially on those chapters in which she attempts to schematize and to find some common mark of holiness, the chapters in which she speaks of the *path* of the saint. "Yes," Fr. Sergius said on this occasion, "This is the path of *this kind* of saint. But there can be others."

"Holiness is not sinlessness."

FULFILLING YOUR CALLING

Once I asked a friend of mine, a beloved student of Fr. Sergius', what holiness was.

"Fulfilling your calling," he answered.

This is a very Orthodox definition. The Church venerates saints of all sorts, precisely because each of them fulfilled a unique "calling."

And there are more saints, of course, than just those whom the Church has already canonized.

One person who knew Fr. Sergius from his time in Prague told me that he could not write a biography of Fr. Sergius because he "knew too much" (he had worked with him on many projects). This is completely wrong! This is nothing more than that same attempt to force everyone into some kind of mold! Such people cannot see holiness where it is at work, where it is born in labor pains, in struggle, in the elements of the world. Instead they have manufactured for themselves some kind of formula for holiness and then set it as a standard against which to judge a living, struggling, trembling human being.

The same person who had said these words about Fr. Sergius' biography nonetheless did write about him (though nothing as formal as a full biography) and tried to "smooth off the rough edges," to present him to people in polished form. But why? Isn't the whole point that in precisely such a life, even despite its sins and inadequacies ("holiness is not sinlessness," in Fr. Sergius' words) you could find such an agonizing, burning, prophetic thirst for Truth, such a boundless search for God, and that such a life concluded in the apotheosis of the Unfading Light with which God glorified him?[8]

FR. SERGIUS LIVED IN THE DESERT

Once, when I read to that same friend an excerpt of mine about how Fr. Sergius died in the desert, he said, "Fr. Sergius *lived* in the desert!"[9]

Yes, this is true.

And on that note, I would like to say that the legend which arose after his death, and even to some extent during the final years of his life, concerning his "success," that he had been an "idol" for many people, was completely false. He was never an "idol" for anyone. People were drawn to him, but people were also "scandalized" by him (and he was persecuted his *entire* life). He often used to say, "Only the lazy are never scandalized." And it wasn't just "enemies" or strangers (although, properly speaking, he had no "enemies"; he often used to say, "I have no personal enemies," and this was something he valued greatly). Even his close friends would suddenly revolt against him and criticize him on more than one occasion.

(I remember one period when Mother Blandina and I revolted against the "problematics" of his theories: "We are sick and tired of going back and forth with these antinomies!" That's how we expressed ourselves—what blindness! We wanted to stand with two legs on firm ground! We wanted assurance, spiritual ease!)

ON THE HUMILITY OF FR. SERGIUS

How important in our days of tempest and chaos are those bright stars in the sky of the spirit who can guide us along the path. How important it is that these "examples" whom we follow speak in the language of our time. Not everyone is able to "read" the hieroglyphs of past centuries. Only to a few is the law of

God so open that this foreign tongue does not get in their way, that through it they can see the Light of the Wisdom of God, which at all times is one and the same. Often, instead of "bread" [cf. Matt. 7:9], such people are given empty content in the form of words that are worn out like faded coins. How readily they employ these words and thus how emptied the words become of their existential, ontological content!

The same thing happens with the concept of holiness—it is understood not according to its essence, but according to the outward forms in which it has appeared. And people begin to mimic these outward forms and take them as the norm. This is seen most clearly in depictions of humility in particular. How *important* are examples when it comes to the virtues! But nowhere is outward imitation of an example more off-key than in the virtue of humility. It is difficult to speak about humility. Perhaps, in order to understand humility, in order that the vastness of its freedom may be revealed to the heart—"And the truth shall set you free" [John 8:32]—it is necessary to understand how humility is connected with love.

Fr. S. never imitated outward forms of humility. His humility was woven into the fabric of his life and was well-earned. The humility of his final years, this was primarily the humility of man before God, of time before eternity. It is linked with dying. So little really matters anymore when you have one foot in the grave. But before that—what a path of humility he walked! How difficult for those whom the Lord has thus singled out to bend the knee. He could not sincerely submit to anyone entirely. And indeed it was unnecessary! But how obediently, and how sincerely did he submit when this was necessary!

FR. SERGIUS DID NOT LIKE SELF-CONFIDENCE

Fr. Sergius did not like self-confidence, it was foreign to him. Often, when something in life was perplexing him, he would say half-jokingly, half-seriously, that self-confident people were some "other species."

"A LITTLE SOMETHING"

We all know how attentive Fr. Sergius was towards others, how he feared offending anyone, even to the point of not expressing his opinion at times. On the name days[10] of those near and dear to him, he would look for every opportunity to mark this special day with "a little something" for that person. "A little something"—here we can see in him what was most elemental, most Russian, most primordial...

In his final years he asked us to remind him of the name days of those in his circle so he would not forget, and we had to help him come up with and find the perfect "little something."

LOVE

What a mystery—human fellowship!

How can an entire spiritual culture have been built upon man fleeing his fellow man! Ontologically, man is not alone. However, in his standing before God there is the ultimate aloneness! Man dies alone.

But love in man is the revelation of God in life, in people.

Yes, what is "love?"...

It is the mystery of life. The mystery of creation.

Fr. Sergius "loved love" in each of its manifestations in people; he contemplated this mystery. In each human love he saw, and contemplated, Love, its sophianic basis. He delighted in it, was inspired by it.

ASCETIC STRUGGLE

Just like they do with holiness, people copy the forms in which ascetic struggle has manifested itself! The ascetic struggle of Fr. S. was a struggle of love, a struggle of life, and not the artificial self-imposition of fetters. How Fr. S. lived everything in life to its limit, how he suffered again and again! He never turned away, never withdrew from painful situations in life (for the Christian this is and should be an ascetic struggle, and not Yoga-like exercises for the attainment of some occultish abilities), he thought, he searched, he agonized...

FR. SERGIUS AND COMFORT

"...In these stone slabs people have bowed down to a different god, and his name is comfort..."—so wrote Fr. S. in his dialogue "At the Feast of the Gods,"[11] describing his first encounter with Europe a quarter of a century before he ended up there again.

The living conditions of Russian refugees were not notable for their comfort: after a short stay in Prague during which he delivered lectures at the university,[12] Fr. S. ended up in Paris, where the circumstances of his life at St. Sergius Representation Church were quite modest.[13] At first there were not even real chairs in the apartment—they had been replaced with uncomfortable iron folding lawn chairs. It was on such a chair that Fr. S wrote his books at his writing desk. He was so used to it that when they got new dining room chairs, Fr. S. kept his former one. Only shortly before the final illness, in light of his intensifying sclerosis and his great fatigue and weariness, did his friends raise the question of purchasing a more comfortable armchair for the writing desk, which served him up to his final days.

But Fr. S. did not shun comfort where it saved time otherwise wasted in overcoming deprivation by expending excessive, unnecessary effort instead of preserving strength for work. And when steam heating was brought into his apartment, he simply took advantage of this convenience and even chuckled a little over those who nearly insisted that it interferes with the spiritual life because it deprives man of the ascetic endurance of cold. The ascesis of Fr. S. was his creative, scholarly work, and in this work he not only did not grow weak but instead grew stronger amid convenience. At the same time, Fr. S. by no means loved to furnish himself with these conveniences, he never fussed about having quiet so that he could work, and he even chuckled a little when he saw this in others; for these situations he had a quip at the ready—"they want to live a 'dacha life'"...

Although his day was always fully booked, especially during summer breaks in the country, when he would always work in the mornings, still he was hardly overprotective of this schedule: the door to his apartment was always open, and everyone who wished could come to him at any moment. When someone would come in the morning hours, which he guarded as time for his work outside of writing his lectures, he would get a little annoyed. Yet he always said, "him that cometh to me I will in no wise cast out" [John 6:37] and received his visitor anyway. And this path—"the labor of love" for people—as a result of years and spiritual growth began to occupy a greater and greater place in his heart, as did the constant, concrete remembrance of God and the sense of His presence in every circumstance. Before he had walked this path, he would force himself, with difficulty, to attend to these interruptions of his work and would say in jest, recognizing his own impatience: "Yes, as a matter of fact, it turns out that I receive as a 'personal enemy' [cf. Matt. 5:44] every person who comes unexpectedly and interrupts my work!" (He would write only in the mornings.)

In his latter years, almost every meeting was for him a joy, yet being torn away from work strongly impacted his writings, and this fact can even explain the many repetitions in his books.

THE LENTEN TRIODION AND PRAYING[14]

Having been brought up in the church from childhood, Fr. S. grew up organically together with its life. While still a little boy—as he used to tell the story—he anxiously awaited when they would sing the canon, "Beneath the waves of the sea"[15] and was afraid to miss it. This sacred and almost childlike attitude towards all the services of Holy Week remained with him for his entire life. While there was much that he criticized about the archaisms and rhetoric of our canons (especially those for the commemoration of certain saints, which were written without any inspiration), the services of Holy Week he singled out and considered particularly inspired. Not long before his final illness he once again recalled with enthusiasm: "'O Lord, the woman fallen into many sins perceived your Divinity'—Exactly so!"[16]

He likewise highlighted not so much the intrinsically tedious content of our services' interminable repetitions as much as the atmosphere they would create—especially our services at the St. Sergius Representation Church—during the first week of the fast [Great Lent]. Although these services greatly wore him down, he would return from church as if from a long journey in unknown lands, having scaled the great heights of the spirit, and would say that the soul in this season breathes the particularly rarified air of these heights. And thus even this private critique of these services in their particulars, which was entirely justified, became somewhat discordant, especially later in his life, with these feelings of his. He recommended treating these Holy Week services with even some superstitious fear: "do not skip them."

But many of our prayers seemed to him burdensome, archaic, unmodern. This was especially true of the rule of prayer for preparation for Holy Communion. We often spoke about this, how burdensome it was and how it did not correspond to our feelings and thoughts before the holy mystery of Communion in the Body and Blood of Christ. Despite this, he never allowed himself any sloppiness or nihilism toward the "rule" and recited it strictly. At the end of his life, when he was very weak, he almost always read them while sitting at his writing desk.

As for the archaic canon of Andrew of Crete,[17] he liked to poke fun at it; but as I mentioned earlier, he valued the atmosphere it created, as he valued the entire atmosphere of the first week of the fast. He even tried to define what the "magic" of this rhythm consisted of, locating it in the mysterious repetition of "Have mercy on me, O God, have mercy on me," in the mysterious sighs of repentance.

MY FIRST TIME MEETING FR. SERGIUS

The first time I saw Fr. Sergius was in Oleiz, an estate near the town of Koreiz, in the second year after his ordination...[18]

Fiery, piercing eyes. He was almost frightening, especially for the youthful, enthusiastic, and naïve young woman that I was at the time. His figure was a bit awkward, a bit ungraceful: it was as if he did not fit into the framework of everyday life. His priestly garb didn't quite "suit" him either; but it was simply hard to imagine him otherwise, to the point that his clothes seemed everyday and ordinary for someone who cut such an all-around exceptional figure. At the same time, there was a sort of touching helplessness and childlikeness that remained with him his entire life. And there was a humility too, which is also not a treasure that can be acquired in a day, at a stroke, but is instead something unceasing, something that unfolds throughout an entire *life*, it is a life of humility, as is the life of every "daughter of Wisdom" (and the "path of Wisdom," in the words of Isaac the Syrian, is never-ending).[19] This humility was expressed, of course, most fundamentally in his putting off the "old man" and putting on the "new man" in the "holy foolishness" of his priesthood [Eph. 4:22–24].[20] Renouncing the halo that comes with being a university professor, he laid his life at the foot of the Altar of God and immolated himself. Everything was so fresh, new, and exciting in this new position. Many people (indeed nearly everyone at that time) still called him "Sergei Nikolaevich," and only a few began to "accept" and "recognize" him as a priest.[21] His appearance almost shocked others, and he was almost always shy and apologetic around them. You got the sense that, in everything, he made his way "without a map," so to speak.

But there were already some souls around him that reached out to him as a priest, and, of course, there were already more than a few "miracles" of human communion in his life at that time. (It was even said that a few of the local guys "converted" under his influence.) Although a long road of trials was waiting to test it, at that time his characteristic humility was already apparent both in trifles and when he would speak of his "writing" as he went to work; almost in a childlike manner did he perform all the church rites with hands that were helpless and nearly trembling (in adoration!). By day, in light of the difficulties with the food situation at that time, he could invariably be found working in the garden. He did this quite helplessly and ineptly, because in childhood he grew up in an urban environment and was not accustomed to such work. At that time, I had a small crisis and sought an escape from the somewhat soothingly-pagan atmosphere of life that drew us in on the southern shore of Crimea. After returning home after visiting the Bulgakovs in Oleiz for the first time, I went back there again two days later, alone (28 km by foot), in order to make my confession to Fr. S. for the first time in my life...

The next day, a brief conversation in the garden. Fr. S. warned against looking too intently for a "teacher," against ascribing to him too much meaning: "for one is your Teacher—Jesus Christ," in the words of the apostle [*sic*] [Matt. 23:10].

FR. SERGIUS AND RUSSIA

It was not by his own will that Fr. S. left Russia—he was expelled. He used to underscore this all the time, saying that he himself would not have left. The first year of his life abroad, he desperately feared "disconnecting from Russia"; he constantly reminisced about all the little details of his life in his final days and months there. Almost every conversation with him would begin like this: "A half a year ago at this time I was doing this and that, or I was in this or that place"; or, "a year ago on this day," and so on. Throughout all the years of his exile, Fr. S. followed with great interest everything that was happening in Russia. Toward every manifestation of the creativity of Russian genius he felt great enthusiasm, and toward scientific discoveries, inspiration and admiration.

He considered his creative, spiritual, ecclesial, and theological work to be connected with all these creative manifestations. He expressed this link through the image of a "tunnel" (his own expression), which people begin digging at two separate ends that must eventually merge.

The church schism that had tormented the Russian Church abroad for so many years Fr. S. accepted as a merely formal reality. He would always say that he never considered himself excommunicated from the Russian Church.[22]

PROMISSORY NOTE

Fr. S. used to say that attendance at church services was like a promissory note.

THAT WE MUST ALSO ENCOUNTER GOD

Unhappy are those who defend an "impersonal" concept of God, as merely the Good and so forth. They are correct in the apophatic sense—the concept of God is incompatible with our understanding and words: we cannot say what "God" is. Yet at the same time, they are incorrect in the sense that there is no religious life without *encountering* God, without seeing the face of God. But one must not seek out this vision according to some external standard or by merely following the example of others. Each person has this vision in his own way, in his own language, within his very self. Or rather, you must *discover* in yourself, you must catch a glimpse of this vision within yourself—and do not claim for it a permanence or an intensity, a brightness or distinctness it does not have. In fact, one shouldn't claim anything at all for it. Rather, sharpen your inner sight, do not pass this vision by unawares. For some, this vision comes easily and often; for others, it is sporadic and rare.

The life of prophets is especially marked by these "encounters." Fr. S. was in a sense a prophet for our days. And in his life, these "encounters" took place not only in those exceptional situations that he himself described in his autobiographical materials, but much more often.[23]

I remember on this score his almost sacred relationship with the places in which he had lived. Once we drove past a place where he had spent a summer. "Here I lived..."—this was said so monumentally, so meaningfully, not with the satisfaction of some personal recollection, no—this was a *fact*, the concreteness of life: here I lived, here I talked with God, here I fell and stood up again, here God raised me up.

London, 1945–1946.

NOTES

NOTES TO TRANSLATORS' PREFACE

1 For selections from his Yalta diaries (1921–1922), see the forthcoming volume by Yury P. Avvakumov and Roberto J. De La Noval, *Ecclesiology in Revolution: The Crypto-Catholic Writings of Sergius Bulgakov, 1921–1923*. In his 1939 essay, "The Sophiology of Death," Bulgakov notes in reference to his journaling that he "had long ago already stopped writing anything down." Roberto J. De La Noval, *The Sophiology of Death: Essays on Eschatology: Personal, Political, Universal* (Eugene: Cascade, 2021), 135n17.

2 Whether Bulgakov ever had plans to publish it is an interesting question that admits only of speculative answers, some of which are provided in the Biographical Introduction.

3 In Prot. Sergii Bulgakov, *Avtobiograficheskie Zametki, Dnevniki, Stat'i* [*Autobiographical Notes, Diaries, Essays*] (Orel: Orlovskoi gosudarstvennoi teleradioveshchatel'noi kompanii: 1998), 175–282. Reprinted as *Protoierei Sergii Bulgakov: Dnevnik Dukhovnoi* (Moscow: Obshchedostupnyi Pravoslavnyi Universitet Osnovannyi Protoiereem Aleksandrom Menem, 2003). The *Diary* was published again as part of the volume *Dela i Dni. Stat'i 1903–1944: Memuarnaia i Dnevniknaia Proza* [*Works and Days. Essays 1903–1944: Prose works from Memoirs and Diaries*] (2008).

4 Published in *Vestnik RSKhD* 174, no. 2 (1996)/no. 1 (1997): 5–51; vol. 175, no. 1 (1997): 20–75; vol. 176, no. 2–3 (1997): 54–70.

5 *Sergej Bulgakov: Zápisky a duchovní deník teolog* (Olomouc: Refugium Velehrad-Roma, 2009).

6 *Sergiusz Bulgakow: Dziennik duchowy*, trans. Monachini Eudokia (Halina Lachocka) (Kraków: Homo Dei, 2014).

7 Aleksandra Vladimirovna Obolenskaya (1897–1974; took monastic vows in 1937). For more on Mother Blandina, see the section "Bulgakov as Spiritual Father: Mother Blandina and Sr. Joanna."

8 *Vestnik RSKhD* 159, no. 2 (1990): 51–83.

9 Among the names of Bulgakov's students and spiritual children are priests, theologians, monastics, iconographers, and martyrs. Some of the better known are Fr. Alexander Schmemann, Mother Maria Skobtsova, Sr. Joanna Reitlinger, Elisabeth Behr-Sigel, Fr. Georges Florovsky, Lev Zander, and Paul Evdokimov.

10 See p. 177.

11 Letter from Bulgakov to Aleksandra Obolenskaya. 20.XII/2.1.1923. *Vestnik RSKhD* 200 (2012): 13.

12 A snapshot of their correspondence can be found in *Vestnik RSKhD* 200 (2012): 10–25. A Russian volume of their correspondence is being prepared for publication.

13 See the volume by Boris Jakim, *Sergius Bulgakov: Apocatastasis and Transfiguration* (New Haven: Variable Press, 1995), which contains Sr. Joanna's account of Bulgakov's pre-death "Taboric" illumination.

14 See Y. N. Reitlinger (Sister Joanna) and Fr. Sergii Bulgakov, *Dialog Khudozhnika i Bogoslova: Dnevniki. Zapisnye knizhki. Pis'ma* [Dialogue of an Artist and a Theologian: Diaries. Written booklets. Letters], ed. Bronislava Popova (Moscow: Nikeia, 2011), 48.

15 In addition to the sketch of Bulgakov's friendship with Sr. Joanna found in our Biographical Introduction, see Sergii Bulgakov, eds. Barbara Hallensleben, Regula M. Zwahlen, Dario Colombo, trans. Mike Whitton, *The Apocalypse of John: An Essay in Dogmatic Interpretation*, for an essay (pp. 339–51) by Bronislava Popova that treats of their relationship and of Bulgakov's theological influence on Reitlinger's art, especially on her frescos in England commissioned by the Fellowship of St. Alban and St. Sergius, which are also reproduced in that volume (pp. 361–89).

NOTES TO BIOGRAPHICAL INTRODUCTION

1 The great Orthodox theologian Fr. Alexander Schmemann, one of Bulgakov's students, was unsparing in his criticism of his teacher's theology: "Bulgakov uses a thoroughly Orthodox terminology, everything is a sort of 'brocade'—at the same time, romantic, almost subjective. 'My' theology—'There! I will impose on Orthodoxy my "Sophia." I will show everybody what they really believe.' And it wasn't imposed on anybody, not because people are ignorant, but because it's unnecessary." From Alexander Schmemann, *The Journals of Father Alexander Schmemann, 1973–1983*, trans. Juliana Schmemann (Crestwood: St. Vladimir's Seminary Press, 2000), 261–62. Yet Schmemann highly regarded Bulgakov as a pastor and a prophet. As Alexis Klimoff writes, "Schmemann concludes that posterity may well judge Bulgakov's charismatic presence, prophetic fervor, and authentic Christian witness as far more significant than what he characterizes as [a] Teutonically elaborate philosophical system" ("Georges Florovsky and the Sophiological Controversy," *St. Vladimir's Theological Quarterly* 49, nos. 1–2 [2005]: 82). See Alexander Schmemann, "Trois Images," *Le Messager orthodoxe* 57 (1972): 2–20, for his glowing words about Bulgakov as priest and pastor.

2 For more on Bulgakov's conversion, see the Theological Introduction.

3 William James, "Great Men, Great Thoughts, and the Environment," *Atlantic Monthly* (October 1880), https://www.uky.edu/~eushe2/Pajares/jgreatmen.html.

4 This is, of course, a claim that must be qualified. Certainly, there had been theologians, meetings, statements, and other points of contact between the Christian East and the Christian West between the Council of Florence and the twentieth century. But it was only under Bulgakov's formative influence that the Eastern Orthodox Church came into real *dialogue* with the Western Churches in the modern period. This is what I mean by encounter. Bulgakov's primary role in this encounter took shape in two primary ways, first in his capacity as dean of St. Sergius Orthodox Theological Institute. Through Bulgakov and his students, this school participated in the rich, interdenominational, theological conversation taking place in Paris through lectures, publications, and classes. It is hard to overstate the importance of

St. Sergius for exposing the Western world to Orthodox Christianity and its theology. Second, Bulgakov facilitated encounter through his tireless work in the bourgeoning Ecumenical Movement, work that would be carried on in different forms by his students. Bulgakov was a major player at the very beginning of the Movement. Additionally, one may also mention his theological work itself, which, following earlier Russian thinkers like Vladimir Solovyov, sought to engage Western Christian thought on its own terms rather than as a mere polemical target.

5 While in Yalta, Bulgakov kept a diary from June 1921 to September 1922. While in Constantinople, he kept a diary from December 1922 to April 1922. Both of those diaries are collected in Prot. Sergii Bulgakov, *Avtobiograficheskie Zametki, Dnevniki, Stat'i* [Autobiographical Notes, Diaries, Essays] (Orel: Orlovskoi gosudarstvennoi teleradioveshchatel'noi kompanii, 1998), 75–172. Bulgakov's daily diary while in Prague is published in two different volumes: Sergius Bulgakov, *Iz Pamiati Serdtsa. Praga (1923–1924)* [*From the Heart's Memory. Prague* (1923–1924)], ed. Alexei Kozyrev and Natalia Golubkova with Modest Kolerov (Moscow: O. G. I., 1998); Y. N. Reitlinger (Sister Joanna) and Fr. Sergii Bulgakov, *Dialog Khudozhnika i Bogoslova: Dnevniki. Zapisnye knizhki. Pis'ma* [Dialogue of an Artist and a Theologian: Diaries. Written booklets. Letters], ed. Bronislava Popova (Moscow: Nikeia, 2011), 95–135.

6 This is a story that has not been told in English in anything but the most basic sketches. The most detailed account of Bulgakov's pre-Paris period is Catherine Evtuhov, *The Cross and the Sickle: Sergei Bulgakov and the Fate of Russian Religious Philosophy: 1890–1920* (Ithaca: Cornell University Press, 1997), but the author does not cover much ground after Bulgakov's ordination to the priesthood. See also Regula M. Zwahlen, "Sergei Bulgakov's Intellectual Journey, 1900–1922," in *The Oxford Handbook of Russian Religious Thought*, ed. Caryl Emerson, George Pattison, and Randall A. Poole (Oxford: OUP, 2020), 277–92. The doctoral dissertation by Sergei V. Nikolaev, "Church and Reunion in the Theology of Sergii Bulgakov and Georges Florovsky, 1918–1940," PhD Dissertation (Southern Methodist University, 2007), discusses the development of Bulgakov's ecclesiological thought in the early 1920s in its first two chapters, but does not provide much in the way of biographical detail.

7 Many of those counted among the *intelligentsia* joined the ascendant Bolshevik party in the late 1910s and early '20s, the party that would rule the Soviet Union after a protracted power struggle with other left-wing political entities. Others, like Bulgakov, rejected Bolshevism and were exiled for their "counter-revolutionary" (often religious) views. Still others stayed in Russian but many were "purged"—imprisoned or executed—along the way. See Evtuhov, *The Cross and the Sickle*.

8 Bulgakov, diary entry, 2/15.VI.1924; in *Dialog Khudozhnika i Bogoslova*, 104–5.

9 Bulgakov, letter to Florensky on 1.IX.1922; in Pavel Florenskii and Sergii Bulgakov, *Perepiska sviashchennika Pavla Aleksandrovicha Florenskogo so sviashchennikom Sergiem Nikolaevichem Bulgakovym* [The Letters of Priest Pavel Aleksandrovich Florenskii and Sergii Nikolaevich Bulgakov], ed. Andronik Trubachev and S. M. Polovinkin (Tomsk: Volodei, 2001), 169.

10 Bulgakov, letter to Florensky on 1.IX.1922, in *Perepiska*, 176.

11 See Hyacinthe Destivelle, *The Moscow Council (1917–1918): The Creation of the Conciliar Institutions of the Russian Orthodox Church*, ed. Michael Plekon and Vitaly Permiakov, trans. Jerry Ryan (Notre Dame: University of Notre Dame Press, 2015).

12 Bulgakov, letter to Florensky on 1.IX.1922, in *Perepiska*, 175. He continued, "I, of course, am not so stupid or naive as to ascribe to myself—or even to you, despite all your supernatural talents and uniqueness—the capacity to meet this goal; it was a task given to us, so it seemed, by the Church, a task born in *ecclesial* consciousness. Faced with so great and miraculous a work, I could not even ask myself whether this was in my power or in our power, because it is, in fact, in the power of One Alone because only the Highest Power can accomplish it" (ibid., 176.)

13 Bulgakov, letter to Florensky on 1.IX.1922; in *Perepiska*, 169–70.

14 Bulgakov, letter to Florensky on 1.IX.1922; in *Perepiska*, 170–71.

15 See the forthcoming translation by Yury P. Avvakumov and Roberto J. De La Noval, along with a translation of Bulgakov's confessional letter to Florensky and much of his Yalta diary.

16 Bulgakov's views on church reunion at this time were strongly influenced by Vladimir Solovyov's. See Vladimir Solovyov, *Russia and the Universal Church*, trans. Herbert Rees (London: G. Bles, 1948).

17 John Paul II, *That They May Be One*: Encyclical Letter, *Ut Unum Sint*, of the Holy Father John Paul II on commitment to Ecumenism, 1995. https://www.vatican.va, paragraph 54.

18 Bulgakov, "Yalta Diary," diary entry, 6.IX.1922; in *Avtobiograficheskie zametki*, 111–12.

19 Bulgakov, letter to Florensky on 1.IX.1922; in *Perepiska*, 176.

20 See Avril Pyman, *Pavel Florensky: A Quiet Genius: The Tragic and Extraordinary Life of Russia's Unknown Da Vinci* (New York: Continuum, 2010).

21 Bulgakov, "Yalta Diary," diary entry, 5/18.VI.1922; in *Avtobiograficheskie zametki*, 106.

22 See Thomas Allan Smith, "Introduction" to Sergius Bulgakov, *Unfading Light: Contemplations and Speculations*, ed. and trans. Thomas Allan Smith (Grand Rapids: Eerdmans, 2012), xxxi.

23 Pavel Florensky, *The Pillar and Ground of the Truth: An Essay in Orthodox Theodicy in Twelve Letters*, trans. Boris Jakim (Princeton: Princeton University Press, 1997).

24 Bulgakov, "Yalta Diary," diary entry, 5/18.VI.1922; in *Avtobiograficheskie zametki*, 107.

25 See e.g., Bulgakov, "Yalta Diary," diary entry, 3.XII.1921; in *Avtobiograficheskie zametki*, 89. He wrings his hands about Fr. Pavel in the Constantinople diary as well, on occasion: 10/23.I.1923; 31.I/13.II.1923.

26 Bulgakov, "Yalta Diary," diary entry, 24.IV.1922; in *Avtobiograficheskie zametki*, 100.

27 Bulgakov, "Constantinople Diary," diary entry, 16/29.I.1923; in *Avtobiograficheskie zametki*, 140–41.

28 He wrote soon after his arrival in Constantinople, "The most grievous and difficult thing awaited me in the ecclesial sphere: an acute and entirely old-fashioned proselytizing encounter with Catholics who also employ proselytizing gimmicks here." From Bulgakov, "Constantinople Diary," diary entry, 2/15.I.1923. Day of St. Seraphim. Constantinople; in *Avtobiograficheskie zametki*, 122.

29 Bulgakov, "Constantinople Diary," diary entry, 31.I/13.II.1923; in *Avtobiograficheskie zametki*, 143. This passage gives a very different take on the notion of the church's "two lungs."

30 See note 4 above.

31 Bulgakov, "Constantinople Diary," diary entry, 4/17.III.1923; in *Avtobiograficheskie zametki*, 155–57.

32 Bulgakov, "Constantinople Diary," diary entry, 13/26.III.1923; in *Avtobiograficheskie zametki*, 160.

33 He wrote in March 1923 that, upon having his heart checked, the doctor told him he may have arteriosclerosis—the same condition from which his mother and father died. Occupied by the task of uniting the churches, he wonders whether he should turn his attention instead to his family, to make sure they would be secure in case he were to die. See Bulgakov, "Constantinople Diary," diary entry, 15/28.III.1923; in *Avtobiograficheskie zametki*, 161.

34 Bulgakov, "Constantinople Diary," diary entry, 19/31.III.1923; in *Avtobiograficheskie zametki*, 161–62.

35 Bulgakov, "Constantinople Diary," diary entry, 31.III/13.IV.1923; in *Avtobiograficheskie zametki*, 165–66.

36 In his guilt, he cried out in one of his diary entries from Constantinople: "I will not give up my Russia, not to anyone and not for anything!" (Bulgakov, "Constantinople Diary," diary entry, 23.II/8.III.1923; in *Avtobiograficheskie zametki*, 151.

37 Bulgakov, "Constantinople Diary," diary entry, 22.IV/5.V.1923, from Vienna *en route* to Prague; in *Avtobiograficheskie zametki*, 171–72.

38 Bulgakov, *From the Heart's Memory*, diary entry 14/27.V.1923; in *Iz Pamiati Serdtsa*, 117.

39 Bulgakov, *From the Heart's Memory*, diary entry, 26.V/8.VI.1923; in *Iz Pamiati Serdtsa*, 122.

40 Bulgakov, *From the Heart's Memory*, diary entry, 11/24.VI.1923; in *Iz Pamiati Serdtsa*, 128. After the Russian Revolution in 1917, Crimea's political status changed several times. It was held by the anti-Bolshevik White Army until November 1920, when it was driven out by the Red Army.

41 Bulgakov, *From the Heart's Memory*, diary entry, 20.VIII/2.IX.1923; in *Iz Pamiati Serdtsa*, 147.

42 Bulgakov, *From the Heart's Memory*, diary entry, 27.ix/10.X.1923; in *Iz Pamiati Serdtsa*, 165–66. Founding members mentioned: A. V. Kartashev, P. I. Novogorodtsev, P. B. Struve, V. V. Zenkovsky, C. C. Bezobrazov, and G. V. Florovsky. See *Bratstvo Sviatoi Sofii: Materialy i Dokumenty 1923–1939* [*The Brotherhood of St. Sophia: Materials and Documents, 1923–1939*] (Moscow/Paris: Russkii Put'/ YMCA Press, 2000).

43 Bulgakov, *From the Heart's Memory*, diary entry, 12/25.XI.1923; in *Iz Pamiati Serdtsa*, 202. On Bulgakov's pervasive sense of shame and inadequacy at this time, see the Theological Introduction.

44 Bulgakov, *From the Heart's Memory*, diary entry, 6/19.XII.1923, St. Nicholas Day; in *Iz Pamiati Serdtsa*, 213–14.

45 Elena Ivanova (neé Tokmakova) Bulgakova (1868–1945).

46 Bulgakov, *From the Heart's Memory*, diary entry, 1/14.I.1924, New Year's Day [Old Style], at night upon returning home from church; in *Iz Pamiati Serdtsa*, 218.

47 Bulgakov, *From the Heart's Memory*, diary entry, 3/16.I.1924; in *Iz Pamiati Serdtsa*, 218.

48 Bulgakov, *From the Heart's Memory*, diary entry, 13/26.I.1924, evening; in *Iz Pamiati Serdtsa*, 223.

49 Many, if not most, of his diary entries from Constantinople and Prague (not the *Spiritual Diary*) discuss Bulgakov's children, especially his son Fedya, who had remained in Russia, about whom Bulgakov and his wife worried constantly.

50 Bulgakov, letter to Florensky on 1.IX.1922; in *Perepiska*, 169.

51 Bulgakov, "Constantinople Diary," diary entry, 31.I/13.II.1923; in *Avtobiograficheskie zametki*, 145.

52 Bulgakov, *From the Heart's Memory*, diary entry, 1/14.VI.1923; in *Iz Pamiati Serdtsa*, 249.

53 Bulgakov, *From the Heart's Memory*, diary entry, 2/14.XII.1923, on the train in Příbram; in *Iz Pamiati Serdtsa*, 208–9.

54 Bulgakov, *From the Heart's Memory*, diary entry, 28.I./10.II.1924; in *Iz Pamiati Serdtsa*, 227.

55 "Truly, in my life the moment has come, and was a long time coming, when *only to myself and in myself* should I search and find myself and my center." From Bulgakov, "Prague Notebook, 1924–1925," diary entry, 11/24.V.1924; in *Dialog Khudozhnika i Bogoslova*, 100.

56 Bulgakov, "Prague Notebook, 1924–1925," diary entry, 2/15.VI.1924; in *Dialog Khudozhnika i Bogoslova*, 104.

57 John of Kronstadt, *My Life in Christ*, ed. and trans. E. E. Goulaeff (London: Cassell, 1897).

58 Alexander Elchaninov, *The Diary of a Russian Priest*, trans. Helen Iswolsky (Crestwood: St. Vladimir's Seminary Press, 1982).

59 See Aleksei P. Kozyrev, "Otets Sergii Bulgakov: Dva Goda v Prage [Father Sergii Bulgakov: Two Years in Prague]," *Filosofskie Pis'ma. Russko-Evropeiskii Dialog* 3, no. 4 (2020): 30–47; Kateřina Bauerová, "Geographical and Imaginary Spaces: Sergei Bulgakov and Joanna Reitlinger in Prague," *Communio Viatorum* 57, no. 2 (2015): 193–209.

60 See Reitlinger and Bulgakov, *Dialog Khudozhnika i Bogoslova*, 137.

61 See e.g. Bulgakov, "Prague Notebook, 1924–1925," diary entry, 18/31.V.1924; in *Dialog Khudozhnika i Bogoslova*, 102.

62 Bulgakov, *From the Heart's Memory*, diary entry, 15/28.IV.1924, Bright Monday; in *Iz Pamiati Serdtsa*, 255.

63 Bulgakov, "Prague Notebook, 1924–1925," diary entry, 11/24.V.1924; in *Dialog Khudozhnika i Bogoslova*, 100. Emphasis in original. Bulgakov's questionable notion that Florensky needed to be the center of attention may owe to his somewhat obsessive attitude toward his mentor.

64 See for example an entry from Reitlinger's spiritual diary from the mid-1930s, at the height of the controversy surrounding Bulgakov's teaching on Sophia: "Sophia is love, Sophia is hope, Sophia is faith. I do not need to *see* Holy Sophia, for I would, perhaps, consider it a delusion (after all, 'walk by faith, not by sight' [2 Cor. 5:7]), but this very faith grants inner, spiritual contemplation, which can be communicated in outward forms—it is a concrete sense of various planes, as it were, spatial representations of non-spatial things." From Reitlinger and Bulgakov, *Dialog Khudozhnika i Bogoslova*, 187.

65 Bulgakov, diary entries, 5/18.XI.1923; in *Iz Pamiati Serdtsa*, 200–2; 24.V/6.VI.1924; in *Dialog Khudozhnika i Bogoslova*, 103; 6/19.X.1924, 11/24.X.1924; in *Dialog*, 115–16.

66 Bulgakov, "Prague Notebook, 1924–1925," diary entry, 6/19.X.1924; in *Dialog Khudozhnika i Bogoslova*, 115–16.

67 Bulgakov, "Prague Notebook, 1924–1925," diary entry, 11/24.X.1924; in *Dialog Khudozhnika i Bogoslova*, 116. See also the entry on the same date in the *Spiritual Diary*. For more on Bulgakov's focus on the need to reconcile oneself with God's will, see the Theological Introduction.

68 He had read portions of his pro-Catholic *At the Walls of Chersonesus* to an Orthodox audience in Prague in December 1923, who met the piece with bewilderment. It earned him the reputation of being insufficiently "churched," a reputation he would fight for years, even after he renounced his former sympathies with papism. "The Lord has humbled me," he wrote after the frosty reception. See Bulgakov, *From the Heart's Memory*, diary entry, Monday, 15.XII.1923; in *Iz Pamiati Serdtsa*, 209.

69 Bulgakov, *From the Heart's Memory*, diary entry, 18.II/2.III.1924; in *Iz Pamiati Serdtsa*, 236.

70 Referencing Eurasianism, he wrote, "I cannot be reconciled and will not reconcile myself to the flightlessness and rudimentariness of the emigration." From Bulgakov, *From the Heart's Memory*, diary entry, 18.II/2.III.1924; in *Iz Pamiati Serdtsa*, 237.

71 See Paul L. Gavrilyuk, *Georges Florovsky and the Russian Religious Renaissance* (Oxford: OUP, 2014), 60–79.

72 Bulgakov, "Prague Notebook, 1924–1925," diary entry, 31.III/13.IV.1925; in *Dialog Khudozhnika i Bogoslova*, 132.

73 Bulgakov, *From the Heart's Memory*, diary entry, 18.II/2.III.1924; in *Iz Pamiati Serdtsa*, 237. Bulgakov wrote similarly in February, 1924: "Everything sounds of mistrust of my ecclesiality; to me, this is the punishment for my secret papism.... I'm getting closer and closer to 'splendid isolation.' But this all obscures a bright joy: yesterday in a letter from Petrograd(!!) I received from my faithful Elizaveta Vasilievna [Bobkova] a piece of the coffin and fleece from St. Seraphim—and I feel this is like a blessing from the Saint and a sort of forgiveness for my sin against Orthodoxy. I gave a piece to Yuliya,

for I feel this is a blessing to her from Him." From *From the Heart's Memory*, 25.II/9.III.1924; in *Iz Pamiati Serdtsa*, 241.

74 See Metropolitan Evlogy (Georgievskii), *My Life's Journey: The Memoirs of Metropolitan Evlogy*, 2 vols. trans. Alexander Lisenko (Crestwood: St. Vladimir's Seminary Press, 2014).

75 Bulgakov, "Prague Notebook, 1924–1925," diary entry, 2/15.VI.1924; in *Dialog Khudozhnika i Bogoslova*, 106.

76 Bulgakov, *From the Heart's Memory*, diary entry, 29.X./12.XI.1923; in *Iz Pamiati Serdtsa*, 197–98.

77 Anastassy Brandon Gallaher and Irina Kukota, "Protopresbyter Sergii Bulgakov: Hypostasis and Hypostaticity: Scholia to *The Unfading Light*," *St. Vladimir's Theological Quarterly* 49, no. 1–2 (2005): 5–46. He wrote in June 1924, "These days, as strength allows, I'm turning over once again questions of Sophia and Her hypostaticity, because I have discovered in myself a shift in understanding, and this will be the main dogmatic question." Bulgakov, "Prague Notebook, 1924–1925," diary entry, 26.V/8.VI.1924; in *Dialog Khudozhnika i Bogoslova*, 103.

78 The works of the "little trilogy" are *The Friend of the Bridegroom* (1927), *The Burning Bush* (1927), and *Jacob's Ladder* (1929), and those of the "great trilogy," *On Divine-Humanity*, are *The Lamb of God* (1933), *The Comforter* (1936), and *The Bride of the Lamb* (published posthumously in 1945).

79 In September 1924, Metropolitan Anthony Khrapovitsky attacked Bulgakov (and Florensky) in a Russian émigré newspaper for supposedly teaching the heresy of Sophia as a "fourth hypostasis" in the Trinity, but retracted his rebuke soon afterwards. See Gallaher and Kukota, "Hypostasis and Hypostaticity," 6n5. Admittedly, Bulgakov did use the problematic language of "fourth hypostasis" in *Unfading Light*, but took pains to emphasize that this was meant only by analogy. Sophia, for him, remained outside of God the Holy Trinity, and is not a hypostatic Person as Father, Son, and Holy Spirit are. See Bulgakov, *Unfading Light*, 217–21.

80 See Gallaher and Kukota, "Hypostasis and Hypostaticity," 26n36.

81 The bishops that he says were opposed to his ideas were Bishop Theopan (Bystrov), a Russian émigré bishop known for his asceticism, Sergii (Korolev), bishop of Prague, and Seraphim (Sobolev), archbishop in charge of the Russian parishes in Bulgaria. See Bulgakov, "Prague Notebook, 1924–1925," diary entry, 21.V/3.VI.1924; in *Dialog Khudozhnika i Bogoslova*, 102–3, in which he expresses gratitude for being under the omophorion of Metropolitan Evlogii Georgievsky. See also "Prague Notebook, 1924–1925," diary entry, 9/22.I.1925; in *Dialog Khudozhnika i Bogoslova*, 126–27.

82 See Bulgakov, "Prague Notebook, 1924–1925," diary entry, 16/29.V.1924; in *Dialog Khudozhnika i Bogoslova*, 101.

83 Bulgakov, "Prague Notebook, 1924–1925," diary entry, 2/15.II.1925, on the train from Příbram; in *Dialog Khudozhnika i Bogoslova*, 128. Emphasis in original.

84 Bulgakov, "Prague Notebook, 1924–1925," diary entry, 2/15.II, on the train from Příbram; in *Dialog Khudozhnika i Bogoslova*, 128.

85 He wrote in March 1925, "I need to strengthen myself on the inside and be prepared for isolation." From Bulgakov, "Prague Notebook, 1924–1925," diary entry, 17.II/2.III.1925; in *Dialog Khudozhnika i Bogoslova*, 129. Bulgakov wrote a month later, "I ride wounded and battered." He received harsh words on his essay "Hypostasis and Hypostaticity" from Nikolai Arseniev, a founding member of the Brotherhood, and Grigorii Trubetskoy, also a member of the Brotherhood. Bulgakov thought it was just a misunderstanding of his thought. "I must go toward everything, whatever the cost, for the confession of truth, if the Lord has enlightened me with it, and in my conscience I cannot see any theological sin. How they have beaten me, both as a theologian and a priest, and a dean. They have judged and condemned [me]! . . . I do not know where this leads: to a teaching ban or removal from the Academy, or a ban on serving—everything, everything is possible, and all the more must I go out to meet it. I, weak and slavish as I am, have such a consciousness of my rightness and, essentially, debt, that I cannot back down from anything" (Bulgakov, "Prague Notebook, 1924–1925," diary entry, 23.III/5.VI.1925 Paris; in *Dialog Khudozhnika i Bogoslova*, 130–31). Bulgakov wrote in the *Spiritual Diary* on the next day, "Grant it to me to joyfully accept the trials and adversities that You give to me to endure for Your Name. Grant me a clear conscience and unwavering firmness to walk the true path of service to You." See diary entry 24.III/6.IV.1925.

86 Bulgakov, "Prague Notebook, 1924–1925," diary entry, 20.III/2.IV.1925; in *Dialog Khudozhnika i Bogoslova*, 130.

87 Bulgakov, "Prague Notebook, 1924–1925," diary entry, 16/29.VI.1925, in Prague; in *Dialog Khudozhnika i Bogoslova*, 135.

88 Bulgakov, "Prague Notebook, 1924–1925," diary entry, 2/15.VI.1924; in *Dialog Khudozhnika i Bogoslova*, 105.

NOTES TO THEOLOGICAL INTRODUCTION

1 The most succinct presentation can be found in Sergei Bulgakov, trans. Patrick Thompson, O. Fielding Clarke, and Xenia Braikevitc, *Sophia, The Wisdom of God: An Outline of Sophiology* (Hudson: Lindisfarne Press, 1993).

2 It is not emphasized enough that Bulgakov's major trilogy is entitled "On the Divine-*Humanity*."

3 Sergius Bulgakov, trans. Boris Jakim, *The Lamb of God* (Grand Rapids: Eerdmans, 2008), 137.

4 Sergius Bulgakov, trans. Boris Jakim, *The Bride of the Lamb* (Grand Rapids: Eerdmans, 2002), 93.

5 *Lamb of God*, 91.

6 Only angels share this distinction with human persons. Bulgakov's extended essay on angelology can be found in English as Sergius Bulgakov, trans. Thomas Allan Smith, *Jacob's Ladder: On Angels* (Grand Rapids, 2010).

7 "The Problem of Conditional Immortality," in Sergius Bulgakov, trans. Roberto J. De La Noval, *The Sophiology of Death: Essays on Eschatology: Personal, Political, Universal* (Cascade Books, 2021), 65.

8 "Natural revelation is based on the very same fact of the presence of God's image in man, who already contains within himself the divine essence,

because of the very manner of his creation." So writes Bulgakov (133) in his chapter contribution to eds. John Baillie and Hugh Martin, *Revelation*, (London: Faber and Faber, 1937).

9 For a short overview of the controversy, see Paul Ladouceur's *Modern Orthodox Theology: 'Behold, I Make All Things New'* (New York: T&T Clark, 2019), 88–91. An English translation of the major texts from the Sophia Affair is currently in progress.

10 *Seven Orthodox Discuss "Sophia"* (*Razgovor semi pravoslavnykh o Sofii*) (Berlin: Izdanie biulletenia *Za Tserkov'*, 1936), 7. This difficult-to-find text was made available to me in a digital transcription by A. P. Kozyrev and Regula M. Zwahlen, as was the text cited in fn 12 below.

11 For more on Arsen'ev's relationship with Bulgakov, see p. 27 of this volume.

12 "A Few More Words on the Sophiological Dispute" ("Eshche neskol'ko slov k sofiologicheskomu sporu") (Warsaw: Sinodal'naia tipografiia, 1936), 10.

13 "[A]s a fallen being, enslaved by the results of sin and caught by the force of necessity, man must pass through the mystery of redemption, in it must restore his god-like nature, regain his lost freedom." Nikolai Berdyaev, trans. Donald A. Lowrie, *The Meaning of the Creative Act* (San Rafael: Semantron Press, 2009), 101.

14 *5/18.IV.1924*

15 Sergius Bulgakov, trans. Thomas Allan Smith, *Unfading Light: Contemplations and Speculations* (Grand Rapids: Eerdmans, 2012), 343.

16 For Bulgakov's pre-*Diary* discussions of creativity and its relationship to human freedom, see Sergius Bulgakov, trans. Catherine Evtuhov, *Philosophy of Economy: The World as Household* (New Haven: Yale University Press, 2000), 143–47; as well as *Unfading Light*, 207–13. A helpful discussion of the idea of creativity in Russian religious thought of the 19th and 20th centuries can be found in Victor V. Bychkov and Oleg V. Bychkov, "Russian Religious Aesthetics in the First Half of the Twentieth Century" in the *Oxford Handbook of Russian Religious Thought*, eds. Caryl Emerson, George Pattison, and Randall A. Poole (Oxford: OUP), 363–78.

17 *5/18.IV.1924*

18 E.g., Sergius Bulgakov, trans. Boris Jakim, *The Comforter* (Grand Rapids: Eerdmans, 2004), 192–94. There are strong parallels here between Bulgakov's sophiological account of creation and Maximus the Confessor's *Logos*-and-*logoi* creation metaphysics. In fact, in *The Lamb of God* (126n6), Bulgakov claims that Maximus' teaching on the divine *logoi* of creation is "essentially a sophiology." For a fuller scholarly exposition of Maximus' metaphysics, see Jordan Daniel Wood, *The Whole Mystery of Christ: Creation as Incarnation in Maximus Confessor* (Notre Dame: University of Notre Dame Press, 2022).

19 *The Comforter*, 202.

20 *10/23.IX.1924*

21 *Unfading Light*, 7–9.

22 *28.V/10.VI.1924*

23 *16/29.XI.1924*

24 *6/19.VI.1925*

25 *10/23.III.1924*

26 *3/16.III.1925*

27 *6/19.VI.1925*

28 *Philosophy of Economy*, 137.

29 *Unfading Light*, 227.

30 Compare Athanasius of Alexandria's discussion of the "divine dilemma" in the early chapters of *On the Incarnation*. Bulgakov's thinking on nature and the relationship between the ideal and the real therein was a natural outgrowth of the decades he spent working in economics. This concern with human economics as a transfiguration of the material world carries over into Bulgakov's theological period, particularly in his theology of the Eucharist. See the cogent analysis by Mark Roosien in "The Common Task: Eucharist, Social Action, and the Continuity of Bulgakov's Thought," *Journal of Orthodox Christian Studies*, 3, no.1 (2020): 71–88.

31 *Unfading Light*, 345.

32 E.g., Alexander Schmemann, *For the Life of the World: Sacraments and Orthodoxy* (Crestwood: St. Vladimir's Seminary Press, 1997).

33 *5/18.IV.1924*

34 The clearest mature articulation of this idea can be found, appropriately, in Bulgakov's 1930 essay, "Icons and Their Veneration." Sergius Bulgakov, trans. Boris Jakim, *Icons and the Name of God* (Grand Rapids: Eerdmans, 2012).

35 *The Comforter*, 203.

36 Sergius Bulgakov, trans. Boris Jakim, *The Holy Grail and the Eucharist* (Hudson: Lindisfarne Books, 1997), 128.

37 *23.XI/6.XII.1924*

38 *27.I/9.II.1925*; *19.V/1.VI.1925*

39 *27.IX/10.X.1925*; Cf. *3/16.V.1925*

40 *27.I/9.II.1925*

41 *16/29.I.1925*

42 Cf. "Tedium is one of the eight deadly vices, and indeed the gravest of them all." John Climacus, trans. Colm Luibheid and Norman Russell, *The Ladder of Divine Ascent* (*The Classics of Western Spirituality*) (New York: Paulist Press, 1982), 163.

43 At times, the melancholic experience covered by the term *acedia* was singled out as a separate vice, *tristitia*, a sorrow distinct from tedium, *taedio*. An overview of *acedia* in the first Christian millennium can be found in the chapter, "Acedia: Madness and the Epidemiology of Individuality" in Peter Toohey's *Melancholy, Love, and Time: Boundaries of the Self in Ancient Literature* (Ann Arbor: University of Michigan Press, 2004), 132–60. For a quite brief though illuminating discussion of the separation of sloth from sorrow as the eight deadly vices became instead seven, see Donald Capps, *The Depleted Self: Sin in a Narcissistic Age* (Minneapolis: Fortress Press, 1993), 41–43.

44 See the Biographical Introduction for more on Bulgakov's relationship with Florensky. It is interesting in this connection to consider Bulgakov's teaching that shame is the inevitable accompaniment to sexual intercourse after the Fall. This line of thinking, heavily influenced by St. Augustine, can be found already in 1918, in the chapter "Sex in the Human Being" in *Unfading Light*, and then again in the Crimean period, in his unpublished essay from 1921, "Masculine and Feminine." Eds. A. P. Kozyrev and M. A. Vasil'eva, *S. N. Bulgakov: religiozno-filosofskii put': mezhdunarodnaia nauchnaia konferentsiia posviashchennaia 130-letiiu so dnia rozhdeniia* (Moscow: *Put'*, 2003), 343–90.

45 Bernard Lonergan's clarification of the relationship between the life lived by the theologian—his authenticity in religious, moral, and intellectual conversions (which come in degrees)—and the theology he produces—the doctrines in his tradition that he will find intelligible, attractive, and worth promoting—leads us to ask the biographical question when reading Bulgakov's writings on self-hatred. There exists, of course, the further question of the authenticity of the monuments of a religious tradition itself as representing and facilitating these basic conversions (Bernard J. F. Lonergan, *Method in Theology* [Toronto: University of Toronto Press, 2013]; on conversions, 223–30; on authenticity and inauthenticity in traditions, 77, 153). Feminist theologians most of all have served the Christian churches by raising the question of the authenticity of their religious traditions with respect to questions of self-love and self-hatred. My analysis in this chapter has benefited from their work, and especially from Elizabeth Antus' "The Doors of the Soul: A Critical Augustinian Account of Self-Love," unpublished dissertation (University of Notre Dame, 2015), which provided some orientation and bibliography for what immediately follows.

46 The phrase "divided self" appears in William James (Capps, op. cit., 87); "depleted self" is from Donald Capps. It is suggestive that the Austrian-American psychoanalyst Heinz Kohut considered Dostoyevsky a transitional figure between the self defined by guilt and the self defined by shame (ibid., 93); compare Bulgakov's comments in his entry on humility (*16/29.VI.1925*): "For people who are gifted and strong, the 'rich,' it is harder to acquire humility, because they tarry longer in the consciousness of their own power, yet such an epiphany inevitably awaits every person on the path of life. But this is not yet humility: rather, it is merely a negative condition, for it that still requires certain positives. In the absence of the latter, this disenchantment with the self poisons the soul with a wicked despondency, with envy, and *then a person's 'underground' emerges*" (italics mine).

47 The German-American psychoanalyst Karen Horney was one of the early theoreticians to develop the notion of the "idealized" versus the "real self" (which would become pivotal for the psychology of shame in the twentieth century), together with the notion that pride was in fact a subsequent and derivative *response* to the acknowledgement of the gap between the ideal and the real. For a theologically and psychologically sophisticated account of pride that builds on Horney's insights, see Terry D. Cooper, *Sin, Pride and Self-Acceptance: The Problem of Identity in Theology and Psychology* (Downers Grove: InterVarsity Press, 2003).

48 "Nothing short of absolute fearlessness, mastery, or saintliness has any appeal for the neurotic obsessed with the drive for glory. He is therefore the antithesis of the truly religious man. For the latter, only to God are all things possible; the neurotic's version is: nothing is impossible to *me*." Karen Horney, *Neurosis and Human Growth: The Struggle Toward Self-Realization* (New York: Norton, 1950), 34–35.

49 Anthony J. Steinbock has argued that shame cannot be experienced in consciousness unless the subject also simultaneously and more fundamentally values and loves herself. "When something emerges to elicit shame, I am moving against a more basic orientation that is sufficient to call me into question. I am not being 'Myself.'" What Steinbock calls "Myself"—one's self given in consciousness as already beloved—is not far from Bulgakov's sophianic self, which in its essence exists as an outpouring of divine love. Anthony J. Steinbock, *Knowing by Heart: Loving as Participation and Critique* (Evanston: Northwestern University Press, 2021), 92–93.

50 *3/16.V.1925*

51 *24.II/9.III.1925*

52 *27.IX/10.X.1925*

53 *27.IX/10.X.1925*

54 *24.II/9.III.1925*

55 *16/29.I.1925*

56 For Bulgakov on the question of eschatology as "personal mood," see "The Foundational Antinomy of the Christian Philosophy of History," trans. Roberto J. De La Noval in *The Sophiology of Death: Essays on Eschatology: Personal, Political, Universal* (Cascade Books, 2021), 1–8.

57 Fyodor Dostoevsky, trans. Richard Pevear and Larissa Volokhonsky, *The Brothers Karamazov* (San Francisco: North Point Press, 1990), 289.

58 *10/23.V.1925*

59 *5/18.VIII.1924*

60 *10/23.V.1925*

61 *18.IV/1.V.1925*

62 The most famous literary depiction of this theological doctrine is C. S. Lewis' *The Great Divorce*. For a literary telling of an eschatological vision akin to Bulgakov's own, see George MacDonald's novel, *Lilith*.

63 *23.VI/6.VII.1924*

64 "The past, alas, we cannot change; we can only lament it. In silent reproach it stands before our conscience and judges us prior to the Dread Judgment." *27.IX/10.X.1925*

65 *15/28.X.1924*

66 For a more detailed study of Bulgakov's development of this theme of eschatological self-judgment, with some constructive additions, see Roberto J. De La Noval, "We Shall See Him as He Is: Bulgakov on Eschatological Conversion" on the website *Eclectic Orthodoxy*.

67 *15/28.X.1924*

68 See Sebastian Brock, *Isaac of Nineveh* (*Isaac the Syrian*): *"The Second Part," Chapters IV–XLI* (Lovanii: Peeters, 1995).

69 *17/30.IV.1925*

70 *6/19.IX.1924*

71 The Great Canon of St. Andrew of Crete, Thursday of the First Week of Lent, Ode 8.

72 *Unfading Light*, 355.

73 "The Judgment... shows to each one their own self in a true light, in the wholeness of their image, given from nature and re-created by freedom, and thanks to this insight, by seeing in themselves the traits of falsehood, they suffer, experiencing the torments of 'Hell.'" *Unfading Light*, 427–28.

74 Consider Evagrius in the *Praktikos*: "Sadness sometimes occurs through the frustration of one's desires, or sometimes it follows closely upon anger." Robert E. Sinkewicz, *Evagrius of Pontus: The Greek Ascetic* Corpus (Oxford: OUP, 2003), 98. If the desire Evagrius speaks of is the desire of self-perfection, expressed either in a positive ideal or in an arrogant self-idealization, then it is natural that sadness should follow upon moral failure. Compare, too, Freud's classic notion of depression as anger turned inwards.

75 As, for example, in Maximus the Confessor's "On the Utility of the Passions" (*Ad Thalassium* 1). St. Maximus the Confessor, trans. Paul M. Blowers and Robert Louis Wilken, *On the Cosmic Mystery of Jesus Christ* (*Popular Patristics Series*) (Crestwood: St. Vladimir's Seminary Press, 2003), 97–98.

76 *17/30.IV.1925*

77 "And now, in my decline, I see how I have spent my whole life in laziness and have not put Your gifts to good use, have not labored for You, for I have indulged in self-pity to no end." *27.I/9.II.1925*

78 *Bride of the Lamb*, 492.

79 *6/19.III.1925*

80 *26.IX/9.X.1924*. These Marian reflections here correspond with the evidence from his archive that Bulgakov was already in 1924 writing what would eventually become his 1927 book on Orthodox Mariology. Sergius Bulgakov, trans. Thomas Allan Smith, *The Burning Bush* (Grand Rapids: Eerdmans, 2009).

81 First antiphon of the Liturgy of St. John Chrysostom.

82 *24.X/6.XI.1924*

83 *21.XII.1924/3.I.1925*

84 *21.XII.1924/3.I.1925*

85 *18.IV/1.V.1925*

86 *21.XII.1924/3.I.1925*

87 Among the more positive meanings of divine election in the *Diary* we find God's election of spiritual friends in our lives (*13/26.I.1925*) and the election of receiving artistic gifts to serve God's tabernacle (*7/20.III.1925*).

88 *22.XII.1924/5.I.1925*

89 *29.X/11.XI.1924*

90 *21.X/3.XI.1924*

91 See the classic study by Dimitry Pospielovsky, *The Russian Church Under the Soviet Regime: 1917–1982* (Crestwood: St. Vladimir's Seminary Press, 1984).

92 *2/15.XI.1924*

93 This, however, does not make God the cause of evil. See note 118 below.

94 See, for example, *Russia and the Universal Church*, trans. Herbert Rees (London: G. Bles, 1948).

95 For Bulgakov on Catholicism see the Biographical Introduction, 5-11; Because Bulgakov abandoned his thesis of the Russian Church's guilt before *Rome* and the universal church does not mean that Bulgakov believed the Russian church bore no blame for the tragedy of the Communist revolution. Indeed, Bulgakov's political philosophy and ecclesiology before his "Catholic temptation" in 1921–1923 already contained a significant critique of the relationship between Russian autocracy and the Russian Orthodox Church's complicity in it. See his pseudonymous "Letters from Russia" reprinted in *S. N. Bulgakov: Trudy po sotsiologii i teologii, Tom 2: Stati i raboty raznykh let* (1902–1942) (Moskva: Nauka, 1997), 3-20. This period of Bulgakov's life is well studied in Evtuhov, op. cit.

96 Sergius Bulgakov, trans. Mike Whitton, *Judas Iscariot: Apostle-Betrayer* (available on Amazon Kindle).

97 Shusaku Endo, trans. William Johnston, *Silence* (New York: Taplinger Publishing Company, 1980), 119.

98 Here Williams expounds the thought of Stanley Cavell. Rowan Williams, *The Tragic Imagination* (Oxford: OUP, 2016), 36.

99 Bulgakov and his immediate family—excepting his son Fedor, "Fedya"—were forcibly exiled from Russia on December 30, 1922, by direct order of the Soviet authorities. For more of the story of these political expulsions on the "Philosophy Steamers," see Leslie Chamberlaine's riveting account in *Lenin's Private War: The Voyage of the Philosophy Steamer and the Exile of the Intelligentsia* (New York: St. Martin's Press, 2006).

100 *11/24.XI.1924*

101 *11/24.XI.1924*

102 See his essay "Apocatastasis and Theodicy" in trans. Roberto J. De La Noval, *The Sophiology of Death: Essays on Eschatology: Personal, Political, Universal* (Eugene: Cascade Books, 2021), 92–103.

103 *11/24.XI.1924*

104 *16/29.VI.1925*

105 *24.VIII/6.IX.1924*

106 *30.V/12.VI.1925*

107 *14/27.II.1925*

108 *20.IX/3.X.1924*

109 *23.V/5.VI.1925*

110 *11/24.X.1924*

111 See *Lamb of God,* 354–60.

112 *23.IX/6.X.1924.* Here we see the roots of Bulgakov's divergence (*The Lamb of God,* 78–79) from Maximus Confessor's teaching that Christ lacked a gnomic will.

113 *28.IX/11.X.1924*

114 *13/26.V.1925*

115 *24.III/6.IV.1925*

116 *13/26.IX.1924*

117 *16/29.IX.1924*

118 To put it in more theoretical terms, God's foreknowledge is identical to God's predestination. On this point, Bulgakov follows St. Augustine explicitly (*de dono perseverantiae,* 41), although he takes Augustine's identification of foreknowledge and predestination to its logical conclusion, one which Augustine (and later Aquinas) were reluctant to grant: that God's predestination in history is a predestination both to grace *and* to reprobation. That is, God's election is one, but its effect is duplex—in those who now receive grace and in the rest who are passed over in history for reasons we cannot discern. For Bulgakov, this selective gift of grace does not make God a cause of evil, but it does make God *responsible* for the consequences of human freedom. "[In Christ,] God tells His creation: 'You are created by My hands. You are My work, and you would not exist if I did not will it. And, since I am responsible for you (*kak tvoi Vinovnik*), I take upon Myself your guilt (*vinu*)'" (*Lamb of God,* 363; translation altered). Further distinguishing Augustine and Bulgakov, however, is that the latter understood this reprobation to be *temporary,* limited to and in the service of God's historical purposes, and so ultimately lifted and reconciled in the universal restoration, when God will be all in all. In this, of course, Bulgakov is much closer than Augustine to St. Paul's own conclusion to Romans 9–11, as well as to the vision of divine election made manifest in the winding comedy that is the book of Genesis. For more on Bulgakov's theology of predestination and his relationship to Augustine's thought, see Roberto J. De La Noval, "'Augustinianism and Predestination' by Sergius Bulgakov," *Journal of Orthodox Christian Studies* 2, no. 1 (2019): 65–99.

119 *14/27.X.1924*

120 See *Unfading Light,* "Freedom and Necessity," 207–14, for Bulgakov's clear and concise discussion of the inviolability of creaturely freedom and its compatibility with divine foreordination in eternity.

121 "One way or another, after all, all causes are logically reducible to their first cause. This is no more than a logical truism. And it does not matter whether one construes the relation between primary and secondary causality as one of total determinism or as one of utter indeterminacy, for in either case all 'consequents' are—either as actualities or merely as possibilities—contingent upon their primordial 'antecedent,' apart from which they could not exist." David Bentley Hart, *That All Shall Be Saved: Heaven, Hell and Universal Salvation* (New Haven: Yale University Press, 2019), 70.

122 "God is love, but the world contains malice, struggle and hatred. The world is full of the immeasurable suffering of creatures. Groans and wails

are borne to heaven, but heaven remains mute and without answer. Such is the kenosis of the Father's love." *The Comforter*, 385.

123 *16/29.XI.1924*

124 *8/21.III.1925*

125 *1/14.VIII.1924*

126 This is how 1 Thessalonians 5:18 reads in the Russian Synodal Version (*za vse blagodarite*).

127 See p. 169.

128 *23.IX/6.X.1924*

129 *13/26.V.1925*

130 *13/26.II.1925*

131 *5/18.IV.1924*

132 *23.IX/6.X.1924*

133 *29.X/11.XI.1924*

134 *4/17.II.1925*

135 *16/29.VIII.1924*

136 *28.II/13.III.1925*

137 *8/21.V.1925*

NOTES TO THE SPIRITUAL DIARY

1 St. Sergius of Radonezh (d. 1392); see note 59 below.

2 These three cities were among the several where Russian émigrés settled, and they subsequently became hubs of Russian intellectual and religious life, especially in connection with the Russian Christian Student Movement (RCSM), for which Bulgakov served as a founder and spiritual leader. Some of the persons listed here likely came to study in Prague from Belgrade and Přerov after their emigration there. Many of these students went on to perform leadership roles in the same RCSM.

3 Bulgakov taught in the Russian Law Faculty at the University of Prague (Charles University) in 1923 until moving to Paris to serve as professor and dean of St. Sergius Orthodox Theological Institute.

4 Nikolai Mikhailovich Zernov (1898–1980): Philosopher and theologian. Zernov served as a secretary of the RCSM (1925–1932) and later as one of the founders of the fellowship of St. Sergius and St. Alban. Lectured at Oxford and became a prolific author, perhaps best known for his book, *The Russian Religious Renaissance of the Twentieth Century* (New York: Harper and Row, 1963).

5 Iosif Rietoriya: We have been unable to find any bibliographical information for Iosif.

6 Vasily Vasilievich Zenkovsky (1881–1962): A philosopher and theologian. Ordained to the priesthood in 1942. Served as president of the RCSM (1923–1962), and later as professor of history, philosophy, and psychology at St. Serge. Became dean of St. Serge after Bulgakov's death.

7 Sofia Mikhailovna Zernova (1899–1972): Sister of Nikolai Zernov. Secretary of her chapter of the RCSM from 1926 to 1931, and later served as secretary of the International Refugee Organization.

8 Ekaterina (Katya) Vladimirovna Obolenskaya (*née* Euler) (1903–2006). A descendant of the famous mathematician Leonhard Euler. Sister-in-law to Aleksandra Oboslenskaya and Andrei Obolensky (see below). Graduated from University of Prague as a doctor of medicine in 1928.

9 Aleksandra (Asya) Vladimirovna Obolenskaya (Mother Blandina) (1897–1974). Sister of Andrei Obolensky and sister-in-law to Ekaterina Obolenskaya (see above). A member of the RCSM from its beginnings, she became a spiritual daughter to and frequent correspondent with Fr. Bulgakov. Took monastic vows in 1937 and assumed the name Mother Blandina. In 1938 became a founding member of the women's monastic community at Moisenay (later the Intercession Monastery). One of the four women who cared for Bulgakov in his final days. Transcribed the *Spiritual Diary*. See the Translators' Preface, p. xviii–xix.

10 Ekaterina (Katya) Nikolaevna Reitlinger-Kist (1901–1989). Sister of Sr. Joanna. A poet active in the Prague "poets' skete" and an architect. A close friend of renowned twentieth-century Russian poet Marina Tsvetaeva.

11 Yuliya Nikolaevna (Sr. Joanna) Reitlinger (1898–1988): Sister of Ekaterina Reitlinger-Kist. Iconographer and spiritual daughter of Fr. Sergius. Lived on the campus of St. Serge. Took monastic vows in 1935, becoming Sr. Joanna. One of the four women who cared for Bulgakov in his final days. Returned to Russia and, near the end of her life, became a spiritual daughter of Fr. Alexander Men'. She is the author of memoirs of Bulgakov that conclude this volume. See the Translators' Preface, p. xviii–xix and Biographical Introduction, p. 17–18.

12 Pavel Ivanovich Novgorodtsev (1866–1942). Russian lawyer and philosopher. Founder and dean of the Russian Faculty of Law at the University of Prague.

13 Georgij Nikolaevich Shumkin (1894–1965). A member of the RCSM, where he served as a mentor to a young Anthony Bloom. Graduated from St. Serge, later was ordained a priest.

14 Arkady Petrovich Struve (1905–1951). Son of Pyotr Berngardovich Struve. Served as secretary for Bishop Sergii of Prague (Korolev, Arkadii Dmitrievich).

15 Sergei Sergeevich Bezobrazov (Bishop Kassian) (1892–1965). Member of the RCSM, later a professor of New Testament and Greek at St. Serge. Future archimandrite, then bishop and member of the episcopal council of Western European Russian Exarchate.

16 Andrei Vladimirovich Obolensky (1900–1979): Son of Andrei Vladimir Andreevich Obolensky, brother of Aleksandra Vladimirovna Obolenskaya, and brother-in-law of Ekaterina Euler. Fought in the White Army during the Russian Civil War and later emigrated with his family to Europe. A painter.

17 A reference to Ekaterina Yakovlevna Kizevetter (née Frauenfelder), wife of the Russian historian, Aleksandr Aleksandrovich Kizevetter (1866–1933), a member of the intelligentsia who, like Bulgakov, was sent into exile on the "Philosophy Steamers" of 1922–1923. A professor of history, he was one of the

founding members of Russian National University in Prague, a university formed by and for Russian émigrés after the Bolshevist Revolution. His wife preceded him in death by nine years. Bulgakov discusses Kizevetter also in the diary he kept concurrently with this one, entitled *From the Heart's Memory*, on 4/7.III.1924. See Sergius Bulgakov, *Iz Pamiati Serdtsa. Praga (1923–1924)* [*From the Heart's Memory. Prague (1923–1924)*], eds. Alexei Kozyrev and Natalia Golubkova with Modest Kolerov (Moscow: O. G. I., 1998), 243–44.

18 Bulgakov is almost certainly referring to Yuliya (later Sister Joanna, in monasticism) Reitlinger. For more on their relationship, see the Biographical Introduction.

19 This dying man was Pavel Ivanovich Novgorodtsev (1866–1924), a well-known Russian lawyer and philosopher who led the Russian law faculty at Charles University in Prague, where Bulgakov was also teaching. See Bulgakov, *From the Heart's Memory*, diary entry 18/31.III.1924; in *Iz Pamiati Serdtsa*, 246–47.

20 Sung each evening at Vespers in the Orthodox Church.

21 Novgorodstev died on this day. See Bulgakov, *From the Heart's Memory*, diary entry 28.III/10.IV.1924; in *Iz Pamiati Serdtsa*, 248.

22 Yuliya Reitlinger finished the two icons that day. See Bulgakov, *From the Heart's Memory*, diary entry 2/15 Apr<il>, 1924, *afternoon*; in *Iz Pamiati Serdtsa*, 250.

23 A reference to the "holy fire" at the Church of the Holy Sepulcher in Jerusalem that is passed between worshippers each year on the eve of Pascha. It is claimed that the flame does not burn or scorch when touched.

24 From April 23/May 6, 1924 to May 11/24, 1924 Bulgakov traveled from Prague, through Serbia, to Budapest and then Vienna. He was probably in Vienna at the time of writing this entry.

25 See Bulgakov's essay "The Name of God" in Sergius Bulgakov, *Icons and the Name of God*, trans. Boris Jakim (Grand Rapids: Eerdmans, 2012), 115–66.

26 This verse is used in the prokeimenon (responsorial psalm) for Vespers every Thursday evening.

27 As can be seen in his later theological works, Bulgakov had a penchant for isolating one attribute of God's and deriving a name for God from it (for example, the term "God-Creator").

28 Psalm 143 is read each day in the Orthodox Church in the services of Matins and Compline.

29 The Povolzhye famine of 1921–1922 that had just killed around five million people was fresh in Bulgakov's memory.

30 This verse is sung repeatedly as a refrain between hymns known as the "Evlogitaria" ("Blessings") at Matins during the vigil service on the eve of Sundays, and on other occasions.

31 The gap between this entry and the previous entry can be explained by Bulgakov's travels. From July 13/26 to 17/30, 1924 he was at the Chateau Argeronne outside Rouen, France for the first meeting of the Russian Student Christian Movement. He then stayed in Paris until July 28/August 10 for a meeting of the Brotherhood of St. Sophia. On the Brotherhood, see the Biographical Introduction.

32 Reading *angelami* for *angely*.

33 Bulgakov writes this entry during the two-week period of fasting that leads up to and prepares for the August 15 Feast of the Dormition of the Mother of God. The celebration of this great feast then lasts for eight days.

34 Bulgakov refers to traditions about the Virgin Mary saving the Russian people from enemies, especially through her icons. One of the most famous examples is the Kazan icon of the Mother of God. During the "Time of Troubles" in the early 17th century, the Polish army invaded Moscow. Attempting to defend their lands, the Russians carried an icon of the Theotokos from Kazan into battle and defeated the Polish army. The Russian victory was credited to the Virgin Mary. The Russian Orthodox Church commemorates the Kazan icon in memory of this event each year on October 22.

35 See note 78.

36 From the litanies of the Divine Liturgy.

37 This psalm is chanted at most celebrations of the Divine Liturgy in the Slavic tradition.

38 Patriarch Tikhon (Bellavin) of Moscow (1865–1925), the first Patriarch of Russia after the re-establishment of the Patriarchate at the All-Russian Council of Moscow in 1917–1918. Having died in 1925 after being tortured by the Soviet authorities, he was canonized in 1989 by the Russian Orthodox Church. Bulgakov had been close to him in the years leading up to the Council, and Patriarch Tikhon personally encouraged Bulgakov's ordination to the priesthood. For Bulgakov's reflections on Patriarch Tikhon, see his speech from April 27, 1925: "The Guardian of the House of the Lord (To the Memory of the Most Holy Patriarch Tikhon)," trans. by D. Mirsky, *The Slavonic and East European Review* 4, no. 10 (1925): 156–64.

39 This verse is used as a communion chant on days commemorating martyrs and other saints.

40 In 1924, Zbraslav was an independent municipality adjacent to Prague. It was joined to the city of Prague in 1974. From September 8 to 14 (new style), 1924, Bulgakov was in Přerov for another meeting of the Russian Student Christian Movement.

41 The Stroganov School, a 16th–17th century school of Russian icon painting, flourished under the patronage of the Stroganov merchant family, thereby acquiring its name. Gavrila Gavrilovich Solodovnikov (1825–1901), one of the wealthiest entrepreneurs and philanthropists of the 19th century, belonged to a family of Old Believers, Russian Orthodox Christians who resisted the 17th-century liturgical reforms instituted under Patriarch Nikon (1652–1666) and thereafter went out of communion with the Russian Orthodox hierarchy.

42 The Feast of the Nativity of the Theotokos is celebrated annually on November 8th.

43 The cathedral of St. Nicholas, a Baroque church located in the old town of Prague, was used by the Russian Orthodox in the late-19th and early-20th centuries.

44 The text reads *David*, but this is either a transcription error or a mistake from Bulgakov's own pen. We have replaced it with "Daniel," as

this is the only fitting prophet for the context, in addition to being a close linguistic neighbor to "David." The references in the psalms (e.g., 42:3; 80:5) to tears replacing food and drink also help explain the mix-up, assuming it is original to Bulgakov.

45 This entry was written two days after the September 14th feast of the Exaltation of the Holy Cross.

46 The term "Only Sinless One" alludes to a hymn sung during the Saturday evening vigil service and spoken by the deacon during the Divine Liturgy after the communion rite: "Having beheld the Resurrection of Christ, let us worship the holy Lord Jesus, the Only Sinless One! We venerate your Cross, O Christ, and we praise and glorify Your Holy Resurrection; for You are our God, and we know no other but You; we call on Your name. Come, all you faithful, let us venerate the Holy Resurrection of Christ! For, behold, through the Cross, joy has come into all the world. Ever blessing the Lord, let us praise His Resurrection. For by enduring the Cross for us, He has destroyed death by death!"

47 This is a reference to one of the vesting prayers said by the clergy before the celebration of the liturgy.

48 See the Theological Introduction for more on Bulgakov's Mariology.

49 "Rejoice, O Unwedded Bride" is the repeated refrain from the Akathist hymn to the Theotokos.

50 This verse is referenced in a chant for the Feast of the Entrance of the Theotokos to the Temple: "Cry out, O David: What is this present feast? Is it for her of whom you sang in the book of the Psalms, calling her daughter, child of God and Virgin, saying: Her companions, the virgins that follow her, shall be mystically led to the King? Let this feast be held in honor by all who cry: The Theotokos has come among us, the mediatrix of our salvation!"

51 An allusion to the Troparion for the feast commemorating the Tikhvin Icon: "Today, O Sovereign Lady, your most venerable Icon has shone upon us in the Heavens like a most radiant sun, enlightening the world with rays of mercy, which Russia has received most reverently as a Divine gift from on high. It glorifies you, O Mother of God, as the Queen of all, and joyfully magnifies Christ our God, Who was born of you. Pray to Him, O Lady Theotokos, that He may preserve all Christian cities and countries unharmed from all the machinations of the Enemy, and that He may save those who with faith bow down before His divine image and your most pure Icon, O Virgin who did not know wedlock."

52 An allusion to the call to prayer at the services of the Orthodox daily office: "Come, let us worship God our King! Come, let us worship and fall down before Christ our King and our God! Come, let us worship and fall down before Christ Himself, our King and our God!"

53 This verse is used in a few places in Byzantine liturgy, including during the service of baptism.

54 In his other diary, two days later, Bulgakov describes an uneasiness about his relationship with Yuliya Reitlinger "in recent days." The present entry may be a reference to these circumstances. See Bulgakov, "Prague Notebook,

1924–1925," diary entry 6/19.X.1924; in Y. N. Reitlinger (Sister Joanna) and Fr. Sergii Bulgakov, *Dialog Khudozhnika i Bogoslova: Dnevniki. Zapisnye knizhki. Pis'ma* [Dialogue of an Artist and a Theologian: Diaries. Written booklets. Letters], ed. Bronislava Popova (Moscow: Nikeia, 2011), 115–16. For more on Bulgakov and Reitlinger's relationship, see the Biographical Introduction to the present volume.

55 Bulgakov alludes to a prayer of confession said immediately before Communion in the Divine Liturgy.

56 In an entry on this same date in his other diary, Bulgakov reports that he has decided to no longer allow Yuliya Reitlinger to attend his lectures at Charles University, and that this was painful for him, yet necessary to preserve peace between himself and his wife, Elena. See Bulgakov, "Prague Notebook, 1924–1925," diary entry 11/24.X.1924; in *Dialog Khudozhnika i Bogoslova*, 116. For more on Bulgakov and Reitlinger's relationship, see the Biographical Introduction to the present volume.

57 Gospel of Thomas, saying 82; translation from Richard Valantasis, *The Gospel of Thomas* (London/New York: Routledge, 1997), 162.

58 A reference to the description of the Holy Spirit in the Nicene Creed: "I believe in the Holy Spirit, the Lord, the Giver of Life."

59 St. Sergius of Radonezh (d. 1392), a 14th-century saint from the region around Moscow, is an important and highly venerated saint in the Russian Orthodox Church. See Pierre Kovalevsky, *St. Sergius and Russian Spirituality*, trans. W. Elias Jones (Crestwood: St. Vladimir's Seminary Press, 1976).

60 Bulgakov had recently completed a book titled *Saints Peter and John: Two First Apostles*, which was published in Russian by YMCA Press two years later in 1926.

61 A lavra denotes a monastic compound with a cluster or complex of cells in whose center is found a church and usually a refectory.

62 The Mongols or "Tatars" conquered the territories of Rus' in the early 13th century and controlled them until the early 16th century.

63 Today, the koukoulion refers to the headdress worn by the primates of some Orthodox Churches (including the patriarch of Moscow) and certain advanced monastics, but Bulgakov invokes the older meaning of the word: the simple monastic hood, or cowl. Evagrius of Pontus (d. 399), one of the first to mention and comment on the cowl, writes, "The cowl (*koukoúllion*) is a symbol of the charity of God our Savior. It protects the most important part of the body and keeps us, who are children in Christ, warm. Thus it can be said to afford protection against those who attempt to strike and wound us. Consequently, all who wear this cowl on their heads sing these words aloud: 'If the Lord does not build the house and keep the city, unavailingly does the builder labor and the watchman stand his guard.' Such words as these instill humility and root out that long-standing evil which is pride and which caused Lucifer, who rose like the day-star in the morning, to be cast down to earth" (Evagrius Ponticus, *The Praktikos and Chapters on Prayer*, trans. John Eudes Bamberger [Kalamazoo: Cistercian Publications, 1981], 13).

64 From the Litany of Completion in the Liturgy of St. John Chrysostom.

65 See the Orthodox "Canon to the Guardian Angel" which elaborates an intimate and emotional relationship between Christians and their guardian angels.

66 "Kind guide" (*dobryi nastavnik*) is a common term for one's guardian angel in the Russian tradition, drawing from litanies in the liturgy wherein the guardian angel is called a "faithful guide" (*vernyi nastavnik*).

67 Quotation of a post-communion petition from the Liturgy of St. John Chrysostom.

68 Russ. *bratotvorenie* is the translation of the Greek *adelphopoíesis*, lit. "brother-making." The term refers to an ancient Christian ritual, typically in the Eastern Christian world, of uniting same-sex friends in a sibling-type spiritual relationship recognized by the Church. But Bulgakov is likely using this term in reference to the difficulties in establishing the Brotherhood of St. Sophia, on which see the Biographical Introduction.

69 Citation of the Great Litany from the Divine Liturgy.

70 St. Seraphim of Sarov (d. 1833) is an important and highly venerated saint in the Russian Orthodox Church. A record of his conversation (whose authenticity is debated) with politician and businessman Nikolai Alexandrovich Motovilov, which the latter first published in 1903, the year of St. Seraphim's canonization, caused a stir in Russian society. See the classic book on St. Seraphim by Valentine Zander, *St. Seraphim of Sarov*, trans. Gabriel Anne (Crestwood: St. Vladimir's Seminary Press, 1975).

71 From the Litany of Completion in the Divine Liturgy.

72 Saint Lucian of Antioch, martyred under the emperor Diocletian in AD 312. According to hagiographical reports, Lucian—imprisoned and without access to any piece of furniture to use as an altar—used his own breast as an altar when he celebrated the Eucharistic sacrifice shortly before his death.

73 A reference to Elizaveta Vasil'evna Bobkova, a woman who had become Bulgakov's spiritual daughter when they met in Simferopol some years earlier. In an entry in his other diary on the same day, he mentions receiving a letter from "Eliz. Vas." that greatly troubled him. See Bulgakov, "Prague Notebook, 1924–1925," diary entry 16/29.XI.1924; in *Dialog Khudozhnika i Bogoslova*, 117–18.

74 A popular saying attributed to St. Seraphim of Sarov. See note 70 above.

75 See the *Life of St. Sergius of Radonezh* in Michael Klimenko, *The "Vita" of St. Sergii of Radonezh: Translation, Introduction, Notes* (Boston: Nordland, 1980), 137.

76 This is probably a reference to a donation of $5,000 given by John R. Mott (a prominent leader in the YMCA and the World Christian Student Federation) in June 1924 for the purchase of the property in which the St. Sergius Institute in Paris would be housed. In his history of the Institute, Donald Lowrie writes, "Without this substantial basis of action, it is doubtful if the still-new emigration would have dared to undertake so large a financial project." One of the founding professors of St. Sergius, Anton Kartashev, is quoted as saying, "Through this generous gift Dr. Mott became the real father and founder of our school" (Donald A. Lowrie, *Saint Sergius in Paris: The Orthodox Theological Institute* [New York: Macmillan, 1951], 7–8).

77 This entry was written the day after the November 21 Feast of the Entry of the Theotokos into the Temple.

78 Also known as Andrew of Constantinople (d. 936). Andrew (a Slav) had a vision of the Theotokos covering Constantinople with her omophorion (mantle) while it was under enemy siege; after the city was saved, the feast day of the "Protection of the Theotokos" was established.

79 Gospel of Thomas, saying 82. See note 57 above.

80 Bulgakov would be taking a long trip to Western Europe in a few days' time. See note 82.

81 Bulgakov here draws one of the four adverbs of the Chalcedonian Definition used to describe how Christ's two natures are united in one hypostasis (unconfusedly, unchangeably, indivisibly, inseparably).

82 Bulgakov went on a long trip to Western Europe from November 27/December 10, 1924 to December 18/31, 1924, stopping in Paris (twice), London, and Canterbury. He evidently did not take his spiritual diary with him on that trip, which explains the lack of entries during that time. He did, however, write frequently in his everyday diary. See Reitlinger and Bulgakov, *Dialog Khudozhnika i Bogoslova*, 118–24.

83 Reading *podvergaetsia* for *vvergaetsia*.

84 An allusion to the stichera hymns at the 9th hour for the Feast of Nativity.

85 An allusion to the hymn "God is with us" sung during the service of Great Compline on Christmas Eve.

86 "Christ is born" is the festive greeting of Orthodox Christians on Christmas and throughout the Christmas season.

87 From the Orthodox prayers before sleep.

88 A *starets* (elder) refers to a revered spiritual guide, usually a monastic.

89 An allusion to an episode from the life of St. Seraphim of Sarov. After overseeing the construction of the refectory for the women's monastery at Diveevo where he was the community's spiritual father, St. Seraphim ordered the construction of a walkable moat. When the sisters informed him they would prefer an enclosure wall, St. Seraphim replied, "How silly you are! This moat will recall and mark out the path which the feet of the Queen of Heaven trod when she walked round the land to take possession of it!" (Zander, *St. Seraphim of Sarov*, 50).

90 Bulgakov alludes to an episode in the life of St. Seraphim in which he spent one thousand consecutive nights on a large rock with arms raised in prayer. Beginning in his thirties, St. Seraphim lived in a hut in the forest about five kilometers from the monastery in Sarov. "His days were spent in various tasks: he dug the ground, erected a fence to protect his dwelling from the incursion of wild animals, prepared the ingredients for his stew-pan (for he lived on his own produce). He brought only a little bread from the monastery to last the whole week and it was known that he shared it with the animals in the forest. He was seen in the company of a huge bear who, meek as a lamb, took its food from his hand" (Zander, *St. Seraphim of Sarov*, 16).

91 Although this greeting is usually offered only in the Easter season in the Orthodox Church, St. Seraphim of Sarov was known to greet people this way throughout the year.

92 On the moat, see note 89 above. St. Seraphim also ordered the construction of a mill at Diveevo. See Zander, *St. Seraphim of Sarov*, 42–45.

93 Although January 7 is the Synaxis (feast) of St. John the Forerunner, Bulgakov quotes from the troparion hymn of the feast of the prophet Elijah: "Angel in the flesh and cornerstone of the prophets, the second forerunner of the coming of Christ: glorious Elijah sent grace from above to Elisha, to dispel diseases and to cleanse lepers. Therefore, he pours forth healings on those who honor him."

94 This psalm is used in the Orthodox hymnography for the feast of Theophany, which celebrates the baptism of the Lord in the Jordan River.

95 An allusion to the Gospel accounts of Christ's transfiguration on Mount Tabor.

96 This psalm is sung each evening at vespers in the Byzantine rite, as part of a series of psalms commencing with Psalm 141, "Lord, I cry."

97 This psalm is sung each Saturday at vespers as part of the normal cursus of Psalms 1–3, popularly known as "Blessed is the man," named after the first verse of Psalm 1.

98 A quotation from the Orthodox hymn, "Open to me the doors of repentance," sung from the Sunday of the Publican and the Pharisee (three weeks before Great Lent) and the fifth Sunday of Lent: "Open to me the doors of repentance, O Giver of life; for my spirit rises early to pray towards Your holy Temple, bearing the temple of my body, wholly polluted. But in Your compassion, purify me by the lovingkindness of your mercy. Lead me on the paths of salvation, O Mother of God, for I have profaned my soul with shameful sins, and wasted my life in slothfulness. But, by your intercessions, deliver me from all impurity."

99 The tenth of twenty-four short evening prayers in many Orthodox prayer books.

100 The "Canon to the Guardian Angel" is a set of petitionary and thanksgiving hymns that is often prayed at home among Orthodox (especially Russian Orthodox) Christians.

101 A reference to the hymn for the September 14 Feast of the Exaltation of the Holy Cross, also sung on the Third Sunday of Lent, known as the Sunday of the Veneration of the Holy Cross: "Before your cross we bow down in worship, O Master, and your Holy Resurrection we glorify."

102 An allusion to the 19th-century poet and playwright Aleksei Konstantinovich Tolstoy's poem, *Begut razorvannye tuchi* ("Scattered clouds rush by").

103 This verse is sung often in the Pascha season, and is also considered by many Orthodox believers to possess a kind of apotropaic effect against demons.

104 The church in which Bulgakov's father—an Orthodox priest himself—served, located in the Russian town of Livny.

105 The son of a Russian Orthodox priest, Bulgakov lost his faith as a teenager while attending the Russian seminary schools for children of clergy, which

were notorious for regularly inspiring atheism in their students. Bulgakov's return to his childhood faith was a long and winding road; according to his autobiographical writings, his "reversion" began in 1895 and was confirmed when Bulgakov entered into sacramental communion with the church in 1908. Nearly a decade later, the Bolshevik Revolution began on November 7, 1917; in 1918, Bulgakov was ordained to the diaconate on June 23rd—the feast of Pentecost—and then to the priesthood the following day—the Day of the Holy Spirit. For more, see the Biographical Introduction.

106 Possibly a reference to Yuliya Reitlinger.

107 Orthodox Christians often bring icons to church to be blessed after they paint or acquire them. The origins of this practice can be traced to the 17th century.

108 A reference to the Marian hymn "In You All Creation Rejoices" sung in the Liturgy of St. Basil the Great: "All creation rejoices in you, O Full of Grace, the assembly of Angels and the race of man. O Sanctified Temple and Spiritual Paradise! O Glory of Virgins! From you, God was incarnate and became a child, our God before the ages. He made your body a throne, and your womb He made more spacious than the heavens. All of creation rejoices in you, O Full of Grace! Glory to you!"

109 Allusion to the Orthodox hymn, "O Heavenly King": "O Heavenly King, the Comforter, the Spirit of Truth, Who are everywhere and fill all things; Treasury of Blessings, and Giver of Life—come and abide in us, and cleanse us from every impurity, and save our souls, O Good One."

110 This is the first of three psalms (Pss. 84–86) to be read each day at the ninth hour in the Byzantine Rite.

111 The refrain of the Canon, a set of hymns sung at the morning service of Orthros, for the September 14 Feast of the Exaltation of the Holy Cross, and the Third Sunday of Lent—the Veneration of the Cross. This entry was written on the eve of that Lenten commemoration in 1925.

112 A reference to the textile covers placed over the paten and chalice as they are carried in procession during the Great Entrance rite, at which the "Cherubic Hymn" is sung: "Let us who mystically represent the cherubim, and sing the thrice-holy hymn to the Life-Creating Trinity, now lay aside all earthly cares, that we may receive the King of all, who comes invisibly upborne by the angelic hosts. Alleluia, alleluia, alleluia."

113 Bulgakov was soon to depart on a short, three-day trip to Paris.

114 See note 38 above.

115 This line is repeated often in the prayers said by Orthodox Christians in preparation to receive Holy Communion.

116 A verse from the Great Prokeimenon, a responsorial psalm verse used on some major feasts.

117 From a hymn sung in the service of Great Compline. See note 85 above.

118 Reading *zazhigaetsia* for *zazhigaesh'sia*.

119 Reading *Svoikh* for *Tvoikh*.

120 This verse is used as a prokeimenon, or responsorial psalm verse, in

the Divine Liturgy on days celebrating certain saints.

121 This is the refrain for the Great Prokeimenon, a responsorial psalm that is used on some major feasts.

122 See note 63 above.

123 A quotation from the eucharistic prayer during the *sursum corda* dialogue preceding the eucharistic prayer in the Orthodox liturgy:

> Priest: Let us lift up our hearts.
> People: We lift them up unto the Lord.
> Priest: Let us give thanks to the Lord.

124 Reading *dvizheniem* for *dvizhenie*.

125 Bulgakov alludes to a popular Orthodox morning prayer. "Grant, O Lord, that I may now love You as once I loved sin itself, and that I may labor for You without laziness as once I labored for Satan the deceiver. Even more I will labor for You, my Lord and God, Jesus Christ, all the days of my life, now and ever, and unto ages of ages. Amen."

126 An allusion to the "underground man" of Dostoevsky's novel, *Notes from Underground*.

127 Bulgakov's reading—that the evangelist Luke was Cleopas' companion on the road to Emmaus—is not a supported view today among scholars.

128 From the Litany of Completion in the Divine Liturgy: "That we may live out the rest of our lives in peace and repentance, let us ask of the Lord."

129 A quotation of the hymn, "Open to me the doors of repentance." See note 98 above.

130 In the Byzantine Rite, the piece of bread that is to become the Body of Christ in Holy Communion is called the Lamb. It is consecrated while resting on a plate or paten called the diskos.

131 An allusion to the hymn, "Let all mortal flesh," sung on the morning of Holy Saturday during the Divine Liturgy replacing the Cherubic Hymn: "Let all mortal flesh keep silent, and with fear and trembling stand. Ponder nothing earthly-minded, for the King of kings and Lord of lords advances to be slain and given as food to the faithful. Before him go the choirs of Angels, with every rule and authority, the many-eyed Cherubim and the six-winged Seraphim, veiling their sight and crying out the hymn: Alleluia, Alleluia, Alleluia."

NOTES TO REMEMBERING FR. SERGIUS

1 This rather loose claim is contradicted later in another one of Reitlinger's reminiscences about Bulgakov ("The Manifestation of the 'Unfading Light'"), where she writes that the stroke occurred sometime overnight from the 5th to the 6th of June. This discrepancy indicates that Reitlinger's point here is simply that Bulgakov met his end without ever ceasing from the ministry entrusted to him. For an English translation of "The Manifestation of the Unfading Light," see trans. Boris Jakim, *Sergius Bulgakov: Apocatastasis and Transfiguration* (Variable Press, 1995).

2 "The Sophiology of Death." An English translation can be found in

Sergius Bulgakov, *The Sophiology of Death: Essays on Eschatology: Personal, Political, Universal*, trans. Roberto De La Noval (Eugene: Cascade, 2021).

3 Sergii Bulgakov, "Khristos v mire," *Zvezda* 1 (1994): 150–78.

4 Bulgakov lost the ability to use his vocal chords as a result of two surgeries he underwent for throat cancer in 1939. Despite managing to teach himself to speak again, with great difficulty, he could no longer celebrate Sunday liturgies, and so his long-time desire to celebrate daily morning liturgies was granted to him by his ecclesiastical superiors.

5 Bulgakov's essay "On the Gospel Miracles" can be found in Sergius Bulgakov, *Relics and Miracles: Two Theological Essays*, trans. Boris Jakim (Grand Rapids: Eerdmans, 2011), 43–114.

6 See Bulgakov, *Unfading Light*, 7–9.

7 We have been unable to locate the book to which Sr. Joanna refers. In her two known books on St. Seraphim, Valentina Zander does not discuss the Curé d'Ars. She does, however, draw a comparison between the two saints in an article published years after Bulgakov's death: Valentina Zander, "Iz dukhovnykh nastavlenii Prep. Serafima Sarovskogo," *Vestnik RSKhD* 53, no. 2 (1959): 25–37.

8 Sr. Reitlinger's writings on Bulgakov's manner of death recount the following event: on the fifth day of Bulgakov's nearly unconscious state after his stroke, Reitlinger (along with three other women taking care of Bulgakov) witnessed his face become "a complete and most real light." This illumination lasted for two hours, though Reitlinger reports that others who visited later also commented on the light streaming from Bulgakov's face. For an English translation of Reitlinger's reflections, see note 1 above.

9 Meaning, the ascetical life.

10 In many Christian traditions, individuals celebrate their "name day," sometimes called "angel day," on date of the church's commemoration of the saint after whom they are named.

11 See the English translation of Bulgakov's "At the Feast of the Gods" in the 1918 collected volume *Out of the Depths (De Profundis): A Collection of Articles on the Russian Revolution*, translated and edited by William F. Woehrlin (Irvine: Charles Schlackes, 1986).

12 The University of Prague, or Charles University, where Bulgakov lectured in the Russian Faculty of Law until his departure for Paris in 1925.

13 Bulgakov lived in the parsonage of the titular church of the St. Sergius Theological Institute while he was dean of the school.

14 The Lenten Triodion is the liturgical book that contains the texts and rubrics for the Lenten and pre-Lenten services in the Byzantine Rite.

15 This is the first line of the hymns of the canon sung on the Friday night service of Holy Week.

16 This is the opening line from the Hymn of Kassiani, a beloved hymn by the ninth-century female hymnographer St. Kassia, which is chanted on the Wednesday of Holy Week:

"The woman had fallen into many sins, O Lord,

yet when she perceived Your divinity,
she joined the ranks of the myrrh-bearing women.
In tears she brought You myrrh before Your burial.
She cried: Woe is me!
For I live in the night of licentiousness,
shrouded in the dark and moonless love of sin.
But accept the fountain of my tears,
as You gathered the waters of the sea into clouds.
Bow down Your ear to the sighing of my heart,
as You bowed the heavens in Your ineffable condescension.
Once Eve heard Your footstep in paradise in the cool of the day,
and in fear she ran and hid herself.
But now I will tenderly embrace those pure feet
and wipe them with the hair of my head.
Who can measure the multitude of my sins,
or the depth of Your judgments, Savior of my soul?
Do not despise Your servant in Your immeasurable mercy."

Trans. Ephrem Lash, https://newbyz.org/lashtriodion.html.

17 The Canon of St. Andrew of Crete is a lengthy, penitential work that is sung during Great Lent in the Orthodox Church. It consists of short, one- or two-sentence meditations on Scripture, punctuated with the chanting of "Have mercy on me, O God, have mercy on me" between each meditation.

18 The year was 1920. Koreiz is a suburb of Yalta, on the Crimean peninsula. Oleiz was the estate belonging to the Tokmakovs, the family of Elena Ivanovna Bulgakova (*née* Tokmakova) (1868–1945), Bulgakov's wife. For more on Reitlinger's relationship with Bulgakov, see the Biographical Introduction.

19 A reference to Isaac the Syrian's thirty-second homily in *The Ascetical Homilies of Saint Isaac the Syrian*, trans. Holy Transfiguration Monastery (Boston: Holy Transfiguration Monastery, 1984), 153.

20 The "holy fool" in the Eastern Orthodox tradition is a saint who performs unexpected and shocking acts, reversals, and provocations, often in order to induce others to repentance. See Sergey A. Ivanov, *Holy Fools in Byzantium and Beyond*, trans. Simon Franklin (Oxford: OUP, 2006).

21 The typical form of address in polite Russian society is to refer to someone by their first name and patronymic, a sort of "middle name" derived from their father's first name. A priest, however, would be addressed with some variant of "Father" plus the first name, or a more tender form of "Father" in Russian, depending on the interlocutor's level of intimacy with the priest.

22 The canonical situation with ecclesiastical jurisdictions in the Russian emigration was extremely complicated almost from the start. In 1930, the Patriarchate of Moscow (headed at that time by vice locum tenens Metropolitan Sergius Stragorodsky) broke communion with Metropolitan Evlogius Georgievsky, the head of Bulgakov's canonical jurisdiction, the Russian eparchy of Western Europe. Soon afterwards Metropolitan Evlogius came under the authority of the Ecumenical Patriarch (Photius II), making his

diocese an exarchate of the Ecumenical Patriarchate. The schism was never resolved in Bulgakov's lifetime.

23 Some, but not all, of Bulgakov's autobiographical materials can be found in Sergius Bulgakov, *A Bulgakov Anthology*, eds. James Pain and Nicolas Zernov (Philadelphia: Westminster, 1976), 3–27.

INDEX

Printed in Great Britain
by Amazon

20465811R00140